# The Science of Academic Writing

# Get the skills you need to succeed!

Student Success books are essential guides for students of all levels. From how to think critically and write great essays to planning your dream career, the Student Success series helps you study smarter and get the best from your time at university.

**Test yourself with practical tasks**

YOUR PROGRESS

**Diagnose your strengths and weaknesses**

min                    max

**Dial up your skills for improved grades**

Visit **www.sagepub.co.uk/studyskills**
for free tips and resources for study success

STUDENT
SUCCESS

# The Science of Academic Writing

## A Guide for Postgraduates

Anne Pertet

**S Sage**

1 Oliver's Yard
55 City Road
London EC1Y 1SP

2455 Teller Road
Thousand Oaks
California 91320

Unit No 323-333, Third Floor, F-Block
International Trade Tower
Nehru Place, New Delhi 110 019

8 Marina View Suite 43-053
Asia Square Tower 1
Singapore 018960

Editor: Kate Keers
Assistant editor: Sahar Jamfar
Production editor: Martin Fox
Marketing manager: Maria Omena-Neale
Cover design: Sheila Tong
Typeset by: C&M Digitals (P) Ltd, Chennai, India
Printed in the UK

**Library of Congress Control Number: 2022941213**

**British Library Cataloguing in Publication data**

A catalogue record for this book is available from the British Library

ISBN 978-1-5297-7993-6
ISBN 978-1-5297-7992-9 (pbk)

This book is written in memory of my late husband, Fred ole Pertet. He continuously inspired and encouraged me to complete the book, which was in draft form at his demise. Fred, you always believed in my ability to succeed in the academic arena. I will be forever grateful to you for critiquing the early drafts and providing honest feedback. This book might never have been written without your constant reassurance, and I regret that you did not live to see it published.

This book is written in memory of my late husband, Fred ole Penel. He continuously inspired and encouraged me to complete the book, which was in draft form at his demise. Fred, you always believed in my ability to succeed in the academic arena. I will be forever grateful to you for critiquing the early drafts and providing honest feedback. This book might never have been written without your constant reassurance, and I regret that you did not live to see it published.

# Contents

# Contents

# Acknowledgements

A book is not simply a product of its author but of a community of formal and informal contributors. This book is a dream I have had for years – it represents self-actualisation. However, my journey to this reality would not have been possible without the support of my friends, family and well-wishers.

First and foremost, I am grateful to God the Almighty for continuously giving me insights as I wrote the book.

I thank Professor Dan Kaseje, the former Vice-Chancellor and currently leading the Research Centre at The Great Lakes University of Kisumu (GLUK). Professor Kaseje planted the original seed for writing this book and the writing journey. He pushed me to teach academic and scientific units when my psyche was on taking research units. His passion for teaching and research excellence inspired the best in me and he has been my mentor, colleague, advisor, and friend.

I specifically want to thank my family. I could not have written this book without their moral support. I appreciate my 93-year-old mother, Leah, who has always believed in me and kept asking me 'have you finished writing?', which motivated me to keep going. To my loving children, Kasaine, Lucy, Soila, Mulwa and Immanuel, and my grandchildren, Sean, Noni and Zoya, I thank you for your patience, endurance, encouragement and understanding as I took some family time to work on the book. This gave me the strength and determination to succeed, finally making this book a reality. A special message to my grandchildren is that if I complete this book, I desire that you believe that you can achieve anything you set your mind to accomplish from the bottom of your heart.

I specifically thank Jai Seaman, Kate Keers and Sahar Jamfar at Sage. Jai encouraged me from the earliest stages when I was struggling to focus. In addition, the trio patiently advised me along the way and provided insightful feedback. I genuinely appreciate their help and inspiration, which led me to achieve my dream of publishing a book with a well-known international publisher.

The book evolved from a series of lecture notes based on my experiences of teaching, supervising, examining, and advising students in research methods, critical reading, and scientific writing classes at undergraduate and postgraduate levels. I am grateful to my students for the insights they conveyed to me during our collective interactions and experiences. It might not be obvious how much I learned from you, but this book is a testament to what our mutual experiences have accomplished, including rewards, when we receive positive examiners' reports and theses that pass the examination.

# Introduction

## About the book

Academic writing is clear, concise, structured, and backed by evidence. It is generally formal and written for scholarly purposes, including class essays, dissertations, and scholarly publications. Failure to complete a doctorate, Master's, or postgraduate diploma can be linked to students' academic writing problems.

Many students and inexperienced researchers find it challenging to fulfil the requirements of writing a thesis and sharing this knowledge by publishing research papers based on the thesis. Even before graduation, some universities may require their student researchers to publish work. Supervisors or other experienced academics often lack the time to guide thesis writing, and many universities, especially in developing countries, do not have Writing Centres that assist students in writing. Thus, there is a need for a book that fills these gaps.

## The audience

This book addresses the needs of the postgraduates studying for a postgraduate degree or diploma that requires an undergraduate degree as part of the entry requirement. These postgraduates can be categorised as postgraduate researchers (PGRs) or postgraduate taught students (PGTs) studying for a Master's, Master of Philosophy (MPhil), doctorate or postgraduate diploma. The book is also helpful for supervisors, faculty, advisors, and those who are beginning to examine Master's and doctorates. It provides a valuable tool for academicians in their research, including the skills of critically evaluating and reviewing published literature or academic articles. The book is written in a style of language that appeals to native and non-native English speakers, especially those who have *English as a second language (ESL)*.

This book mainly focuses on quantitative methods, but also has critical sections on qualitative research. It supports postgraduates in the long journey deemed necessary for writing a thesis that meets the examiner's requirements. It helps them to produce a logically structured, coherent, well-argued thesis that permeates from the introduction to the conclusion. The need for assistance with writing is significant given that most postgraduate students work independently after completing their coursework.

## The author

The author is a university professor specialising in preventative and community health. She has over four decades of experience in research that integrates health and social sciences theories and methods. She holds a bachelor's degree in education, a Master's in community health, and a doctorate in child health. She also has vast experience teaching undergraduate and postgraduate students in research methods, scientific and academic writing, and thesis preparation. Her motivation to write this reader-friendly handbook grew out of her encounters with students who found writing their theses particularly challenging and is based on the experience she has gained through teaching, supervising, and examining theses.

She is passionate and committed to community and public health research.

## Pedagogical features

The book is reader friendly and its pedagogical features include: discussion-based exercises, using real sample texts and including examiners' comments to spark conversations between students and lecturers; practical examples, illustrating key discussion points; a checklist; and an annotated list of references for further reading. Together, these features make it an invaluable, student-driven, self-learning reference book for new and experienced researchers alike.

The book is written from the examiner's perspective, given that they are the most prominent audience for a thesis. Thus, it focuses primarily on the *thesis as a final product that satisfies the examiner's prerequisites*. As a result, the book moves away from the advice/instructional genre and lengthy lectures that tell the reader precisely what to do, and focuses instead on approaches that promote critical thinking.

### Discussion-based exercises

*Discussion-based exercises* are the primary pedagogical approach used in this book. Discussion texts drawn from the social and behavioural sciences make the content engaging and interactive for a teaching environment. The discussion approach promotes critical thinking, enabling students to use the higher cognitive learning levels of analysis, evaluation, and application of **Bloom's taxonomy**, thus forcing them to put together an argument. In this book, the texts for discussion are excerpts from a draft chapter of a thesis or a section of a thesis chapter *before* it is submitted for examination. The rationale for using unexamined drafts is that they contain unedited examples of writing pitfalls that a student can learn from. The examiner's comments are included to act as a 'key' to guide students in critiquing the texts provided for discussion.

Individually and independently, the student analyses and evaluates the text's strong and weak aspects and provides reasons to support their judgements and suggestions for improving the text. This step is valuable and relevant for students studying independently, since they may not be able to participate in class-based discussions unless the teaching is in a virtual environment. In the classroom setting, lecturers can adapt the discussion-based exercises for use in small group or whole-class work. Once students have completed the exercise individually, groups of three or four students can discuss a specific question or topic together, sharing their ideas and assessments of the text. The group discussion encourages participation from all students.

Group discussions can be based on various sources, such as assignments from the week's reading, class lectures, or additional evidence that supports students' views and suggestions. These discussions provide students with an opportunity to re-examine and apply what they have learned to monitor their progress in writing their thesis. By engaging in group discussions, students can explore multiple viewpoints, develop critical thinking skills, and gain a deeper understanding of the topic.

## The lecturer's use of the discussion exercises

The lecturer can initiate discussions about the real-example texts, with a prompt that ensures the students understand the lecturer's expectations of what they are tasked to do. The basis for the discussion, for example, may be relevant to something that has arisen in class, or from an assignment or a lecture, or simply be an extract from the real-example text. The lecturer can point students to a specific piece of evidence or a quote in the real-example text that is related to this discussion or to one of examiner's comments, which are listed at the end of each exercise. The lecturer can ask the students to examine the selected text, paraphrase it, and state their understanding of the concept, or what interpretations or inferences they make about the quote or comment.

Then, looking at the text, the students can be asked whether they think these comments apply to the text or quote (Yes/No). The lecturer can ask students to defend their yes/no response, giving them clear directions for defending or explaining their answers, such as *'Why or why not?'*. Next, the students discuss how they can improve the text or the different ways the text might have been presented/articulated by providing their own version of the text. Finally, the lecturer can ask the students whether they have any other comments about issues that were not captured by the examiner's comments. If students respond with brief answers, the lecturer can follow up or prompt them with questions such as *'Can you tell me more?'*, *'Why do you say that?'*, or *'How did you come to that conclusion?'*.

## Practical suggestions and examples

The book presents practical examples for writing the various sections of all the required chapters in your thesis. These examples provide valuable tips and illustrations that strengthen the writing of actual thesis chapters.

## Common pitfalls

The book identifies common pitfalls and mistakes that students make when writing each chapter of their thesis. By reviewing the list of pitfalls, students can correct mistakes that undermine the quality of their work. This will help them to produce a high-quality thesis that meets academic standards.

## Checklist

Checklists offer students a way to organise their thesis, gauge their progress, and assess whether they have met all the requirements of the thesis. The checklist used in the final chapter of this book is derived from a comprehensive source that enables students to reflect and self-critique their theses. It is available online and can be downloaded for free.

## Suggestions for further reading

Each chapter ends with a selection of references for further reading. Brief synopses of each text are provided. These resources are helpful to the reader, providing additional information on the subject matter of the chapter.

# The organisation of the book

This book is divided into two parts. Part I has three chapters that act as an *aide-mémoire* for reference while writing the actual thesis chapters.

Chapter 1, 'Enhancing Academic Writing', suggests ways to improve your writing style for clear communication. It provides an overview of the critical issues to consider in academic writing. These issues include grammatical accuracy, sentence structure, conciseness, linking sentences, and continuity in representing ideas. The chapter also considers paragraph structure, linking paragraphs, and coherence and flow between chapters.

Chapter 2, 'Developing an Academic Argument', introduces the different writing genres in academic writing and how they can be applied in thesis chapters. It offers practical suggestions to develop arguments commonly used in theses.

Chapter 3, 'Critical Review of the Literature and Building a Theoretical Framework', illustrates ways of critically reviewing the literature to identify gaps in knowledge, and offers tips on developing a theoretical framework that guides the research and demonstrates how literature is integrated into the various chapters of the thesis.

Part II of the book focuses on how to write the six chapters of the thesis.

Chapter 4, 'Writing the Introduction Chapter', presents information on introducing the research problem identified from the critical literature review and its significance. It shows how to write the purpose statement and a problem statement.

Chapter 5, 'Writing the Literature Review', discusses how to present synthesised information from the critical review literature, including the theoretical framework. It illustrates how to organise the literature review, and explain its scope, trends, and concerns, as well as how your research adds to the literature.

Chapter 6, 'Writing the Methodology Chapter', discusses various research designs and methods (quantitative, qualitative, and mixed methods) that can be used in your research and how to present them. It also discusses ethical considerations and writing about the limitations of the methodology.

Chapter 7, 'Writing the Results Chapter', describes ways to present quantitative statistical data and qualitative findings from the data collected in the methodology chapter. It focuses on reporting descriptive statistics and correlations and regressions in quantitative methods. It also demonstrates how non-textual formats can be used to summarise results.

Chapter 8, 'Writing the Discussion Chapter', demonstrates how to present a summary and interpretation of the results. It explains how the results add to the knowledge of previous studies and how they can be generalised to other contexts. It includes writing about the limitations of your research (e.g., limited sample size).

Chapter 9, 'Writing the Conclusion and Recommendations Chapter', shows how to present the thesis's contribution to research, indicating what the research achieved and explaining how it brings new understanding to the research problem. It offers ways to convey the research implications for theory, practice, and policy, and to set out future research directions.

Chapter 10, 'Finalising the Thesis', focuses on the final processes that need to be done before submitting the thesis for examination. It includes sections on writing the title and abstract, and compiling tables of contents, tables and figures, abbreviations, etc. It stresses the importance of editing for clarity, language, and style, as well as checking and formatting references, and ends with a checklist to ensure nothing is overlooked.

# PREPARING TO WRITE YOUR THESIS

# 1

# Enhancing Academic Writing

This chapter provides an overview of the crucial issues to consider while writing one's thesis. First, the chapter explicitly covers the grammatical accuracy needed in **academic writing**. It emphasises sentence structure, conciseness, linking, and continuity. Next, the chapter considers the paragraph structure and, finally, it looks at coherence and flow between chapters.

Scientists use academic writing to communicate highly scientific information from their research to others. In addition, academic writing is used in scholarly publications and at universities. For example, a university student uses academic writing in essays, research papers, research proposals, and theses or dissertations. All these documents should be well structured and written in language that communicates clearly.

Research from different contexts and across various universities, both at home and abroad, shows that students face challenges in producing academic writing, especially in English, which may not be their first language but which has emerged as the lingua franca for most academic discourse. This challenge starts from the proposal writing stage and persists to thesis writing (Ali Al-Khairy, 2013; Cumming, Lai, & Cho, 2016; Hei & David, 2015; Komba, 2015; Manchishi, Ndhlovu, & Mwanza, 2015; Qasem & Zayid, 2019; Yeh, 2010). The problem of low English proficiency, such as poor grammar and an inadequate vocabulary, has been shown to negatively affect student writing. While the abundance of software that is available to assist in this issue might indicate that this is not a significant issue, it does not lessen the critical challenge of developing confidence in conveying an academic voice and the difficulty in organising and expressing ideas.

The empirical literature suggests that traditional academic writing techniques may not adequately address postgraduate needs in research writing. Students are rarely offered systematic instruction in high-level academic writing, which is the most pressing need during thesis writing. Courses designed for assisting in academic writing were shown to be inadequate, and students are left to grope around for ways to survive the research writing task (Yeh, 2010). Furthermore, many books that could supplement universities' efforts in this area focus on English writing and include complicated terminologies, English jargon, colloquialism, and conversational language that is difficult to comprehend, especially for students whose native language is not English (Qasem & Zayid, 2019). In the remainder of this chapter, we will cover some of the basics that are needed in good academic writing.

# Grammatical accuracy

## Word-level grammar

Grammar is the way words are arranged to construct proper sentences. This section explicitly covers the grammatical accuracy needed in academic writing, especially in writing a thesis and academic papers. The writing should be error-free in terms of grammar, punctuation, and spelling. In other words, it should be grammatically accurate to influence the readers' impression of the thesis. Sloppy presentation, poor spelling, and grammatical errors distract the examiner's concentration on the actual content, questioning the student's competence and the quality of the thesis.

Word-level grammar explains how to use verbs and tenses (both passive and active voice), adverbs, nouns, and first-person pronouns, while sentence-level grammar covers words, phrases, and clauses.

## Active and passive verbs

In academic writing, you use your voice to show the reader what you are thinking, your views, and how you have engaged critically with the topic being discussed.

The subject acts in sentences written in the active voice, while in a sentence written in the passive voice, the subject receives the action. In other words, passive voice emphasises the action rather than the actor. Active verbs are recommended over passive verbs in academic writing as active verbs are more direct and less wordy. If you want to emphasise what is occurring or the action rather than who is doing it, you can use the passive voice.

The voice used in academic writing depends on the university department or disciplinary area. Some traditions (such as the more positivist methodologies) value writing that is more objective, where the student's voice does not stand out. In contrast, other disciplines, such as anthropology, demand a writing style that is more expressive and allows more room for individual observations.

---

## Example: Active and passive voice

Active: Researchers showed that high blood cholesterol could cause heart attacks.

Passive: It was established that heart attacks could be caused by high blood cholesterol.

---

## The subject–verb agreement

The subject and the verb need to agree because subject–verb agreement unites a sentence. The subject and verb should be placed close together at the beginning of the sentence to make it easier for readers to follow the ideas. Do not insert extra words or phrases to describe the subject between the subject and verb.

---

## Example: Subject–verb agreement

Subject–verb disagreement: The patient's blood sugar levels [subject/the actor] taken six hours after the insulin injection [extra words] decreased [verb] by 50%.

Subject–verb agreement: The patient's blood sugar levels [subject/the actor] had decreased [verb] by 50% six hours after the insulin injection [extra words].

---

## Use of tenses in academic writing in chapters

This section explains how tenses are explicitly used in thesis chapters. You should be consistent in the use of tenses. For example, use the same tense within the same paragraph or in adjacent paragraphs of a document. Furthermore, past tense is used to recount past events, such as the study's purpose, literature review, methodology chapters, and the results chapter.

## Example: Past tense

Our study aimed to test approaches that can be used to improve ARV medication adherence by persons living with HIV/AIDS. [purpose] Studies conducted by Demartoto & Adriani (2016) showed a relationship between the perceived seriousness of the disease and compliance with medication. [literature review] We used an analytical research design to collect data from 36 randomly selected patients in a health facility. [methodology] These results indicated a significant negative correlation between the perception of the seriousness of the disease and antiretroviral therapy adherence. [results]

The present tense states the research objectives, discusses the results' implications, and presents conclusions.

## Example: Present tense

This study investigates perceptions about the severity of disease progression and its influence on adherence to antiretroviral (ARV) medication. [objective] The results support Safri, Sukartini, and Ulfiana's (2013) study, which showed that perceived seriousness significantly affects compliance to take medication. [implications] Therefore, perception of the seriousness of the disease is an influential factor in medication adherence. [conclusion]

The present perfect tense describes something that began in the past and continues to the present, and is appropriate for literature reviews and descriptions of a procedure if the discussion is on past events.

## Example: Present perfect tense

Several cohort studies conducted over several years have confirmed the benefits of medication in improving the quality of life of people living with HIV/AIDS (Del Romero et al., 2010; Musicco et al., 1994).

The future tense describes how you intend to accomplish your research in the future. It is used in the proposals and methodology chapter.

> ## Example: Future tense
>
> Using random sampling, we shall enrol HIV/AIDs patients attending a comprehensive care unit at the health facility who were over 18 years and not critically ill. [proposal stage]

## Pronouns

Pronouns are words that stand in for nouns and can refer to specific people and things (e.g., I, you, it, him, their, this) or to non-specific people and things (e.g., anybody, one, some, each). First-person pronouns (I, we) may be used in academic writing, depending on your field, but second-person pronouns are best avoided. You can avoid using second-person pronouns (you, yours) in your academic writing by using 'one' instead of 'you' and 'one's' instead of 'yours'. For example: 'You should use your medicines as directed' is stated as 'One should use one's medication as directed.'

Avoid pronouns such as 'this', 'that', 'these', and 'those' when referring to someone or something in the previous sentence. Instead, repeat the noun, such as 'this test', 'that trial', 'these participants', and 'those reports'. This approach avoids introducing ambiguity in your text. Likewise, avoid ambiguity by using a personal pronoun rather than the third person. For example, instead of saying 'the literature being reviewed', replace it with 'the authors reviewing the literature'.

Avoid using too many prepositional phrases, such as 'there is ...' and 'there are ...', because they obscure the main subject and action in a sentence.

In addition to following grammar rules, it is important to consistently apply conventions regarding writing numbers, introducing abbreviations, capitalising terms and headings, and spelling and punctuation used in UK and US English.

## Sentence-level structure

This section focuses on the sentence (grammar and sentence structure) as the basic unit of academic writing. A sentence can be either a simple, compound, or complex sentence. Simple sentences have three parts, usually in this order: a subject (someone or something acting, a noun or a pronoun), a verb (an action word or a state-of-being word, such as 'to be' or 'to feel'), and words to complete the thought.

## Example: Simple sentence

The evidence in this study [subject] indicates [verb] a shortage of drugs in the facility [completes the thought].

A compound sentence has two connected thoughts of equal importance. Each clause has equal weight in terms of ideas, which are equally important. A comma and a linking word, such as 'and', 'but', or 'or' (conjunctions), join the clauses to form the sentence.

## Example: Compound sentence

The evidence [subject] of this study indicates [verb] a shortage of drugs in the facility, but [a comma and a linking word] the findings were insufficient to conclude that policy reform is needed [complete the thought].

A complex sentence has a complete base but adds additional information, which can be placed in brackets or separated with other punctuation, such as commas. In a complex sentence, the different elements of the sentence cannot stand alone.

## Example: Complex sentence

The evidence [subject] of this study (which was quantitative) [additional information] indicates [verb] the shortage of drugs was insufficient to conclude that policy reform is needed [complete the thought].

The average number of words per sentence can range from 8 for a very easy and simple sentence to 20 for a complex or compound sentence. However, these thresholds are guidelines, not set limits. Sentences with more than 30 words are often difficult to follow and confuse the reader. Therefore, break long sentences into multiple sentences to ensure readability and comprehension. A mix of short and long sentences maintains interest and comprehension; thus, long sentences may be necessary occasionally. Long sentences also help to avoid monotony. Short sentences (not more than 25 words) are easier to comprehend than long ones. Therefore, vary sentence lengths to help readers maintain interest and comprehension. Direct, declarative sentences with simple, common words are usually the best.

## Conciseness

Conciseness is essential in academic writing. Conciseness, which is the opposite of wordiness, helps to clarify sentences. Make sentences concise by eliminating redundant words (wordiness), overuse of the passive voice, and combining too many ideas into one long sentence. Use a new sentence for each new idea. Jargon or specialist language makes writing more concise and accurate but generally targets an academic audience that is familiar with the terminology. Also, avoid inflated phrases that use several words where just one or two are sufficient. For example, 'Age appears to have a consequence [inflated] on adherence to medication' can be simply expressed as 'Age appears to affect adherence to medication'. Avoid redundancies, which occur when the same idea is expressed twice, and use only essential words to convey meaning. For example, avoid saying 'compete with each other' instead of 'competing', 'due to the fact that' instead of 'because' or 'since', and 'in connection with' instead of 'about'.

Wordiness uses too many words to make a point, obscures main points, and impedes a grasp of ideas.

---

### Examples: Wordiness

Wordy sentence: I will now begin this section by making a number of observations concerning antiretroviral medication issues.

Concise sentence: I begin by making several observations about antiretroviral medication.

---

Most writing software can give alternative words or phrases to prevent wordiness.

## Punctuation and transitioning

This section illustrates how punctuation marks and transitional words contribute to continuity and showing the relationship between ideas.

For good academic writing, you should be fully aware of how punctuation is used in sentences.

## Punctuation

Punctuation primarily indicates pauses in thought and emphasises specific ideas or thoughts, making writing straightforward and understandable for readers. In addition, punctuation marks show continuity in the presentation of ideas, and they help to strengthen arguments made in the text. Punctuation marks include abbreviations, apostrophes, brackets, capital letters, colons, commas, dashes, ellipses, exclamation marks, hyphens, italics, underlining, parentheses, quotation marks, and semi-colons. The most common punctuation marks are the period, comma, and semi-colon.

**Commas** [,] mark pauses between clauses within a sentence or are used to separate three or more items in a list. Commas are placed around subordinate clauses that add extra information to a sentence. For example:

Jansen, a nutritionist, was a great scientist.

More books, journals, and student theses need to be stocked in the library.

**Semi-colons** [;] represent a pause and are more distinctive than a comma. The semi-colon is used to separate the independent clauses of a compound sentence. It uses coordinating conjunction, such as 'and', 'or', 'for', 'so', and 'yet'. The clause before and after the semi-colon should be independent. In other words, a semi-colon connects extra independent parts of a sentence. For example:

The health research conference is top-rated; researchers from all over the globe attend it each year.

A semi-colon is also used in lists that already have commas. For example:

Next, the reader presents the author's purpose, rationale and context for the study; the research methodology and data-gathering procedures; and the findings of the research.

**Colons** [:] introduce elements of lists. The colon is used when two related clauses follow a sequence of thought. For example:

There are three types of Rhetorical appeals: Ethos, Pathos, and Logos.

A colon can also be used to connect two sentences when the second sentence summarises, improves, or explains the first. Both sentences should be complete. Colons should not be used this way too frequently as they can interrupt the flow of the writing. For example:

> The study focused on four demographic variables: age, sex, marital status, and occupation.

**Capital letters** are used to start a sentence. They are also used when the previous sentence ends with a question mark or an exclamation mark, or if the sentence ends with a clause in parentheses (brackets).

**Exclamation marks** [!] show surprise or excitement at the end of a sentence. The use of exclamation marks is not recommended in academic writing.

**Periods**, or **full stops** [.], are used to indicate the end of a sentence. They are placed at the end of an abbreviated word (e.g., Prof.), or after certain abbreviations of time (e.g., 5:00 p.m.). The most used abbreviation forms in science are 'et al.', and 'etc.', which stands for 'et cetera'. Three periods in a row are called an ellipsis, which indicates that entire words or complete subordinate clauses have been cut out of a quote.

**Question marks** [?] are used at the end of a sentence to show a direct question. For example:

> What is the topic of your thesis?

**Apostrophes** ['] are used to show ownership of something. If the 'owning' noun is singular, the apostrophe comes before the 's' (e.g., 'the researcher's findings'), but if there is more than one 'owning' subject, such as several researchers, the apostrophe is placed after the 's' (e.g., 'the researchers' findings'). An apostrophe is also used to show that letters have been left out of a word (e.g., 'can't' instead of 'cannot'). These are called contractions. It is best to avoid contractions in academic writing.

**Brackets** [( )], also called parentheses, add information to a sentence when the sentence can still make sense without the added information. The added information brings something extra or interesting to the sentence. For example:

> Students should (intentionally) avoid grammatical errors in their essays.

**Dashes** [–] are also an indicator of additional information. A dash can indicate a pause, especially for effect at the end of a sentence. They can also be used instead of brackets. A dash used before a phrase sum-marises the idea of a sentence. For example:

Beliefs and motivation – these are concepts used to define perceived behavioural control.

Subjective dashes used before and after a phrase or list add extra infor-mation in the middle of a sentence. For example:

Conceptual frameworks define the concepts – building blocks – of a theory.

**Hyphens** [-] are used to join two words that together form one idea (e.g., 'health-related' or 'self-confidence'). They are also used to join prefixes to terms (e.g., 'non-controlled environment'), and when writing com-pound numbers (e.g., 'one-eighth').

**Quotation marks** ['...'] are used to mark the beginning and end of a phrase to show that the text is taken from another source and you are repeating the exact words used by the original writer. Punctuation is placed after the closing quotation mark if it is not part of the quoted matter. For example:

Alison defined critical review as 'developing an argument designed to convince a particular audience'. She found that 'The level of sugar intake is not related to hyperactivity in children'.

---

### Example: Full stops, commas, semi-colons, and colons

A patient needs to adhere to medication; [semi-colon] otherwise, [comma] they risk developing complications. To collect information on adherence and com-plication, we used a questionnaire that consisted of three parts: [colon] prescriptions, clinical conditions, and blood screening [commas marking a list].

---

## Transitioning

Apart from using punctuation, another way to achieve continuity is through transition words that show the relationships between ideas. Transition words usually appear at the start of a new sentence or clause (followed by a comma). They express how this sentence or clause relates to the previous one. However, transition words can also appear in the middle of a clause.

Transition words and phrases link or connect different ideas in the sentences. To ensure continuity, present ideas through transition words which maintain the flow of thought and link together different ideas in the text to help the reader understand the logic of the thesis. You need to choose a word or phrase to match the logic of the relationship or connection you are making. For example, a *logical relationship* uses words such as 'but', 'consequently', 'conversely', 'even so', 'however', 'nevertheless', 'therefore', and 'thus'. Words such as 'next', 'after', 'while', and 'since' are used for time links. Words used for cause and effect are: 'therefore', 'similarly', and 'moreover'. If you want to give another example to make the same point, you can use words that imply emphasis or similarity, for example, 'nevertheless', 'furthermore', 'indeed', and 'also'.

---

## Example: Transition words in a paragraph

Studies conducted in France (a developed country) indicated a correlation between medication adherence and barriers to accessing treatment. Conversely, [link] we conducted a comparable study in Kenya (a developing country). However, our study showed no correlation between medication adherence and barriers to treatment. Therefore, evidence on the perception of barriers and adherence remains inconclusive.

---

# Paragraphing

This section focuses on developing a paragraph structure. A paragraph comprises a group of connected sentences that support one main idea or a 'controlling idea', irrespective of its length. Information in each paragraph is connected to the ideas before and after a paragraph. Internal paragraph transition means moving from one sentence to the next within paragraphs. Words can indicate the relationship between different sentences; for example, 'because' indicates a reason is coming next, while 'for example' indicates that an example will follow.

There are no set rules for the length of paragraphs, but the general guideline is that a paragraph should have a minimum of two or three sentences and a maximum of five or six sentences, and be between 100 and 200 words long, but should not exceed 500 words. A paragraph cannot consist of only one sentence. Readers are more responsive to shorter paragraphs and will understand the document better if paragraphs are concise. Conversely, paragraphs that are too long are likely to distract the reader's attention. Long paragraphs can be split into two or more paragraphs, each with only one main idea, using a logical place to break them.

If a paragraph shifts to a different aspect of the same subject, use transition words to connect the paragraphs. Highlight differences or conflicts using words such as 'in contrast', 'however', 'yet', and 'on the other hand'. Expand on ideas in the previous paragraph using words like 'in addition' and 'furthermore'

A paragraph starts with an opening, also called the topic sentence(s), which indicates the contents of the paragraph and ends with a concluding sentence. A good topic sentence should be specific enough to give a clear sense of what to expect from each paragraph's content. The topic sentence leads to a few sentences that further develop and support it. All sentences following the topic sentence expand or explain the topic sentence with a statistic or example(s). Make sure every sentence refers to or reinforces the topic sentence. After expanding the main idea, you can then present supporting evidence that supports the main point.

Although topic sentences are usually placed at the start of a paragraph, they can sometimes come later, for instance, when indicating a change of direction in the paragraph's argument. Topic sentences are also used to transition smoothly between paragraphs to show the connections between ideas. Sometimes topic sentences are used to introduce several paragraphs. In this case, start with a transition sentence summarising the paragraphs.

The concluding sentence in a paragraph draws together or wraps up the paragraph by summarising the information that elaborates the main idea. You can restate words or phrases from the topic sentence using different sentence structures. End the paragraph with a transitional hook that ties to the following paragraph or section. Repeat this process for all the other paragraphs until all the evidence is covered. A new paragraph starts when a new idea is introduced. In a thesis, paragraphs are arranged logically around thematic or sub-thematic section headings or sub-headings.

## Example: A paragraph

Adherence to ARV medication of ≥95% 'suppresses the replication of HIV and prevents the infection's progression to acquired immunodeficiency syndrome (AIDS). [topic sentence] HIV/AIDS is a lifelong condition that requires strict adherence requirements. These requirements mean taking all the medicines as prescribed, in the correct dose and quantity, at the right time through the correct route while observing dietary restrictions (Sahay et al., 2011). [explanation] Poor medication adherence has been associated with less effective viral suppression, drug resistance and reduced survival (Bangsberg et al. 2006; Nachega et al. 2007). [evidence] However, although complex, and many patients find it challenging to achieve the recommended adherence levels. [summary and transition into the next paragraph] Medication adherence effectively delays the progression of HIV/AIDS.

# Connecting chapters

Students face challenges connecting chapters and maintaining a coherent common thread while writing theses. This section illustrates how to connect chapters to achieve a coherent and logical flow. A logical flow helps the reader to move from one sentence to the next, one paragraph to another, and one chapter to the next. Thus, cohesion should begin from the sentences in the paragraphs that make up the chapters. Examiners look for a well-structured, coherently written, and logically arranged thesis that follows a 'common theme'. They scrutinise whether the thesis is written as a coherent whole or is merely a collection of chapters.

The first paragraph at the beginning of each chapter's introduction is a recap of the previous chapter. It is followed by introducing the current chapter's critical message or purpose. The chapter ends with a brief concluding paragraph that summarises the chapter's primary information or points. In other words, it pulls the chapter's key points together and shows the chapter's contribution to the thesis. Finally, the last sentence of the concluding paragraph has a transitional hook that ties into the subsequent chapter.

Professor Pat Thomson of the University of Nottingham, UK (Thomson, 2014), gives a valuable guide on connecting chapter introductions through a simple **link, focus, and overview frame**. The frame enables the reader to see coherence and flow between chapters by linking the previous chapter's contents to the current chapter.

The next example demonstrates how to connect chapters using Professor Thomson's frame. The first paragraph of the chapter recaps the previous chapter. The second paragraph focuses on the content and significance of the current chapter. The third paragraph outlines how one will achieve the aim in the previous paragraph. It is a statement of the contents of the chapter in the order that the reader will encounter them, not simply stated as topics but demonstrating how they build the internal chapter.

---

### Example: Connecting chapters

In the previous chapter, I focused on the general characteristics of academic writing. I provided skills to improve academic writing, including grammatical accuracy, organisation, and ideas. [link]

This chapter further discusses argumentation, which is the most critical aspect of academic writing in thesis writing. Finally, the chapter offers practical suggestions and explanations for developing arguments and explains how the argument runs through chapters. [focus]

I begin by presenting different writing genres in chapters and offer practical suggestions and explanations for developing the Rogerian and Toulmin arguments. I go further to explain how these arguments run through the chapters. Finally, I demonstrate how to write a persuasive thesis statement. [overview]

---

## Plagiarism and research integrity in academic writing

Plagiarism is a misdemeanour in academic writing that involves copying sections of text from a source without indicating it is a quotation or supplying a proper citation. Plagiarism is considered academic dishonesty and a publishing crime. It presents another author's original work, words or ideas, language, thoughts, or expressions as your own work without acknowledgement. Copying other people's work is regarded as a breach of ethical standards regardless of the source of published or unpublished material, whether in manuscript, printed, or electronic form. Universities and lecturers treat plagiarism cases seriously. To avoid plagiarism, you must acquaint yourself with the policies, guidelines, and code of conduct relating to plagiarism and research integrity that apply to your discipline and institution.

This section presents some critical forms of plagiarism that are often committed by students when writing theses. These types include direct plagiarism, copying and pasting, paraphrasing, and source-based plagiarism.

Direct plagiarism is the most typical form of plagiarism, when words, sentences, phrases, whole essays, entire research papers, or other students' work or theses are directly copied without citations or crediting the source. Other direct plagiarism includes reprinting diagrams, illustrations, charts, pictures, or other visual materials, including reusing or reposting any electronically available media, such as images, audio, or video, without attributing the source. Penalties for direct plagiarism can be severe and include dismissal from an institution.

The second form of plagiarism is copying and pasting sections of other people's writing without citing them as the source or improperly citing the source, which is considered content theft. If you do want to reproduce an author's exact words in your text, signal it as a direct quote by using double ("…") or single ('…') quote marks around the quotation. If you insert your own words into a direct quotation or change anything in that quotation, indicate this by placing square brackets [ ] around the word(s) you have inserted or changed. If, for example, words are misspelt in the text, place [sic] after the misspelt or otherwise seemingly incorrect word or expression. 'Sic' communicates that 'this is how it appeared in the source'. Cite the author and publication year next to the quotation, and include the full reference entry in your references section.

A third common form of plagiarism is when a researcher paraphrases other people's work without proper citation. Grey areas in plagiarism include using the words of a source too closely when paraphrasing (where you should have used quotation marks), using someone's ideas without citing them, or changing only a few words from the source when summarising or paraphrasing. Furthermore, changing the sentence structure or using synonyms is still plagiarism. It is advised that you use the original quote and quotation marks instead of paraphrasing too closely. Reproducing your own writing by summarising or reporting on past work instead of writing new text on the same topic is referred to as self-plagiarism, and, whether intentional or not, is just as detrimental as stealing from others. The rule is always to rewrite.

The fourth form of plagiarism is source-based plagiarism. It is when the researcher has more than one source of information but only references one source and leaves out the others. Source-based plagiarism also includes quoting non-existent or incorrect sources, fabricating or manufacturing information such as study findings, or presenting misleading statistics.

Fortunately, multiple plagiarism checking tools are available and they can identify if text is plagiarised. These software options include checking for structure, synonyms, and even paraphrasing.

# Conclusion

Chapter 1 has addressed the many challenges that students face in writing English and argues that most of the current literature does not adequately address students' needs in academic writing. The development of an **academic argument**, which is the most crucial part of thesis writing, is discussed in Chapter 2.

---

## Exercise: Critiquing a text

### Instructions

Discuss to what extent the examiner's comments apply to this text, supporting your argument with examples of words, phrases, or sentences from the text. (Refer to the section on Pedagogical features — 'Discussion-based exercises' — in the Introduction of this book for more details on completing this exercise.)

### Text: Treatment of HIV/AIDS

Infection with Human Immunodeficiency Virus (HIV) leads to the destruction of immunity, which leads to increased morbidity and mortality rates among People Living with HIV/AIDS (PLWHA). Antiretroviral (ARV) drugs suppress the replication of HIV and prevent the progression of the infection to acquired immunodeficiency syndrome (AIDS) and death.

Treatment of HIV/AIDS with antiretroviral drugs became available in the early 1990s globally, but most patients developed resistance and became ill or died. A breakthrough occurred with the introduction of effective combination therapy of ARVs drugs, which dramatically improved morbidity, mortality, and quality of life among PLWHA hence transforming HIV from a terminal illness to a manageable chronic disease. Although ARVs are not a cure for HIV, they are very effective in controlling the virus and can even reduce the level of the virus to a point where it is no longer possible to detect any in the blood. Those patients who develop resistance make treatment with ARVs difficult because they may transmit the drug-resistant virus, which requires second-line treatment, which is more expensive, have a range of side effects. The decision to change a person from first-line to second-line remains challenging, especially if viral load testing equipment is not available. If too many patients progress to second-line

---

therapy, the increased costs involved will limit access to treatment for many people who would have benefited from first-line therapy. Also, Treatment resistance can occur for an entire class of ARV drugs rendering them ineffective, and lastly, the resistant viral strain of HIV can be transmitted to newly infected individuals who will have fewer effective treatment options from the start of their HIV infections.

Therefore, every effort should be made to ensure patients achieve a high level of adherence (>95%) to ARVs treatment to delay the emergence of drug-resistant, ensure cost-effectiveness in ARV access, and enable individuals to be treated for many years with first-line ARVs.

This increases their risk of getting opportunistic infections and developing drug resistance, leading to second-line regimens, which are costly, not readily available, and have more side effects.

**Examiner's comments**

- There are numerous presentation errors, including grammatical, spelling, formatting, and typographical.
- It is difficult to understand what is being presented as the writing lacks clarity, and sentences are not concise.
- There are too many wordy sentences, and paragraphs are hard to follow as they do not flow logically.
- There are several flow issues, the sentences within the paragraphs are not correctly linked, and there is no transitioning in the paragraphing.
- The text ends abruptly with no attempt to summarise it.
- The text does not match the title of the topic.
- The candidate's style and language are of a high standard, and the presentation is grammatically sound and free from plagiarism.
- The text is well written, with very few clerical errors, and the style and layout are good.

# Further reading

Bastola, G. K. (2018). Teaching a five-paragraph essay. *Journal of NELTA*, 23(1–2), 174–178. https://doi.org/10.3126/nelta.v23i1-2.23365

This article helps students to write paragraphs with a beginning, middle, and end. It gives an example of a five-paragraph essay. The first paragraph is an introduction, followed by three paragraphs of the essay's body. Finally, the fifth paragraph is the Conclusion. It also incorporates the importance of the thesis statement.

Bloch, J. (2012). *Plagiarism, Intellectual Property and the Teaching of L2 Writing.* (Series: New perspectives on language and education.) Bristol: Multilingual Matters.

This book discusses the current and historical relationship between plagiarism and intellectual property law and how they can be forthrightly taught in an academic writing classroom.

Davies, P. (1999). Paragraphs. In *70 Activities for Tutor Groups.* Abingdon: Routledge. https://doi.org/10.4324/9781315264080

This book describes the basic rule of thumb of paragraphing: one idea to one paragraph and transitions to a new idea.

Evans, D., Gruba, P., & Zobel, J. (2014). *How to Write a Better Thesis.* New York: Springer. https://doi.org/10.1007/978-3-319-04286-2

The book's emphasis is firmly on a clear and logical structure, which is the key to a good thesis. It gives concrete examples of common structural problems, including ways to avoid them, and offers a checklist to help stay on track.

Gilmore, J., Strickland, D., Timmerman, B., Maher, M., & Feldon, D. (2010). Weeds in the flower garden: An exploration of plagiarism in graduate students' research proposals and its connection to enculturation, ESL, and contextual factors. *International Journal for Educational Integrity, 6*(1), 13–28. https://doi.org/10.21913/ijei.v6i1.673

This study discusses the rates and potential causes of plagiarism and offers solutions to address plagiarism among the ESL population in Master's and doctoral programmes. Participants plagiarised, in part, because they lacked an awareness of the role of primary literature in the research process. The study found that plagiarism was more common among research participants who had English as a Second Language (ESL) .

Glasman-Deal, H. (2009). Unit 4: Writing the Discussion/Conclusion. In *Science Research Writing for Non-Native Speakers of English.* London: Imperial College Press. https://doi.org/10.1142/p605

This book provides a step-by-step guide for structuring the various sections or chapters of a research paper or thesis. In addition, it has many useful tables with frequently-used phrases in academic writing.

Gopen, G. D., & Swan, J. A. (1990). The science of scientific writing. *American Scientist.* Retrieved from https://cseweb.ucsd.edu/~swanson/papers/science-of-writing.pdf

This paper presents a methodology for improving the quality of scientific writing by understanding the expectations of readers. It outlines seven structural principles for making scientific writing more comprehensible to readers.

Hyland, K., & Shaw, P. (Eds) (2016). *The Routledge Handbook of English for Academic Purposes*. Abingdon: Routledge. https://doi.org/10.4324/9781 315657455

This handbook provides an accessible, comprehensive introduction to English for Academic Purposes (EAP), covering the main theories, concepts, contexts, and applications of applied linguistics and language skills. It is an essential reference for advanced undergraduate and postgraduates.

McGee, I. (2017). Paragraphing beliefs, pedagogy, and practice: Omani TESOL teacher attempts to hold it all together. *International Journal of Applied Linguistics*, 27(2), 383–405. https://doi.org/10.1111/ijal.12136

This book contains suggestions on paragraphing for the TESOL (Teachers of English to Speakers of Other Languages) community. The author provides pedagogical guidance on paragraphs by investigating the writing and beliefs of Omani teachers.

Swales, J., & Feak, C. (2012). *Academic Writing for Graduate Students* (3rd edition). Ann Arbor, MI: University of Michigan Press. https://doi.org/10.3998/mpub.2173936

This textbook is designed to help non-native speakers of English with their academic writing. The book helps students to tailor their writing for their academic genre and target audience.

Sword, H. (2012). *Stylish Academic Writing*. Cambridge, MA: Harvard University Press.

Sword's analysis of peer-reviewed articles covers a wide range of fields. It explores writing practices in academia and provides tips on how to make writing more accessible to larger audiences.

Thody, A. (2013). *Writing and Presenting Research*. London: Sage.

This book is an invaluable introductory guide on how to report research. It is easy to follow and has checklists, style variations, examples, and reflection points.

Thomson, P. (2014). connecting chapters/chapter introductions. *patter*. https://patthomson.net/2014/01/16/connecting-chapterschapter-introductions/

Students' primary challenge when writing a thesis is connecting one chapter to another. Thomson gives a valuable guide on connecting chapter introductions through a simple framework – link, focus, and overview.

University of Chicago (2017). *Chicago Manual of Style* (17th edition). Chicago, IL: University of Chicago Press.

This book is a style guide for American English which covers grammar, usage, citations, document preparation, and formatting.

Wallace, M., & Wray, A. (2016). *Critical Reading and Writing for Postgraduates*. London: Sage.

The book focuses on the critical reading process. The authors show postgraduate students and early-career academics how to read and write critically.

Wallwork, A. (2011). *English for Writing Research Papers*. New York: Springer. https://doi.org/10.1007/978-1-4419-7922-3

This guide is based on a study of referees of journal editors of papers written by non-native English speakers, based on abstracts by PhD students, and teaching hours of teaching researchers. It gives reasons why articles written by non-native researchers are rejected because of problems with English usage.

Washington University. (2014). Paragraph Development. *Notes*. Available at https://faculty.washington.edu/ezent/impd.htm

This guide provides advice on developing and organising a research paper in the social sciences.

# 2

# Developing an Academic Argument

Chapter 1 provided skills to improve academic writing. This chapter introduces types of **writing genres** and offers practical suggestions and explanations for developing arguments commonly used in theses – these arguments include Rogerian and Toulmin arguments. The chapter further illustrates how to mix different genres in chapters. Other writing genres, such as those used in journalism, essays, and blogs, are not the book's focus as they are not appropriate for academic writing.

## Types of writing genre

A thesis comprises multiple genres, including descriptive writing, arguments, and accounts: the argument is the dominant genre. This section describes different writing genres and how they are used in the specific thesis chapters. Descriptive writing presents the situation as it stands, without any analysis or argument – it helps set the background within which an argument can be developed.

An account is a text that presents what happened, retells an event or an experience, or describes what others did. Two types of accounts that occur regularly in scholarly texts are personal accounts and factual accounts. In personal accounts, the author retells events/activities they have been involved in. On the other hand, a factual account recalls details of a particular event or sequence of events. It does not indicate any analysis, evaluation, or critique of the components. Accounts help to clarify which details to include in the discussion, but they do not substitute for the explanation, critique, or argument (Ramage, Bean, & Johnson, 2015).

An argument in a thesis challenges a broadly accepted assumption by raising a question or a hypothesis, or extending previous knowledge in some way. The argument is described in more detail in the following section as it is the dominant genre in a thesis.

## Mixing genres in the chapters

The different chapters of the thesis will use mixed genres. For example, the introduction chapter provides an account and summary of the topic and presents the background of the problem. It shows why the problem is significant and needs to be studied (argument). The literature review chapter presents a summarised account of other researchers' findings on the problem and the argument that there is inadequate knowledge to understand or solve the problem. The methodology chapter recounts the methodological approaches and data collection methods used. It presents a convincing argument of why the chosen approach and data collection methods stand a strong chance of answering the research question. The chapter argues that the methods used to investigate the problem were appropriate and robust to provide valid answers to the problem's unresearched aspects. The results chapter recounts findings and themes, and provides graphs and evidence that support the argument. The discussion chapter summarises (describes) and interprets the results, discusses other researchers' findings, and argues for the contribution the research has made to the topic. Finally, the conclusion chapter summarises the whole thesis, and discusses its contribution to knowledge, and the next steps.

## The academic argument

The literature shows that although students do not seem to have issues with the descriptive, recounting, and summaries genres, they have challenges developing academic arguments. Consequently, their academic argument, which makes the most significant contribution to thesis writing, is typically its weakest link. Thomas Reid, an excellent philosopher of the eighteenth century, coined the proverb 'a chain is as strong as its weakest link' in 1786. The saying means that a chain's strength depends on its weakest link. In other words, the person or thing making the least contribution to the group's collective achievement is its weakest link (Cuneo & van Woudenberg, 2004).

Gruber defines a thesis as an extended argument that 'must demonstrate logical, structured, and defensible reasoning based on credible and verifiable evidence presented in such a way that it makes an original contribution to knowledge, as judged by experts in the field' (Evans, Gruba, & Zobel, 2014). Craswell and Poore (2011), on the other hand, define an academic argument as a credible, evidence-based defence of a position on a complex issue, such as a 'thesis', that uses logic and evidence from the literature. Parker defines a 'position' taken as 'the point of view arrived at on completion of critically assessing the relevant literature'.

An argument provides the reader with an indication of why the argument is persuasive and convinces them to examine a problem or issue differently or to consider a new solution. In addition, its claims must be arguable, i.e., another person can disagree or have a different perspective regarding the claim. Thus, an argument can be challenged. Each chapter contributes to thesis development. An argument is different from a 'fact'. A fact is demonstrated or verified as genuine or is generally accepted as a truth based on a professional, well-versed opinion in a field. Thus, it is usually not verifiable.

The basis of the claim(s) made in the argument depends on the robustness of the evidence. This robustness emanates from the methods employed, including data collection and analysis. The student can evaluate a claim's robustness based on knowledge of the most relevant previous studies, the most applied, unique approaches and the theories used, especially those that are significantly outstanding, including their advantages and disadvantages. In addition, a claim is based on the author's beliefs, assumptions, and potential biases, which may influence the interpretation of their results. Therefore, there is a need to consider whether the assumptions on which the claims are based are acceptable and, consequently, whether the claims that flow from these assumptions are convincing, and whether the author's view is potentially biased. These assumptions are grouped into three core philosophical approaches: epistemology, ontology, and axiology. **Epistemology** is a theory used to generate evidence from relevant sources in a particular field of inquiry. **Ontology** is a fundamental belief about what exists and can be studied and what people know. **Axiology** is the study of judgement about values, i.e., what is wrong or right about what exists, what is worth studying to make an impact and who is affected by it. Axiology, for example, shows how the people involved in or affected by research should be treated.

## The degree of certainty and generalisation

The degree of certainty and generalisation (low, high, tentative) with which a claim is made is based on robust and appropriate evidence.

Generalisations about the practicability of the findings to other contexts should have sufficient supporting evidence to sustain the degree of certainty with which a a claim is made, including the strength of counter-evidence and how papers published after the study could impact the claim. The student should argue whether their interpretation applies to other cases or whether there are other possible interpretations of these claims that have not been considered.

The degree of certainty of a claim is usually expressed with caution. For example, this can be expressed as 'it can be argued…', 'this study suggests that…', '… maybe the case', 'arguably', 'this indicates…', or 'this may indicate…'.

## Writing a thesis statement: Exerting a position when making claims

Many of the problems in thesis writing can be traced to students' inability to write a persuasive thesis statement. This section focuses on writing a persuasive thesis statement that asserts a position. The thesis statement helps to organise ideas and assists the reader to follow the argument. A persuasive thesis statement is critical in any argument and indicates to the reader the direction the thesis will follow. An argument is usually the main idea in academic writing, and is often called a 'claim' or 'thesis statement'. A thesis statement conveys a claim or argument that is defendable and sufficiently narrow to be successfully supported with evidence. It captures the author's position and reason for the position.

The statement has a main point, main idea, and central message.

The thesis statement announces the debatable point of view or claim (argument) in one or two sentences that express the main idea or one central message asserting the author's position. The literature review provides empirical evidence to support that position, demonstrating that the argument is based on research. Therefore, the student needs to understand the issue or problem before generating a thesis statement. The position that emerges through discussion, interpretation, and evaluation of the sources requires critical thinking. Assume that the reader is an authority on this topic and is aware of where the conversation stands currently.

This position can be challenged or opposed by others. In other words, the position taken is debatable, and other scholars can disagree with it. Therefore, the student should consider counterarguing or addressing possible arguments against their thesis. The counterargument is the flip side of the claim. In other words, the student should be aware of the opposing argument(s) that the reader might pose against their argument.

## Ways to write a thesis statement

There are three main approaches to writing a thesis statement. The simplest method is to turn the topic or prompt into a question and then answer that question.

---

### Example: Posing a question to identify a thesis statement

Question: What are the most significant factors influencing medication adherence?

Answer/thesis statement: Patient-related factors are the most significant factors in influencing medication behaviour.

---

This statement tells the reader that the thesis focuses on patient-related factors and medication adherence.

The second way to create a thesis statement is to state the main opposing point of view and evidence, and then refute or cast doubt on that view.

---

### Example: Presenting the opposing view in order to refute it

While healthcare providers have been found to play a role in patient medication adherence, patient factors remain the most influential determinants of medication adherence.

---

The third way to compose a thesis statement is to introduce the main point and explain how it will be substantiated.

---

### Example: Introducing the main point and supporting evidence

Medication adherence is improved by focusing on patient-related factors. Collaborative approaches that address the patients' perceptions of the disease and treatment have more positive outcomes.

---

A rule of thumb is to place a thesis statement at the end of the introductory paragraph of the introduction chapter to give the reader a sense of the thesis's direction.

## Types of arguments used in thesis-driven writing

This section focuses on the three basic structures or types of argument: the Toulmin argument, the Rogerian argument, and the Classical or Aristotelian argument, the latter of which is a mode of persuasion by the spoken word. The Toulmin and Rogerian arguments are the core upon which most academic, thesis-driven writing is based. The assertiveness in a thesis depends on the type of argument; for example, in a Toulmin argument, a thesis statement emphasises one side of the issue. In contrast, in a Rogerian argument, the thesis statement reflects both sides of the issue.

### Toulmin model of argument

The Toulmin model is the core upon which most academic, thesis-driven writing is based. Stephen Toulmin, a contemporary philosopher, identifies several features of an academic argument. These include a claim (the central assertion), evidence to support that claim, a warrant (an assumption that the claim is reasonable), counterclaims (statements that contradict or oppose the initial claim), and rebuttals (negations of the counterclaim) (Brockmeier, 2006; Ehninger, 1960).

**Claim/thesis statement**: The thesis statement in Toulmin's argument makes a claim about a main idea that you are attempting to defend by presenting a persuasive argument of your position. Thus, the thesis statement announces the debatable point of view. It should aim to do this in one or two sentences.

**Evidence supporting the claim**: The claim is supported by presenting as many evidence paragraphs as needed to prove it. However, choosing the best or most substantial evidence is advisable if the space is limited. Successful arguments marshal sufficient evidence to support a claim and demonstrate that it is better than alternative claims. It is a 'win win' argument, presenting a stronger case than the opposing view.

**Warrant/reason**: Warrants link claims and evidence. Warranting is providing support of the claims by reasoned argument, based on sufficient and appropriate evidence and ample grounds to convince the reader to accept the claim. For example, the first sentence of the paragraph establishes a reason to support the claim and content of the paragraph. Subsequent sentences provide the evidence that supports the reason. Finally, the paragraph concludes by reinforcing the claim and rationale.

**Counterarguments**: Counterarguments are alternative or opposing positions to any argument or position. They reflect the positions that the opposing side might argue about the issue. Including a counterargument paragraph when writing a thesis demonstrates an understanding that other positions exist, and it strengthens your argument. The counterargument paragraph includes the opposing argument, but it will also explain why the counterargument is incomplete, weak, or flawed, and not backed up by examples or evidence to support the position. The paragraph is closed by restating why your argument is stronger than the identified counterargument.

**Rebuttals**: A rebuttal is a response to the counterclaim. The rebuttal usually addresses the main opposing perspective on the position and provides evidence that casts doubt on that view. The rebuttal paragraph begins with a reminder of the opposing argument by stating its main points and explaining how it differs from the argument. For example, you can challenge the currency of the evidence and present and explain why the evidence does not hold up.

---

### Example: A Toulmin argument

Patient-related factors are better predictors of medication adherence than provider-related factors. [thesis statement]

There is empirical evidence that patients' perceptions of a given disease to a particular treatment or procedure predict patient adherence to the therapeutic regimen (Rosenstock, 1974; Safri, Sukartini, & Ulfiana, 2010). [evidence] These findings indicate that a patient is likely to adhere if they believe the drug reduces its seriousness or severity and probability of dying from the disease. This reasoning is supported by one of the most common theories used in explaining treatment adherence behaviours (Rosenstock, 1966), which posits that medication adherence is based on a patient's beliefs and perceptions rather than only on medical advice. [warrant/reasoning] On the other hand, the World Health Organization (WHO) (2003) defines adherence as a 'person's behaviour with agreed recommendations from a health care provider'.

---

## Rogerian model of argument

Carl Rogers, a renowned psychologist, proposed the Rogerian argument as an alternative approach that is less adversarial than the Toulmin argument. The Rogerian argument finds common ground between opposing positions, recognising their strengths and weaknesses. A strong Rogerian argument presents the problem and clearly understands the opposing position. In Rogers' model, opposing views are addressed by establishing common ground, acknowledging the contexts in which the opposing position is applicable, and stating how these two positions can enhance each other. Thus, successful arguments provide a compromise that satisfies both sides. The Rogerian argument is most useful when an issue is highly polarised or where there is genuine principled opposition, but collaboration is required. In most cases, it is usual to present only two or three differing positions.

In a Rogerian argument, shared goals are identified and common grounds are created to reach an agreement. Whereas the Toulmin argument focuses on winning, the Rogerian model seeks a mutually satisfactory solution.

The steps of a Rogerian argument include: introducing the problem, stating the opposing position, stating your position, searching for the middle ground, and reaching a conclusion.

First, the Rogerian argument introduces the problem, which addresses the topic being discussed or the problem being solved. Second, a statement of the opposing position is presented, showing that the writer understands and acknowledges the opposition's viewpoints. This explanation may take several paragraphs. Third, the writer presents their position on the issue without dismissing the other side. This explanation may also take several paragraphs. Fourth, the writer brings the two sides together, helping the reader to see their position for the middle ground, which will form the key focus of the write-up and may take several paragraphs. Finally, the writer concludes by reminding the readers of the balanced perspective and clarifying how both views contribute to the argument.

---

### Example: A Rogerian argument

Medication adherence refers to continually taking medications as prescribed. It is an 'active, voluntary, and collaborative involvement of the patient in a mutually acceptable course of behaviour to produce a therapeutic result' (Delamater, 2006; Morisky, 1988). [introducing the problem]

Most physicians believe that non-adherence is due to lack of access or poor memory and is often an intentional choice by the patient (Chan et al., 2010) or the patient's failure to follow healthcare providers' recommendations (Chesney, 2000). [statement of opposition]

---

Patients' perceptions of a given disease to a particular treatment or procedure are more predictive of patient adherence to the therapeutic regimen (Demartoto & Adriani, 2016; Rosenstock, 1974; Safri, Sukartini, & Ulfiana, 2010). [your position]

We are cognisant that healthcare providers' actions and relationships are also determinants of medication adherence. While healthcare providers' actions and relationships with patients are recognised as determinants of medication [adherence], there is evidence that interventions will be ineffective if they do not involve the patient (Nieuwlaat et al., 2014; Laws et al., 2013). Physicians' ability to predict patient adherence to medication is limited and inaccurate in identifying non-adherent patients in clinical practice (Zeller, Taegtmeyer, Martina, Battegay, & Tschudi, 2008). In addition, patients are reluctant to share the details of their less-than-optimal medication-taking behaviour with their healthcare providers. Therefore, health providers might not accurately portray the patients' adherence patterns (HCPs) (Wabe, Angamo, & Hussein, 2011). [your position]

Treatment outcomes tend to be more positive when patients and their doctors share similar beliefs about patient participation and when patients and physicians desire more patient involvement (Jahng, Martin, Golin, & DiMatteo, 2005). Therefore, patients and providers influence adherence decisions and should work together to improve treatment adherence. Individuals' beliefs about the doctor–patient relationship significantly impact their decision to non-adhere to prescribed medication (Stavropoulou, 2011). [bringing the two sides together]

Therefore, encouraging and supporting patients to take their medications should be a joint effort between the healthcare provider and the patient and requires innovative approaches focusing on the patient and the [healthcare] provider. [conclude the argument]

## Classical or Aristotelian argument

The Aristotelian style of argument was developed by the famous Greek philosopher and rhetorician. Aristotle described three strategies (sometimes called rhetorical appeals) that writers and speakers use to make their arguments convincing. In other words, they are modes of persuasion by the spoken word. These strategies include *logos* (an appeal to logic), *ethos* (appeals to credibility), and *pathos* (appeals to emotion). Ethos depends on the speaker's character, pathos puts the audience into a specific frame of mind, and the logos provides the proof or apparent proof, which is conferred by the words of the speech itself.

Pathos (appeal to emotion) convinces an audience by creating an emotional response to an impassioned plea or a convincing story. Arguments based on pathos encourage readers to make decisions based on emotions, such as anger, pity, fear, sympathy, compassion, disappointment, love, sadness, and resentment, to convince the audience of their argument. Pathos can be used in grant applications to demonstrate how the project connects to the broader community through values, engagement, and disciplinary or cultural norms.

---

### Example: Pathos

The teaching staff have worked against everything this university has tried so hard to build, and they do not care whether the institution goes down in the process. They are the enemy, and they will not stop until we are all finished. [an administrators' speech]

---

Ethos (sometimes called an appeal to ethics) is used to convince an audience of the authority or credibility of the persuader. Ethos uses the writer's credibility and character to make a case and gain approval. The writer uses their position as the expert, an authority, or the right person to give their arguments. The writer states their experience and credentials using specific, concrete examples that display the depth of knowledge. Ethos is displayed in a speech or in writing by demonstrating the writer's expertise or pedigree.

---

### Example: Ethos

My three decades of experience as a researcher, educational qualifications, and teaching experience speak for themselves.

---

Logos (appeal to logic) persuades an audience with reason, using facts and figures to rationalise a position. It relies on the reader's sense of reason. Arguments based on logos involve claims and evidence that establish skill in reasoning. Academic discussions are mostly logos-driven because academic audiences respect logic and evidence. In the grant application, this can be a concise review of the literature, a need for the study, relevant details explaining the reason for the study, and acknowledging the study's contributions to the field.

## Example: Logos

Patients living with HIV/AIDS have inadequate knowledge of medication adherence. Action research, a methodological approach used by social scientists worldwide, will be used to raise awareness of HIV/AIDS medication.

Besides these academic writing genres, other writing genre typologies include blogs and journalism, which use colloquial, emotive language that is not appropriate for academic writing.

## Ways of presenting an argument

This section explains options for presenting an argument, including a topical strategy, following chronological order, and using the strongest point first and the weakest point last (known as 'strongest–weakest').

The first method of structuring is the topical structure, which begins with the ideas and issues currently in the news. In a topical method, information is arranged in order of relevance or importance regarding current events, such as issues currently impacting society, and then moves to other issues that might not be presently relevant but still support the argument.

## Example: Topical strategy

The argument on the importance of handwashing and disease prevention would start from a topical issue that is currently relevant. In 2020/2021, that could be adherence to handwashing in relation to Covid-19 prevention. The argument can then refer back to earlier handwashing protocols, such as handwashing that is focused on the prevention of diarrhoea.

The second method is to structure the argument in chronological order, or in order of time sequence. This method begins the argument at the earliest time frame; for example, discussing examples from the earliest documentation that support the argument, then advancing the argument as time progresses, with the final examples being from the most recent works. Chronological order is an effective method because ordering the examples and main ideas following a sequence of time stresses how the main point has persisted through history, emphasising the importance of the argument.

## Example: Chronological order

An argument that washing hands to prevent coronavirus spread is effective could begin by quoting earlier studies that have used handwashing as a disease prevention strategy. It could then move chronologically through other studies on this topic and end with the studies relating specifically to Covid-19.

The final method to structure an argument is based on the strongest and weakest points. This method begins with the most robust point of the argument and ends with the weakest point. In most cases, people tend to remember the first detail mentioned in an argument. Thus, it is advisable to begin with the strongest reasons and then use weaker points to back the stronger points.

## Example: Strongest–weakest

In this presentation, the argument focuses on the key points of evidence from scientific research experiments and verifiable evidence (which represents strong evidence), followed by evidence from an empirical study based on observations, including abstract ideas (which represents weaker evidence).

## Exercise: Critiquing an argument

### Instructions

Discuss to what extent the examiner's comments apply to this text, supporting your argument with examples of words, phrases, or sentences from the text. (Refer to the section on Pedagogical features — 'Discussion-based exercises' — in the Introduction of this book for more details on completing this exercise.)

### Text: Motivation and HIV/AIDS medication adherence

Intrinsic motivation is the most effective and sustainable way to improve ARV medication adherence considering HIV/AIDs is a lifelong condition.

Intrinsic motivation originates from within the individual, while extrinsic motivation arises from outside. Because it originates from within the individual and controls their action, external forces with minimal individual control determine extrinsic motivation.

Extrinsic motivation comes from outside, i.e., a person does something to gain an external reward. For example, social networks or support groups of people living with HIV/AIDS provide psychosocial support that reduces self-stigma and enhances disclosure, contributing to increased adherence levels. Additionally, intrinsic motivation requires a higher degree of individual effort based on individual behaviour and characteristics. Therefore, it is typically a more effective long-term method for achieving goals and achieving responsibilities such as adherence. Finally, intrinsic motivation is the most effective way to improve ARV medication adherence for people living with HIV/AIDS. Thus, I argue that intrinsic motivation leads to more sustainable behaviour, which is the set of deliberate and practical actions that result in medication adherence. Therefore, my position is that external motivation is the most effective way to improve ARV medication adherence. Thus, intrinsic motivation is the most effective and sustainable way to improve ARV medication adherence.

**Examiner's comments**

- The candidate does not explicitly describe their central claim, and the thesis statement is not an arguable point of view or claim (argument).
- The candidate has problems creating a clear argument, inserts too many unqualified personal opinions, and presents material that is irrelevant to the topic or argument developed.
- The central claim is not related to the thesis statement or supported by evidence or theory.
- The candidate has demonstrated the ability to develop and structure the arguments that make up the thesis.
- The candidate acknowledges other scholars' counter-evidence.

# Further reading

Kamler, B., & Thomson, P. (2014). *Helping Doctoral Students Write: Pedagogies for Supervision* (2nd edition). London: Routledge. https://doi.org/10.4324/9781315813639

This book offers a framework to help doctoral students produce clear and well-argued dissertations. It is illustrated with actual postgraduate students' writing. The book also deals with the challenges of writing arguments. Although not written as a self-help manual, the book gives examples and sufficient detail to act as a guide for readers while writing their thesis.

Ramage, J. D., Bean, J. C., & Johnson, J. (2015). *Writing Arguments: A Rhetoric with Readings* (10th edition). New York: Pearson.

This book's primary purpose is to integrate a comprehensive study of argument with a process approach to writing. It treats arguments as a means of personal discovery and clarification, and as a way of persuading audiences.

University of Arizona (n.d.). Template for writing an argumentative thesis. *Thesis Generator*. Available at https://writingcenter.uagc.edu/thesis-generator

The University of Arizona provides a template that helps students to formulate an argumentative thesis statement.

Wingate, U. (2012). 'Argument!' Helping students understand what essay writing is about. *Journal of English for Academic Purposes*, *11*(2). https://doi.org/10.1016/j.jeap.2011.11.001

This article presents research into undergraduate students' concepts of argument, the difficulties they experience with developing arguments, and the type of instructions they receive from their teachers. The findings show that students' incorrect concepts of an argument are caused by inadequate knowledge of what an argumentative essay requires, particularly the need to develop their own academic debate position.

# 3

# Critical Review of Literature and Building a Theoretical Framework

The previous chapter focused on developing an academic argument that requires asserting your position and using empirical evidence to support that position. This chapter focuses on a **critical review of the literature**, which is undertaken to accumulate the evidence that supports a claim or argument. It also includes tips on developing a theoretical framework. In this book, Chapters 3, 5 (Writing the Literature Review), and 8 (Writing the Discussion Chapter) complement each other.

## Critical review of the literature

A critical review is an evaluation of a text. It can be carried out as a single exercise, but it is part of the preparation for writing a literature review in a thesis. The critical review provides a detailed description, analysis, and interpretation of a text, assessing the main ideas and arguments of the text and its value within the existing literature. Conversely, a literature review is a critical review in which the student analyses and evaluates many sources, including books and scientific articles, specifically related to a particular research topic. The literature review is an analysis and synthesis of information generated from the critical review. It provides evidence of existing knowledge and identifies gaps in research (i.e., unexplored or under-researched areas), problems that remain unsolved, emerging trends, and new approaches, narrowing down areas for further research. In other words, a literature review points to what has been accomplished in and what is missing from previous studies. The review also helps to identify concepts, theories, and models that can be used to develop a theoretical and conceptual framework for generating hypotheses and research questions to inform a new study. It also helps to identify the methodological approaches that are most appropriate for the new study – particularly any unusual approaches – identifying their advantages, disadvantages, and applicability. The literature review includes less detailed information on each source than a critical review of a single book or article.

There is a significant difference between a critical review of the literature and an **annotated bibliography,** in which the student compiles a brief synopsis or commentary on each text they have consulted while they work on their thesis. Creating an annotated bibliography is a helpful note-taking method and allows you to keep a record of your reading. In addition, it allows you to summarise the viewpoint of each source and demonstrate how the source is relevant to your research. Thus, maintaining an annotated bibliography as you work not only is a vital way to record what you have read, but also provides a quick, ready-made overview of sources related to the topic.

A descriptive annotation describes sources and summarises their arguments and ideas, while evaluative annotations go into more detail and provide the researcher's perspective on each source. For example, they may assess the strength of the author's arguments and describe how the source is helpful or unhelpful to the research. Annotations vary in length from a couple of sentences to several paragraphs when summarising and evaluating a book. A good guideline is to write about 50 to 200 words for each source.

An annotated bibliography is different from a standard bibliography or list of references. A standard bibliography or list of references provides publication details of the sources referred to in scholarly work. Whereas the list of references only includes works cited in the thesis, a bibliography may contain other material of interest that is not explicitly referred to in the text of the thesis.

## Identifying the research problem and research question

One of the most critical outcomes of a critical review is identifying a research problem or central research question. A research problem is a specific issue or challenge to investigate or study. The research problem commences when a person does not fully understand or is curious about a phenomenon, and wants to explore it further. First, the researcher must select a topic of interest, then they decide on the phenomenon they want to explore, and finally, they need to decide on a particular problem to research. Sometimes terms can be used interchangeably in research, but it is important to differentiate between subject, topic, and research problem. These terms are different in a thesis and might mean different things.

A subject of study is a broad area of interest. An example of such a subject is HIV/AIDS. It incorporates many areas of study, including prevention, management, and treatment. The researcher may choose HIV/AIDS as a research subject, but they will need to read widely on the topic to come up with a researchable problem – perhaps treatment adherence – and, ultimately, a researchable question.

It is important that, as a researcher, you choose a topic that you are passionate about and that you have adequate knowledge, expertise, and skills in the subject. At this stage, you are just searching for ideas and your critical review of the literature will help you pinpoint your interests, find gaps in the research, and even a specific research question. Avoid choosing a topic that is too recent, too ambiguous, or too specialised, because it might be challenging to find published material on the subject. Of course, if you are undertaking a doctoral thesis, your research will be breaking new ground and the lack of published material will not be an issue. Once you have narrowed the topic down sufficiently, you need to find a researchable problem or question. Identifying the research problem will provide you with a rationale for selecting relevant articles from your critical review of the literature that contributes to answering the research question.

## The research questions

The research question should be answerable within the limitations of the research project, in terms of time, money, and the researcher's expertise. The sample size and accessibility of the research site are key considerations if the project is to be feasible and completed within the designated time contraints. Resources invested in the research should also be worthwhile, given the results, i.e., the research needs to be cost-effective. The question should also be a priority and relevant to the scholarly community and programmes, e.g., it should inform policy and practice or address past research or practice shortcomings. Finally, the question should also be politically and culturally acceptable and a high national priority, i.e., it needs to be applicable. A question can be modified if you discover through the literature review that you have defined it too narrowly or too broadly.

Master's students are usually advised to address a substantive topic in their field of inquiry instead of developing or testing a theory or trialling/testing a new method of data collection or analysis, which is mainly a reserve for doctoral students. Note that research can be time-consuming and frustrating; the researcher can continually hit dead ends, which sometimes might take them back to square one.

## Identifying sources of information

After identifying the research questions, the next step is to identify various published literature in the research field that shapes what is known about the problem. Thus, multiple search approaches are required. These searches include books, computerised databases, and websites. Generally, books are more reliable sources than web-sites. Journals are considered credible sources for academic writing. However, some influential academic journals are more reliable than others – the journal's quality can be assessed by consulting the extensive Journal Quality List, which is regularly updated and free to access. The Journal Quality List ranking includes information from several years of the list's history. In addition, well-known sources for finding journal articles online include JSTOR, Science Direct, Oxford Academic, EBSCO, PubMed, Google Scholar, and Cochrane and Campbell systematic reviews. Most websites lack credibility as they might come from biased, unprofessional experts, and persons or publications with a commercial interest.

In addition to the above sources, researchers can also identify research by reviewing donor reports, special interest group programmes, news-papers, and government policies, programmes, and strategic plans. University libraries have databases of research that have been conducted so far, including archived theses and thesis proposals. This preliminary exploration will help the researcher to see whether anyone has conducted a similar study. It is a way to avoid duplication in research, but can also help to identify gaps in the research literature on a topic.

Ensure that the sources are credible. To evaluate sources' credibility and reliability, California State University developed the Currency, Relevancy, Authority, Accuracy, Purpose (CRAAP) test that evaluates the credibility of sources. The information should be current (i.e., the most recent research), relevant (i.e., relevant to and appropriate for your research), authoritative (i.e., the information was published in a reputable source and the author has a track record in the field), accurate (i.e., the source of information, including the motive for publishing it, is accurate and honest), and have purpose (i.e., the reason this information was published is valid and useful).

For accuracy, check whether the reference list is up to date and contains the most recent research and coverage. A current review usually covers the last five years and any landmark studies before this time if they are significant in shaping the field's direction. If studies conducted before the past five years that are not landmarks are included, you need to defend why these studies were chosen rather than the more current ones. At some point you need to decide when to stop collecting new resources and focus on writing up your findings.

After locating an article, check its relevance by skimming through the abstract, introduction (the first few paragraphs), and conclusion to understand its general purpose, content, and usefulness. Then, if the article is relevant to your topic, download the complete article and take notes. The notes will form your annotated bibliography, and allow you to keep track of the full source details and any key citations so that you avoid plagiarism – this is the beginning of the writing process. Finally, note key concepts, theories, models, methods, frameworks, innovative approaches used, and the results and conclusions of the study.

There is no guideline on the specific number of articles to cite for each type of thesis. The general guidance is to read enough to understand the topic's core concepts to saturation but stop when new articles do not add much to what has been read. The core literature might be apparent in the first 5–10 articles; therefore, it is recommended to start with the most recent landmark publications. A rule of thumb for a PhD is to read about 150 articles, and for a Master's thesis, perhaps about 30–50 articles (Petre & Rugg, 2010).

## Summarising, paraphrasing, and quoting sources

Once you have read through the individual sources and taken notes, you need to incorporate these notes into the written work by paraphrasing, summarising, synthesising, or quoting. These approaches can be combined depending on what you are trying to achieve. Do not copy and paste other people's ideas, but illustrate how they have developed their arguments, ideas, and opinions. Examples of summarising, paraphrasing, or quoting are given in this section.

## Summarising sources

Summarising condenses the key points, ideas, or arguments of the source. The researcher explains the significance of the source in their own words but avoids presenting too much detail, such as examples and unnecessary background that is unrelated to their research question.

Begin the summary with an introductory sentence that states the title and author of the text. Next, summarise the article's main ideas, including only those related to your research question. The summary should contain the ideas of the original text only or the underlying meaning of the article, but not your opinions, interpretations, deductions, or comments. Finally, a summary of the text must be written in your own words, so avoid copying phrases and sentences from the article unless they are direct quotations.

Provide details or summaries of individual studies or articles based on their comparative importance in literature: give more weight to the studies that are considered more authoritative. Use quotes sparingly to emphasise a point but not as a substitute for a summary. When summarising, develop headings and subheadings by themes, not by individual theorists or researchers.

## Paraphrasing sources

While summarising involves condensing other authors' passages in the researcher's own words, paraphrasing involves rephrasing the source material without changing its meaning. As a result, paraphrasing is often about the same length as or shorter than the original text. In other words, the researcher expresses someone else's ideas in their own words without changing the author's idea or argument.

Paraphrasing begins by reading the passage to understand its meaning fully. The researcher then writes their own version of the text, without referring to the original text, noting the key concepts, relevant themes, or points, and remembering to cite the source. To avoid plagiarism, the researcher must not use wording similar to the original text or follow a similar sentence structure. Instead, they must use their own words to capture the essence of the text.

Tips for paraphrasing! Start the first sentence at a different point from that of the source, use synonyms, or change the sentence structure, for example, from active to passive voice or vice versa. Alternatively, break the information into separate sentences. Always compare the paraphrased text with the original passage and adjust phrases that remain too similar or have the same structure.

## Quoting sources

Quoting is copying other authors' text word for word. It is a precise replica of the original, as the author has written it. It must always be placed in quotation marks and properly attributed in the text – by author name, publication date, and the page number of the quotation. Avoid using too many quotes or incorporating a quote without explaining the argument's significance or point.

Paraphrasing is better than quoting in academic writing because it dem-onstrates the student has an understanding of the source, making their work more original. The examples below are from a text that cites an article by Weinberg and Kovarik entitled 'The WHO clinical staging sys-tem for HIV/AIDS' (2010, pp. 203–204).

---

### Example: Direct quotation

The WHO system for adults 'sorts patients into one of four hierarchical clinical stages ranging from stage 1 (asymptomatic) to stage 4 (AIDS). Patients are assigned to a particular stage when they demonstrate at least one clinical condition in that stage's criteria. Patients remain at a higher stage after they recover from the clinical condition which placed them in that stage' (Weinberg & Kovarik, 2010: 203). For example, asymptomatic patients with persistent gen-eralised lymphadenopathy of at least two sites for longer than six months are categorised as being in stage 1, where they can remain for several years. 'Clinical findings included in stage 2 (mildly symptomatic stage) are unex-plained weight loss of less than 10 percent of total body weight and recurrent respiratory infections' (ibid.), and a range of dermatological conditions.

---

### Example: Paraphrased text

The WHO system assigns HIV patients to one of the four hierarchical clinical stages of infection when they demonstrate at least one clinical condition in that stage's criteria. A patient remains at this stage until they recover from the clinical condition that placed them there. Stage 1 includes asymptomatic patients or patients with persistent generalised lymphadenopathy in at least two sites for longer than six months. They can remain in this stage for several years. Patients in stage 2 demonstrate several clinical manifestations, such as unexplained weight loss of less than 10 per cent of total body weight and recurrent respiratory infections and a range of dermatological conditions (Weinberg & Kovarik, 2010: 203–204).

---

**Example: Summarised text**

HIV/AIDS progresses from being asymptomatic to enlargement of one or more lymph nodes in at least two sites for longer than six months. This stage progresses to mild clinical manifestations, including unexplained weight loss of below 10 per cent of total body weight, recurrent respiratory infections, respiratory infections, and a range of dermatological conditions.

---

## Managing sources of information

### Using a summary table or matrix

This section demonstrates how to manage sources using a summary table or matrix. A literature review summary matrix is a table in which the researcher records and organises their notes from each source. They can use it to identify relationships between sources, trends, patterns, theories, methods, or results. For example, it can indicate whether specific methodological approaches change over time, or identify questions or concepts that reappear throughout the literature, such as conflicts, debates, and contradictions. It also helps the researcher to notice where the sources disagree or diverge, and whether instrumental theories or studies have changed the field's direction.

Tables can be created initially in an Excel spreadsheet and then copied into a Word document. An Excel spreadsheet enables you to sort findings by the author, year, the aims or purpose of the study, research methods, concepts, theories or models, key terms used, variables, measurements, summaries of research results, important statistics, key conclusions, and recommendations. In addition, the spreadsheet enables you to compare and contrast different sources, to see how they are related to or differ from each other. For example, you can observe differences in methodology and the types of conclusions arrived at using these methodological approaches. Since the information is arranged in columns, it gives you a valuable overview of all these aspects at a glance.

An example summary table is given in Table 3.1. You can add as many categories of information as you want to adapt the matrix to your needs, thus creating a practical and indispensable resource for organising your research project. As you complete the matrix, be sure to take full notes in the form of an annotated bibliography for each source, including full citation details of the sources to avoid plagiarism. Further guidance on creating and using matrixes can be found in Garrard (2017) and Scott (2000).

**Table 3.1** An example of a summary table/matrix: ARV medication and health beliefs

| Source (author & date) | Main purpose | Geographical setting | Research design | Sample | Variables | Analysis | Findings | Implication |
|---|---|---|---|---|---|---|---|---|
| Nabunya et al., 2020 | The association between family factors and ART adherence self-efficacy | Uganda | Document review | HIV-positive adolescents | Socio-demographic household characteristics, family cohesion and child–caregiver communication | Multivariate analyses of variance | Family cohesion and child–caregiver communication were significantly associated with adherence self-efficacy to ART | Need to strengthen family cohesion and communication within families |
| Xin Gao, 2000 | Establish the relationship of disease severity, health beliefs, and medication adherence | Hospital setting, USA | Cross-sectional study design Self-administered questionnaire | 150 HIV/AIDS adults | Disease severity, regimen complexity, perceived susceptibility, perceived severity, perceived benefits, perceived barriers, medication adherence, and demographic variables | Multivariate analyses of variance | No significant differences in patients' perceptions of the severity of HIV/AIDS across three disease stages | Intervention targeting patients and healthcare providers to improve adherence |
| Safri et al., 2010 | Determinants related to medication adherence by pulmonary tuberculosis was used in this study | Hospital setting | Descriptive analytic design | 66 TB patients | Perceived susceptibility, perceived seriousness, perceived benefits, perceived barriers, cues to action, medication adherence | Chart and narrative | No relationship between all variables with medication adherence | Patients need intensive education on the treatment of pulmonary tuberculosis disease to improve adherence |

*(Continued)*

**Table 3.1** (Continued)

| Source (author & date) | Main purpose | Geographical setting | Research design | Sample | Variables | Analysis | Findings | Implication |
|---|---|---|---|---|---|---|---|---|
| Nutor et al., 2020 | Establish whether attitudes and beliefs influence intention to adhere to antiretroviral therapy (ART) | Hospital setting, Zambia | Observational analytic research with cross-sectional design | 150 HIV-positive breastfeeding women | Attitude, behavioural beliefs, income, knowledge, place of residence, age | Generalised modified Poisson regression models | In adjusted models, women in the weak adherence intention group were more likely to be older, have less knowledge about HIV transmission, and have a more negative attitude towards ART | Effective and appropriate ART counselling for pregnant and breastfeeding women |
| Demartoto et al., 2016 | Association between knowledge, perceived seriousness, perceived benefit and barrier, and family support on adherence to antiretroviral therapy (ART) | PHC Manahan Surakarta | Observational analytic research with cross-sectional design | 36 HIV/AIDS patients | Perception of the seriousness, perception of the benefits and barriers, family support | Logistic regression | Positive correlation between the perception of the seriousness of the disease, the perception of benefits and barriers, and family support with adherence to antiretroviral therapy | N/A |

## Using a synthesis matrix

After summarising and evaluating sources, you need to arrange them in a way that helps you to see how they relate to each other. Whereas students might have no difficulty in summarising sources, they can struggle to adequately synthesise knowledge from these sources and express it in their writing. For example, students do not distinguish different authors' viewpoints or arguments, and tend to list authors' viewpoints separately or one after the other (in the form of an annotated bibliography). They also present details that are irrelevant to their line of argument, or describe the idea/argument without connecting it to the significance of their own research topic, argument, or main point.

While a literature review summary matrix helps you to record and organise notes from each source, a synthesis matrix is a table that organises notes according to thematic categories. Synthesising goes beyond summarising or paraphrasing articles. It combines literature from multiple sources and fits it together. In other words, it uses information from several sources to create new ideas based on the analysis of sources. Sound synthesis puts information from these sources together in a way that shows connections and relationships, thus evaluating information to form new ideas or insights. Finally, synthesis identifies gaps in the literature by highlighting areas where more research is needed.

A synthesis matrix is useful, for example, when dealing with scientific sources that make various arguments about a topic. In each of these sources, you can highlight what the text argues about the topic, noting where the authors' findings diverge or converge with other sources, and you can include their conclusions and recommendations for further research. A synthesis matrix helps you to sort your thoughts, note important points, and think through the diverse arguments that are presented.

You can record your *sources* across the top of the chart, and list the main points or arguments along the side of the chart, or vice versa. When completed, the matrix provides a visual representation of the main ideas found in the literature and any overlaps. A completed matrix helps you to integrate all the different resources, facilitating the synthesis of information on a specific topic. From this matrix, you can identify authors who have similar or differing views.

The synthesis matrix is vital when writing the literature review chapter of your thesis. This is the chapter where you synthesise previous studies related to your research problem or question, and inform the reader of the current state of the research in the topic, i.e., the contradictions, inconsistencies, controversies, and similarities in the body of research, and, most importantly, the knowledge gaps you have identified. The main body of the chapter will include your key points, where you can use headings and subheadings to organise your arguments chronologically, methodologically, or thematically. Thematic themes are mostly used in theses. An example of a synthesis matrix is given in Table 3.2.

# The importance of the critical review

Information emanating from the critical review is crucial in all the chapters of the thesis, not just in the introduction and literature review chapters.

In the introduction chapter, a critical review presents the justification for investigating the particular topic or issue that constitutes the focus of an inquiry. In other words, the critical review is key to unearthing the problem. The central question of the research emanates from the literature review, although it can change during the investigation as your literature review evolves. A critical literature review will identify gaps in knowledge and is often the foundation for a theoretical framework that explains the research theories, showing that the study is grounded in established ideas. It delineates various theoretical positions and provides the conceptual framework for generating hypotheses and research questions.

In the methodology chapter, the critical review enables the student to contemplate how other researchers investigated similar topics. It helps them to identify and justify appropriate methodological approaches, and to support the argument that their research is supported by empirical knowledge. In the discussion chapter, evidence from the review supports claims about research findings. The literature review provides the interpretation and evaluation of the existing research. A reflection on how the theoretical framework and data collection methods may have impacted the results/ findings are also based on the literature reviewed. In the concluding chapter, the warranting claims of a study's significance are supported by empirical research from the review and the theories and models used.

The reference list of the literature sources demonstrates the student's accuracy and completeness, which indicates the thoroughness of the investigation.

## Developing a theoretical framework

A theoretical framework outlines the theory or model and concepts guiding the study. A solid theoretical framework provides the rationale for researching a particular research problem and establishes the structure that guides the research and interpretation of the findings. In most traditional research, the theoretical framework evolves from the literature review. It is developed by reviewing previously tested knowledge of the variables and their relationships.

**Table 3.2** An example of a synthesis matrix: ARV medication and health beliefs

| Source (author & date) | Themes | | | | | |
|---|---|---|---|---|---|---|
| | Perceived severity of illness | Perceived barriers | Perceived Susceptibility | Perceived benefits | Overall individual beliefs |
| Xin Gao, 2000 | No relationship between the stage of HIV/AIDS and medication adherence. This might be due to uniformly high perceptions of disease severity across different stages of the disease. | Monetary and non-monetary barriers did not significantly affect medication adherence | Positive correlation of perceived susceptibility-inaction and medication adherence. However, no relationship found with susceptibility-action. | No relationship between perceived benefits and medication adherence | |
| Safri et al., 2010 | No relationship between the perceived severity of pulmonary tuberculosis and medication adherence | No relationship between perceived barriers and medication adherence | No relationship between perceived susceptibility and medication adherence | No relationship between perceived benefits and medication adherence | |
| Nutor et al., 2020 | N/A | N/A | N/A | N/A | Overall behavioural belief was significantly related to antiretroviral therapy adherence but remained insignificant after adjusting for covariates such as age, knowledge of transmission, and district locality |
| Demartoto et al., 2016 | Positive correlation of perception of the seriousness of the disease and antiretroviral therapy adherence | Positive correlation of barriers and antiretroviral therapy adherence | N/A | Positive correlation of perception of the benefits and antiretroviral therapy adherence | N/A |

## Theories

Theories explain phenomena, draw connections, and make predictions. A theoretical framework is derived from a theory or model explaining a particular problem or phenomenon. In addition, a good theory or model helps to provide a framework on which more knowledge can be built. Most importantly, it establishes a sense of structure that guides the research – or theoretical frameworks.

During the critical literature review, the researcher explores what theories and models other researchers have developed, and evaluates, compares, and selects the most relevant theories for developing their own theoretical framework. The framework lays the foundation to support the analysis, interpretation of results, and generalisations. By 'framing' your research within empirical knowledge, you demonstrate the rationale behind your choices.

## Concepts and constructs

Building a theoretical framework involves evaluating and explaining relevant theories identifying key concepts, and explaining how the research fits in. 'Theoretical framework' and 'conceptual framework' are sometimes used interchangeably. However, a conceptual framework is usually used as a map in the theoretical framework that defines the concepts – or building blocks – which are the primary elements of a theory or model. Groups of concepts are called a model. Models draw on several theories to help us understand a specific problem in a particular setting or context, and are often informed by more than one theory. Unlike a theory, a model does not need to explain why it is suitable to be useful. Concepts might have multiple definitions, hence, the need to define them in the theoretical framework.

Constructs are concepts that have been developed or adopted for use in a specific theory. Variables are the operational forms of constructs. They describe how constructs are measured in a specific situation, based on the research design. The research design determines what to measure, which statistics to use, and how findings are interpreted. A quantitative conceptual framework leads to the formulation of hypotheses and research questions that can be empirically tested.

You can integrate the theoretical framework into a literature review chapter in a thesis or dissertation or include it as a separate chapter if the research deals with complex theories. Although there are no fixed rules for structuring a theoretical framework, a good option is to construct each section around the research question or key concepts.

## Steps of developing a theoretical framework

Students face significant challenges in identifying a theory or model that 'fits' their particular issue or problem, or the most appropriate theory or combination of theories for multiple factors influencing their research problem. The first step in developing a theoretical framework is to pick out the key terms from the research problem and research question.

---

### Example: Key terms from the problem statement and research question

Key terms are italicised.

Many HIV/AIDS patients do not take their medication as instructed, leading to ARV non-adherence [research problem]. Healthcare providers believe that *self-efficacy* will significantly improve *medication adherence*.

---

The key terms in this example are 'self-efficacy' and 'medication adherence'. The next step is to look for the definition of these concepts and conduct a literature review to determine how other researchers have defined and drawn connections between these key concepts. Consider what theoretical constructs and theories have been devised in other research studies. Determine whether they offer an appropriate theoretical framework for your own study.

Another tip is to use your thesis title, research problem, or central research question and add the words 'theory', 'model', 'theoretical framework', and 'conceptual framework' one at a time to search for ideas from other researchers.

Next, compare and critically evaluate the approaches that different authors have proposed. Determine and justify the most relevant theories, models, and concepts, and explain why others are unsuitable for your research. Theories can be combined from different fields to build a unique framework for more complex research projects or at the doctoral level.

Finally, after discussing different theories, models, and concepts, establish the definitions that best fit your research and why this is the case. For example, if you want to test a theory in a specific context, use the theory as a basis for interpreting the results, critique or challenge a theory, or combine different theories in a new or unique way. You can also use a theoretical framework to develop hypotheses.

Although the final draft of a theoretical framework is not long – probably one page – it takes a long time to write. Therefore, read and keep drafts of versions before settling on a particular theory or model that fits into your work. Sometimes, a theory that initially seemed helpful may lead to a deadend, while other ideas and concepts that were not considered valuable initially may become more advantageous. Also, as you develop the theoretical framework, you might identify an alternative or combination of theories that help you to understand the problem better and that might challenge the original theory or model.

Combining ideas from different scholars has the advantage that one theory might have shortcomings that the other addresses, but this procedure takes longer as it requires more thorough drafting before understanding how they all work together. Combining different theories is expected for a doctoral thesis, as it requires a higher level of cognition.

There are debates about whether to place the theoretical framework in the introduction chapter or the literature review chapter. If the whole thesis is on theories or models and perspectives that explain how things work, the theoretical framework can be discussed as a separate chapter; otherwise, it is placed in either the introduction or the methodology chapter, depending on the university or department.

**CONCEPTUAL FRAMEWORK**
**HEALTH BELIEFS RELATED TO ART MEDICATION ADHERENCE**

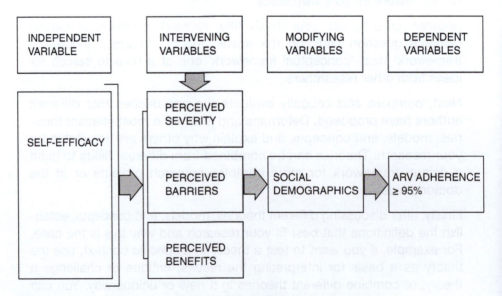

**Figure 3.1**  Health beliefs related to ART medication adherence

Figure 3.1 is an example of a conceptual framework that focuses on medication adherence (as a dependent variable), self-efficacy (as an independent variable) and disease severity, perceived barriers, perceived benefits, and self-efficacy (as the intervening variables). Social demographics are also considered to be modifying variables.

# Conclusion

This chapter has focused on the critical literature review, which includes identifying and evaluating the credibility and reliability of information sources. It illustrated how to skim through the sources for relevance, organise sources using a summary table or matrix, and synthesise a matrix to compare multiple sources and identify gaps in knowledge. The chapter also demonstrated how to develop a theoretical framework that leads to the successful formulation of research questions and testable hypotheses, which are addressed in the introduction chapter.

## Exercise: Critiquing a theoretical framework

### Instructions

Discuss to what extent the examiner's comments apply to this text, supporting your argument with examples of words, phrases, or sentences from the text. (Refer to the section on Pedagogical features — 'Discussion-based exercises' — in the Introduction of this book for more details on completing this exercise.)

### Text: Impact of self-efficacy on medication adherence in HIV/AIDS patients

This study investigates the impact of self-efficacy on medication adherence in HIV/AIDS patients based on Bandura's social cognitive theory. Social cognitive theory posits that human motivation and action are influenced by the interplay of cognitive, behavioural, and environmental factors (Bandura, 1986). Self-efficacy is a cognitive factor that refers to an individual's belief in their capabilities to exercise control over their functioning and events that affect their lives (Bandura, 1977). In the context of medication adherence for HIV patients, self-efficacy refers to an individual's belief in their ability to adhere to their medication regimen. Medication adherence is the behavioural factor, and the environmental factors include factors such as social support and the physical environment.

*(Continued)*

The Health Belief Model (Ellickson et al., 2003) is another popular theoretical framework that has been used to explain medication adherence and self-efficacy. This model primarily focuses on cognitive factors such as perceived susceptibility, perceived severity, perceived benefits, and perceived barriers. Social cognitive theory offers a more comprehensive and predictive theory of human behaviour by studying the interplay of cognitive, behavioural, and environmental factors. Social cognitive theory explains how self-efficacy influences behaviour, while the Health Belief Model focuses on beliefs and attitudes towards health behaviour.

**Examiner's comments**

- The candidate effectively uses Bandura's social cognitive theory to guide their research on the impact of self-efficacy on medication adherence for HIV patients.
- The candidate provides a clear description of Bandura's social cognitive theory and explains why it is a better fit than the Health Belief Model for their research question.
- In addition to the Health Belief Model, the candidate should elaborate on other theories or models which they considered for their research.
- The candidate should describe how the conceptual framework will guide their data collection and analysis strategies.

# Further reading

Garrard, J. (2017). *Health Sciences Literature Review Made Easy: The Matrix Method* (5th edition). Burlington, MA: Jones & Bartlett Learning.

This book provides students with a foundation and the tools they need to evaluate articles and research effectively. It covers constructing a research study effectively, managing a quality literature review, and using a review matrix to write a synthesis.

Grant, C., & Osanloo, A. (2014). Understanding, selecting, and integrating a theoretical framework in dissertation research: Creating the blueprint for your 'house'. *Administrative Issues Journal: Connecting Education, Practice, and Research*, 4(2), 12–26. https://doi.org/10.5929/2014.4.2.9

This article demonstrates how to apply a theoretical framework in a thesis. It explains the steps for selecting and integrating a theoretical framework to structure all aspects of the research process.

Hart, C. (1998). *Doing a Literature Review: Releasing the Research Imagination* (2nd edition). London: Sage.

This book focuses on reviewing research literature. It provides examples of a range of techniques that can be used to analyse ideas and find arguments in research. In addition, the book includes explanations, discussions, and examples of how to analyse other people's ideas and identify ideas that contribute to the body of knowledge on the research topic.

Kelly, L., & Snowden, A. (2020). How to synthesise original findings back into the literature: A reintroduction to concurrent analysis. *Nurse Researcher*, *28*(2). https://doi.org/10.7748/nr.2020.e1710

The article reintroduces 'concurrent analysis' (CA). To illustrate the technique, the authors use a synthesis of relevant literature with findings from a doctoral study of patients' experiences with vascular access devices.

Kivunja, C. (2018). Distinguishing between theory, theoretical framework, and conceptual framework: A systematic review of lessons from the field. *International Journal of Higher Education*. https://doi.org/10.5430/ijhe.v7n6p44

This paper distinguishes between theory, theoretical framework, and conceptual framework, presenting the purposes for and development of a theoretical framework.

Molasso, W. R. (2006). Theoretical frameworks in qualitative research. *Journal of College and Character*, *7*(7). https://doi.org/10.2202/1940-1639.1246

This article introduces early researchers to theoretical frameworks, defining their role in qualitative research, including finding and using a theoretical frame. The book also provides background on the nature of theoretical frameworks and their importance in qualitative research.

Petchko, K. (2018a). *How to Write about Economics and Public Policy*. Oxford: Elsevier. https://doi.org/10.1016/b978-0-12-813010-0.00004-1

This book has several chapters that present model literature reviews from published and unpublished papers. These chapters include organising literature reviews to make statements about the state of current knowledge, identifying other authors' arguments and theoretical positions, and common problems students may have when reviewing academic literature. In addition, the book describes elements of a theory, explains its role in research, and explains the difference between thesis, theoretical framework, theoretical perspective, theory, model, and suggestions for where to place them.

Scott, C. (2000). Health science literature review made easy: The matrix method. *Canadian Journal of Public Health/Revue Canadienne de Santé Publique*, *91*(1).

This paper explains how to plan and manage a search, and select and organise documents for a review using a review matrix to write a synthesis.

University of Wisconsin-Madison (n.d.). *How to Write Critical Reviews*. Madison, WI: The Writing Center, University of Wisconsin-Madison. Retrieved 20 April 2022, from http:// wisc.edu/writing/Handbook/CriNonfiction.html

This article provides guidelines on identifying, summarising, and evaluating the ideas presented in the research literature. It also gives tips on how to structure the introduction, body, and conclusion sections of your critical review.

Wakefield, A. (2015). Synthesising the literature as part of a literature review. *Nursing Standard, 29*(29), 44–51. https://doi.org/10.7748/ns.29.29.44.e8957

This article suggests ways to synthesise and critique research literature and synthesise the research. It explores the critiquing process by breaking it down into seven sequential steps. The article explains how the literature review is shaped to generate a logical and reasoned debate.

# WRITING YOUR THESIS

PART
II

WRITING YOUR THESIS

# 4

# Writing the Introduction Chapter

The chapters in Part I have covered the essentials of academic writing and demonstrated how to identify knowledge gaps that need further research by undertaking a critical review of the literature. The chapters in Part II will lead you through the process of writing each chapter of your thesis. This chapter is about writing the Introduction, which introduces the research problem and explains what led to the investigation of the study and what the research aims to achieve. The introduction chapter of your thesis discusses the problem statement and establishes the central focus of your study.

## Purpose of the introduction chapter

Although the introduction chapter is the first chapter of a thesis, it is finalised after all the other chapters have been written. Thus, the last chapter in a thesis is the final draft of its introduction. It is often rewritten several times — since some rethinking and redrafting are necessary as the thesis develops. After completing each chapter, it is necessary to periodically revisit the introduction chapter to ensure you stay focused on the thesis's central focus and to find out whether you need to revisit the original premise.

The structure of the introduction chapter may vary across disciplines, and universities might have different requirements, but the content remains the same in all theses. The chapter should be simple enough to make it easy for readers to understand the general background of the research problem. Information from the introduction chapter is tied to the literature review and the conclusion chapter. In some universities, the introduction chapter might also include a definition of terms or specialised terms.

The structure of the introduction chapter is as follows: the introduction paragraph; the main body of the chapter, containing various sections and subsections, which comprises the context and background of the research problem, the purpose statement, the statement of significance, the problem statement, and the definition of terms; and the concluding paragraph.

## Introducing the chapter

The first paragraph of the thesis is usually the introductory paragraph, whose goal is to let readers know what to expect from the thesis. The first sentence or topic sentence of the paragraph is a 'hook', which can be a research question or a statistic that arouses the reader's interest in one to two sentences. The hook is followed by one or two sentences about the specific focus of the thesis or why the topic is essential. Finally, a thesis statement is the last sentence of the introduction paragraph and contains a transitional link to the first paragraph of the main body of the chapter. It is recommended that this introductory section be no longer than two pages.

### Example: Writing the introductory paragraph

Medication non-adherence is a significant health problem, sometimes called an 'invisible epidemic'. [topic sentence/hook] Medication adherence is 'the extent to which a patient's behaviour in taking their medication corresponds to agreed recommendations by their health care provider' (Sabate, 2016). These requirements mean taking all the medicines as prescribed, in the correct dose and quantity, at the right time, through the correct route while observing dietary restrictions (Sahay et al., 2011). [focus of the thesis] Adherence to this complicated, routine and lifelong treatment requires sustained motivation and self-efficacy. [thesis statement]

## Main body of the introduction chapter

The main body of the introduction chapter comprises the context and overview of the research problem, a purpose statement, and a statement of significance, and ends with a problem statement and a definition of terms.

## Context and overview of the research problem

This section establishes the research territory by situating the research in a broader context. The context provides an overview of the topic, including recent developments and their importance, and provides enough detail for the reader to have a foundational understanding of the research area and the current context in which the research lies. After presenting an overview of the topic, narrow the focus and highlight the specific research problem.

The description of the problem can include: (a) the causes or factors contributing to the problem; (b) the extent and distribution of the problem at the local, national, or international levels; and (c) the characteristics of the population groups affected.

Next, report on the solutions that have been tried, how well they have worked, and any alternative courses of action or solutions. You need to present just enough information to contextualise the study. Nevertheless, keep the information simple; avoid technical detail at this stage. Include references to the most important scientific articles related to the topic. The context and background of the problem, which usually take 2–4 pages, lead to the problem statement.

---

### Example: Writing a context and overview of the research problem

The HIV medicine called antiretroviral therapy (ART) is a combination of daily medications that stops the virus from reproducing and helps protect CD4 cells or T cells. The medication involves a complicated routine that makes it a challenge to reach the recommended medication adherence levels to suppress the replication of HIV and prevent the progression of the infection to acquired immunodeficiency syndrome (AIDS). The recommended cut-off value for patient adherence to antiretroviral therapy (ART) should be ≥95% or preferably 100% (Apisarnthanarak & Mundy, 2010; WHO, 2002). Non-adherence, the primary cause of treatment failure in PLWHA, is a risk for opportunistic infection that results in inadequate HIV viral suppression leading to clinical disease progression and development of resistance to ARVs drugs. [overview of the problem]

Though ARVs are accessible, by the end of June 2020 only an estimated 68% of adults, 53% of children, and 85% of pregnant and breastfeeding women living with HIV received antiretroviral therapy, indicating the need to motivate people more. [the extent of the problem]

*(Continued)*

---

Sustained motivation and self-efficacy have been identified as the most prominent and significant determinants of adherence to the socio-cognitive theory (Holmes, Hughes, & Morrison, 2014). Therefore, there is a need to focus on self-efficacy as an aspect of medication adherence. Sustained motivation is the will to perform a specific behaviour, such as taking medication. Self-efficacy is a self-judgement of one's ability to perform a task. Therefore, there is a need to focus on self-efficacy as an aspect of medication adherence. [suggested solutions]

## The purpose statement

The purpose statement, which flows from the overview of the problem, is stated in one or two sentences. While the overview of the research problem identifies the problem to be solved, the purpose statement identifies what the research aims to achieve. Sentences of the purpose statement begin with a phrase such as 'The primary purpose of this investigation was to…'.

The purpose statement can focus on a variety of issues. For example, the purposes of the study could be: to identify patterns and trends in the field or tackle trending new issues; to extend, expand, develop, or test a theory; to replicate research tried elsewhere; to apply a particular technique in a new area; to add new knowledge (at PhD level); or to test a hypothesis.

### Example: Writing a purpose statement

The study aimed to develop an effective adherence-enhancing intervention to increase self-efficacy and, consequently, behaviour changes related to medication adherence using motivational interviewing.

## The statement of significance

At the proposal stage, this section is referred to as the justification of the study section. However, having undertaken the study, the results have become available so in the introduction chapter to the thesis it is referred to as the 'significance' of the research. One way to think of the significance of the research is to equate it with potential impact or how it adds value to the population, community, society, technology, and field of research. Therefore, when writing this section, always refer to the problem statement that contains what the thesis will contribute to knowledge. Another way to think of a statement of significance is that it gives a 'voice' to the people who are not heard, or who are silenced or rejected in society, or it addresses potentially new audiences, practitioners, or users. In other words, the statement of the research's significance could be who stands to benefit from the research. For example, the beneficiaries could be academicians, a funding agency, or a research group.

There is no single way of writing a perfect significance statement, and it depends on the subject or disciplinary area. However, the statement should be less than 500 words in length when written for a thesis (thus, a minimum of three to four paragraphs).

---

### Example: Writing a statement of significance

This study presented empirical evidence of motivational interviewing, which doubles as a counselling approach to enhance adherence. Persons living with HIV/AIDS go through the counselling process, gain the confidence to take all the prescribed medicines and maintain long-term after the counselling experience. The Motivation Interviewing (MI) approach can be incorporated into HIV/AIDS treatment programmes, and staff can use it in their HIV/AIDS promotion activities. The study will serve as reference material to guide future researchers who wish to extend the methodological approach to other fields of study.

---

## Problem statement

A problem statement in a thesis is a clear, precise, well-articulated statement that establishes the study's central direction and lays the foundation for everything that follows. It must be written in your own words and contain no references. It states the specific problem or research focus, suggests how it may solve the problem, and convinces that currently there is insufficient knowledge available to explain or solve the problem. The problem statement has at least four elements: (a) an overview of the research problem, including the statement of significance; (b) a purpose statement; (c) a central question or hypothesis; and (d) the theory and methods used.

To write a problem statement, begin by introducing the problem being investigated, establishing its magnitude, the population affected by the problem, and why the problem is significant enough to warrant formal research. In other words, you are establishing the basis of the need for the research. Next, argue that there is insufficient knowledge to explain or solve the problem based on existing knowledge, which you have examined in your literature review. Finally, end with a research question or hypothesis that points to the methodology used in your study, which guided all subsequent stages of inquiry, analysis, and reporting. The problem statement for a thesis or dissertation should be about 150–300 words, or three to four paragraphs, or a one-page section (Ellis & Levy, 2008; Jacobs, 2011; Miles, 2019).

---

## Example: Writing a problem statement

HIV medication involves a complicated routine, making it a challenge to reach the recommended medication adherence levels of ≥95% that is necessary to suppress the replication of HIV and prevent the progression of the infection to acquired immunodeficiency syndrome (AIDS). Non-adherence, the primary cause of treatment failure in PLWHA, is a risk for opportunistic infection, resulting in inadequate HIV viral suppression leading to clinical disease progression and development of resistance to ARVs drugs. [overview of the problem] The study aimed to develop an effective adherence-enhancing intervention to increase self-efficacy and, consequently, behaviour changes related to medication adherence using Motivational Interviewing (MI). [purpose statement]

We hypothesised that there was no significant difference in medication adherence in the group of patients using Motivational Interviewing and those using conventional counselling approaches. [central question or hypothesis]

The experimental study was guided by Bandura's theory of self-efficacy (Bandura, 1977), which states that self-efficacy is a more powerful determinant of behavioural changes because it is rooted in the core belief that one has the power to produce the desired results. [theory and methods]

---

## Definition of terms

While your thesis is written for knowledgeable peers, it is good practice to define technical terms, especially if they are conceptual in nature or have more than one meaning. Include a paragraph to introduce this section before listing the terms and their definitions. A definition of terms does not need to be too detailed. In some universities, the requirement is that the introduction chapter includes definitions of concepts, variables, and terms. In others, the definition of terms is placed in the preliminary sections of a thesis.

According to the American Psychological Association (APA), abbreviations are used for clear communication with the audience. Therefore, do not write out standard abbreviations, such as units of measurement and the names of states. 'Commonly understood' terms, or those with no source, can be listed without citations, but do support definitions with scholarly sources, always citing those sources. Do not use Wikipedia or dictionaries to define terms as it is not appropriate for formal academic research and writing. Operational definitions are defined in the methodology chapter. Each definition may be a few sentences to a paragraph.

---

### Example: Defining terms

'Medication adherence' is defined as the 'the extent to which a patient's behaviour in taking their medication corresponds to agreed recommendations by their health care provider' (Sabate, 2016).

'Self-efficacy' is the person's belief in their capabilities to exercise control over their functioning and events that affect their lives (Bandura, 1977).

---

## Concluding the introduction chapter

The concluding statement wraps up all the main points of the introduction chapter. The first sentence of the conclusion paragraph restates the thesis claim or central question, but it is best to paraphrase it or express it in a different way so it does not appear repetitive. For example, if one starts with the subject or purpose and ends with the argument, then reverse it by beginning with the argument and ending with the subject or purpose of the study.

Include one or two paragraphs summarising what the chapter has achieved, highlighting key themes and ideas that unite the chapter, the new questions or issues that have been identified, and where they will be dealt with in the thesis. Close with an insightful sentence, which ties in with the topic sentence and links to the next chapter. Thus, the last sentence hints at how the literature review chapter helps to answer the research questions.

The concluding section of the introduction chapter should be about 1–3 paragraphs.

## Example: Writing a concluding paragraph

Sustained motivation and self-efficacy are crucial in adherence to the complicated lifelong HIV treatment. [restated thesis statement] We introduce a Motivational Interviewing approach (described in the methodology chapter) and self-efficacy, which proved to be the most powerful motivating factor for behavioural change (described in the literature review). These findings can be useful in planning HIV/AIDS treatment programmes and serve as reference material to guide future researchers (described in conclusion as a contribution to knowledge).

## Roadmap or signposting to subsequent chapters

The final part of the introduction chapter is the roadmap, where a paragraph briefly signposts the content of the remaining chapters. Signposting flags up important ideas in a general way, giving the reader an idea of the shape of the thesis by outlining the remaining chapters. Remember, it is an outline, not a summary. This section should be no more than one or two pages.

## Example: Writing a roadmap

The introduction chapter explains the research problem, medication adherence, and its associated factors. The literature review chapter focuses on what is known about the research problem and related factors and gaps in knowledge on these issues, including the theoretical framework guiding the study. Finally, the methodology chapter discusses the experimental design using Motivational Interviewing to address the knowledge gap. These chapters are described in more detail in their respective sections.

The length of the introduction depends on the size of the entire thesis. Generally, however, if you aim for a length between 5% and 7% of the total, this is likely to be acceptable.

## Common pitfalls of the introduction chapter

The following points are some of the key mistakes students make when writing the introduction chapter.

- Information that is not directly related to the problem of the study is included in the introduction, and irrelevant information that should be in the literature review is introduced in the introduction chapter.
- Students fail to state or provide a scientific justification – primarily, how the problem exists in the study area or the trend that has led to the problem.
- The problem statement is unclear, and writing consists of over-generalised statements unrelated to the problem.
- Although the 'common theme' begins in the introduction, the actual thesis deviates from the research question or does not relate to it directly.

## Example: Introduction chapter: Motivation and ARV medication adherence

### The introduction

Medication non-adherence is a significant health problem, sometimes called an 'invisible epidemic'. Medication adherence is 'the extent to which a patient's behaviour in taking their medication corresponds to agreed recommendations by their health care provider' (Sabate, 2016). These requirements mean taking all the medicines as prescribed, in the correct dose and quantity, at the right time, through the correct route, while observing dietary restrictions (Sahay et al., 2011). Adherence to this complicated, routine and lifelong treatment requires sustained motivation and self-efficacy.

### Context and overview of the research problem

The HIV medicine called antiretroviral therapy (ART) is a combination of daily medications that stops the virus from reproducing and helps protect CD4 cells or T cells. The medication involves a complicated routine that makes it a challenge to reach the recommended medication adherence levels to suppress the replication of HIV and prevent the progression of the infection to acquired immunodeficiency syndrome (AIDS). The recommended cut-off value for patient adherence to antiretroviral therapy (ART) should be ≥95% or preferably 100% (Apisarnthanarak & Mundy, 2010; WHO, 2002). Non-adherence, the primary cause of treatment failure in PLWHA, is a risk for opportunistic infection that results in inadequate HIV viral suppression leading to clinical disease progression and development of resistance to ARVs drugs.

Though ARVs are accessible, by the end of June 2020 only an estimated 68% of adults, 53% of children, and 85% of pregnant and breastfeeding women living with HIV received antiretroviral therapy, indicating the need to motivate people more.

*(Continued)*

Sustained motivation and self-efficacy have been identified as the most prominent and significant determinants of adherence to the socio-cognitive theory (Holmes, Hughes, & Morrison, 2014). Therefore, there is a need to focus on self-efficacy as an aspect of medication adherence. Sustained motivation is the will to perform a specific behaviour, such as taking medication. Self-efficacy is a self-judgement of one's ability to perform a task. Therefore, there is a need to focus on self-efficacy as an aspect of medication adherence.

## Purpose statement

The study aimed to develop an effective adherence-enhancing intervention to increase self-efficacy and, consequently, behaviour changes related to medication adherence using motivational interviewing.

## Significance of the study

This study presented empirical evidence of motivational interviewing, which doubles as a counselling approach to enhance adherence. Persons living with HIV/AIDS go through the counselling process, gain the confidence to take all the prescribed medicines and maintain long-term adherence after the counselling experience. The Motivation Interviewing (MI) approach can be incorporated into HIV/AIDS treatment programmes, and staff can use it in their HIV/AIDS promotion activities. The study will serve as reference material to guide future researchers who wish to extend the methodological approach to other fields of study.

## Problem statement

HIV medication involves a complicated routine, making it a challenge to reach the recommended medication adherence levels of ≥95% that is necessary to suppress the replication of HIV and prevent the progression of the infection to acquired immunodeficiency syndrome (AIDS). Non-adherence, the primary cause of treatment failure in PLWHA, is a risk for opportunistic infection, resulting in inadequate HIV viral suppression leading to clinical disease progression and development of resistance to ARVs.

The study aimed to develop an effective adherence-enhancing intervention to increase self-efficacy and, consequently, behaviour changes related to medication adherence using Motivational Interviewing (MI).

We hypothesised that there was no significant difference in medication adherence in the group of patients using Motivational Interviewing and those using conventional counselling approaches.

The experimental study was guided by Bandura's theory of self-efficacy (Bandura, 1977), which states that self-efficacy is a more powerful determinant of behavioural changes because it is rooted in the core belief that one has the power to produce the desired results.

## Definition of terms

'Medication adherence' is defined as the 'the extent to which a patient's behaviour in taking their medication corresponds to agreed recommendations by their health care provider' (Sabate, 2016).

'Self-efficacy' is the person's belief in their capabilities to exercise control over their functioning and events that affect their lives (Bandura, 1977).

## Concluding the chapter

Sustained motivation and self-efficacy are crucial in adherence to the complicated lifelong HIV treatment. We introduce a Motivational Interviewing approach (described in the methodology chapter) and self-efficacy, which proved to be the most powerful motivating factor for behavioural change (described in the literature review). These findings can be useful in planning HIV/AIDS treatment programmes and serve as reference material to guide future researchers (described in conclusion as a contribution to knowledge).

## Roadmap or signposting to subsequent chapters

The introduction chapter explains the research problem, medication adherence, and its associated factors. The literature review chapter focuses on what is known about the research problem and related factors and gaps in knowledge on these issues, including the theoretical framework guiding the study. Finally, the methodology chapter discusses the experimental design using Motivational Interviewing to address the knowledge gap. These chapters are described in more detail in their respective sections.

## Exercise: Introduction chapter

### Instructions

Discuss to what extent the examiner's comments apply to this text, supporting your argument with examples of words, phrases, or sentences from the text. (Refer to the section on Pedagogical features — 'Discussion-based exercises' — in the Introduction of this book for more details on completing this exercise.)

*(Continued)*

**Text: Barriers associated with adherence to antiretroviral (ARV) drugs among persons living with HIV/AIDS**

## Introduction

This chapter introduces the study and describes the following areas concerning the study topic: Background of the study, the significance of the study, problem statement, the purpose of the study, research hypotheses, study objectives and justification.

## Background of the study

Infection with Human Immunodeficiency Virus (HIV) leads to the destruction of immunity, which leads to increased morbidity and mortality rates in People Living with HIV/AIDS (PLWHA). Antiretroviral (ARV) drugs suppress the replication of HIV and prevent the progression of the infection to acquired immunodeficiency syndrome (AIDS) and death (Bartlett & Gallart, 2005). Although ARVs are not a cure for HIV, they are very effective in controlling the virus and can reduce the level of the virus to a point where it is no longer possible to detect any in the blood (Aspelling et al., 2006). A combination of such treatments is referred to as Antiretroviral Therapy (ART).

Adherence to ARV refers to the timely intake of the correct dose of prescribed ARV pills through the right route while observing dietary restrictions (Sahay et al., 2011, Bangsberg et al., 2006, Carter, 2005). Studies have found that adherence of >95% can suppress HIV to undetectable levels (Seth et al., 2012, WHO, 2006, Paterson et al., 2000). Unfortunately, such high levels of adherence are challenging to achieve among PLWHA, and most patients have been reported to be non-adherence (Aspelling et al., 2006, Hardon et al., 2007).

## Significance of the study

Non-adherence is believed to be the primary cause of treatment failure in PLWHA. In addition, those patients who develop resistance make ARVs difficult because they may transmit the drug-resistant virus, which requires second-line treatment, which is more expensive. If too many patients progress to second-line therapy, the increased costs involved will limit access to treatment for many people who would have benefited from first-line therapy. Adherence level of 95% and above to antiretroviral therapy (ARVs) is strongly correlated with both immunologic and virologic success.

Unfortunately, achieving this high level of adherence can be very difficult considering it is a lifelong treatment and many changes occur within the individual over time. These changes may interfere with treatment adherence among the individuals on ARV treatment and lead to non-adherence. Non-adherence to ARVs leads to treatment failure and the emergence of resistant viruses with eventual exhaustion of treatment options. Therefore, adherence to ARV treatment is currently the only factor that can be controlled to prevent the development of drug resistance and can limit future treatment choices for HIV patients.

Therefore, every effort should be made to ensure patients achieve a high level of adherence (>95%) to ARVs treatment to delay the emergence of drug-resistance.

## Problem statement

Non-adherence to ARV leads to the development of ARV viral resistance, decreased CD4 lymphocyte count, increasing opportunistic infections and finally, death. Though adherence levels of 95% and above have been recommended because they suppress HIV replication and improve immunity, many patients do not achieve this high level of adherence.

Comprehensive Care Clinic records in the study area show that the number of PLWHA who are non-adherent has been increasing, and currently, 64% PLWHAs are not adhering to their treatment. Thus, it is against this that the study sought to establish various barriers associated with ARV adherence among adult PLWHAs.

## Purpose of the study

This study aimed to assess barriers associated with ARV adherence among adults living with HIV/AIDS to come up with relevant and timely recommendations for improving practical ARV adherence among adult PLWHA. Thus, the specific objective of this study was to assess barriers to treatment adherence among adults living with HIV/AIDS.

## Justification of the study

Different factors influence ARV adherence and differ depending on different set-ups, contexts and times; this necessitates ongoing studies to establish factors associated with ARV adherence among PLWHA in different contexts to develop relevant, practical and timely strategies for intervention. Therefore, practical strategies to improve adherence can only be developed using context-specific studies.

## Assumptions, limitations, and scope (delimitations)

This study's main limitation was that it was quantitative and lacked the qualitative research component to explain the quantitative findings.

(Continued)

### Concluding the chapter

The findings generated from this study will make several contributions to both knowledge and understanding of barriers that contribute to non-adherence among adult PLWHA. In addition, identification of barriers to ARV adherence will assist in developing a relevant, timely and practical intervention that will help improve ARV adherence among the patients on ARVs to improve the quality of their life.

### Examiner's comments

- The introduction is explicit, to the point, and indicates that the problem was of significance.
- The candidate demonstrates sufficient knowledge of the inquiry area and has situated the problem appropriately in this broader field.
- The thesis's objective is too ambitious, so the candidate made several disconnected original contributions.
- The thesis does not have a clear and concise problem statement that argues the problem was worth investigating.
- The thesis does not have a specific central research question or a well-formulated hypothesis, or predictions that the research is designed to address.

## Further reading

Bloomberg, L., & Volpe, M. (2012). *Completing Your Qualitative Dissertation: A Roadmap from Beginning to End*. Thousand Oaks, CA: Sage. https://doi.org/10.4135/9781452226613

This book examines how to write research problems, purpose statements, and research questions, and to devise a research design. It discusses collecting data, supporting your analysis, and writing up. The authors provide an integrative summary discussion and an annotated bibliography at the end of each chapter, and comprehensive checklists throughout.

Bourke, S., & Holbrook, A. P. (2013). Examining PhD and research masters theses. *Assessment and Evaluation in Higher Education*, 38(4), 407–416. https://doi.org/10.1080/02602938.2011.638738

This paper analyses the importance of 12 indicators for assessing the quality of PhD and Master's theses. Examiners generally rated the relative importance of these indicators similarly for both the PhDs and Masters, but they gave higher gradings for all contribution indicators for PhDs.

Ellis, T. J., & Levy, Y. (2008). Framework of problem-based research: A guide for novice researchers on the development of a research-worthy problem. *Informing Science: The International Journal of an Emerging Transdiscipline*, *11*, 17–33. https://doi.org/10.28945/438

This article demonstrates the importance of a well-articulated, research-worthy problem statement as the centrepiece for any viable research. It examines some problem statements and proposes a template for crafting a compelling statement.

Gill, P., & Dolan, G. (2015). Originality and the PhD: What is it and how can it be demonstrated? *Nurse Researcher*, *22*(6), 11–15. https://doi.org/10.7748/nr.22.6.11.e1335

This article outlines how doctoral candidates can identify, formulate, and articulate their contributions to knowledge. In addition, it clarifies what constitutes originality in the PhD.

Golding, C., Sharmini, S., & Lazarovitch, A. (2014). What examiners do: What thesis students should know. *Assessment & Evaluation in Higher Education*, *39*(5), 563–576. https://doi.org/10.1080/02602938.2013.859230

The authors identify 11 examiner practices, detailing how examiners read and judge a thesis. They emphasise the importance of writing in a reader-friendly way.

Jacobs, R. L. (2011). Developing a research problem and purpose statement. In T. G. Hatcher & T. S. Rocco (Eds), *The Handbook of Scholarly Writing and Publishing*. San Francisco, CA: Jossey-Bass, pp. 125–142. https://experts.illinois.edu/en/publications/developing-a-research-problem-and-purpose-statement

This chapter discusses the problem statement in research and the logic for constructing problem statements. It discusses the implications of placing greater attention on the problem statement.

Miles, D. A. (2019). Problem statement development: How to write a problem statement in a dissertation. *Doctoral Network Conference*. https://www.academia.edu/39588741/ARTICLE_Problem_Statement_Development_How_to_Write_a_Problem_Statement_in_A_Dissertation

The paper outlines conceptual models and tools for developing problem statements. It is useful for researchers and doctoral students who find writing a dissertation and theses challenging. The author includes a template to help develop a problem statement.

# 5

# Writing the Literature Review

While Chapter 3 focused on how to review literature critically, this chapter discusses how to present synthesised information from the critical review literature, including the development of a theoretical framework. It illustrates how to organise the literature review and explain its scope, trends, and concerns.

## Purpose of the literature review chapter

The literature review chapter is written once the researcher has gained an understanding of the existing literature. It is an integral part of a thesis as it is the foundation on which the study is built. It is the foundation for a theoretical framework that discusses the theories, models, key concepts, research questions, or hypotheses. It also gives an overview of the research design, which determines the methodology and results, and it provides evidence to support claims made in the Discussion chapter. The literature review demonstrates how the current research brings new insights on the topic and explains how the theoretical framework may have impacted the findings.

Before writing the literature review chapter, you will have critically reviewed the literature, thus gaining the state of knowledge on the specific topic, synthesised the literature, and identified a knowledge gap that the research question addresses. Specifically, you will have:

- highlighted and summarised the definitive studies and noted the overall trends in what has been published about the topic, including conflicts, theory, methodology gaps, and new perspectives or scholarship;
- isolated the thematic areas and what the different literature argues on each theme or sub-theme;

- grouped authors who presented different conclusions or results using similar methods, and, in this way, identified inconsistencies where related research yielded different results. The grouping could also include controversies or considerable disagreement among scholars.

Now all this comes together in your literature review chapter. In the literature review, you are not expected to address every argument or perspective concerning the topic, but rather to select and defend those perspectives that are pertinent to your research question.

The literature review chapter is written in the past tense.

## Introducing the literature review chapter

The introduction section of the literature review introduces the purpose and organisation of the chapter, and provides the reader with a roadmap of its contents. Next, it outlines the topic, including any terminology, and explains the scope of the literature review. Finally, it presents the researcher's stance or point of view or position, such as their opinion about trends and concerns in the field and what was lacking. Like any other chapter in the thesis or dissertation, it should have a clear, logical structure which includes an introduction, the main section, and a conclusion.

The introductory paragraph restates the central problem or research question. Then, it provides the scope of the literature review; for example, the review only covered a specific geographic region, or specific populations, or specific periods of time.

The topic sentence could be your position or opinion about the trends and concerns, historical background, study results, statistics, conflicts, theory, methodology, empirical evidence, or gaps in research and scholarship. The topic sentence is followed by an overview of the way the chapter is organised, or a statement of the main topic discussed throughout the literature review, but without arguing for a position or opinion. Finally, the last sentence contains a brief transition to the content of the main body of the chapter, where the details are discussed.

---

### Example: Writing an introduction to the literature review

Many HIV/AIDS patients do not take their medication as instructed, leading to ARV non-adherence. [research problem] Successful treatment of HIV/AIDS

---

involves a complicated, optimal, long-term routine, and medication adherence requires sustained motivation. [topic sentence] The purpose of this chapter is to present a review of studies conducted within the past ten years on motivation as related to medication adherence (only peer-reviewed articles and journals are presented). [scope of literature] The main body of the literature review is organised thematically, i.e., it discusses self-efficacy, social support, and health beliefs related to HIV/AIDS medication adherence. [organisation] We argue that self-efficacy is the most powerful motivating factor for behavioural change and present extensive empirical evidence to support this claim. [position] Details of these themes are discussed in the main body of the chapter. [transition to the main body]

# The main body of the chapter

## Organising the chapter

There are several ways of arranging the literature review chapter, depending on whichever best provides the 'review' for the specific type of research. These include a chronological approach (discussing papers in the order in which they were published), a methodological approach (where the focus is on the methods used in different papers), and a thematical approach (where the focus is on the different themes of the papers).

The thematic approach is often used in theses and that is the approach described in detail in this chapter. But first, we will look briefly at the chronological and methodological approaches.

## Chronological approach

The most straightforward organisational approach is tracing the development of a topic over time, following the patterns, turning points, and key debates that have shaped the direction of the field of inquiry. This is the chronological approach and it aims to interpret how and why these developments occurred.

Organising the literature chronologically means you begin with the first publications or studies in the field of inquiry and progress to the most recently published work. This option makes it easy to discuss the developments and debates in the field as they emerge over time. It also highlights which research has significantly impacted the current understanding of the topic and how discoveries and theories have evolved or developed. Scholars often use it in history or to explore change over time.

## Methodological approach

In a methodological approach, the chapter is organised by the research method used, for example, qualitative, quantitative or mixed methods designs. Studies using the same approach are discussed together. This option is useful when drawing research from various disciplines or critiquing different methods. The methodological approach focuses on how existing research has been conducted. It can form the basis of the arguments in the discussion chapters of your thesis for choosing research methods. If your sources are from different disciplines or fields that use diverse research methods, you can compare the results and conclusions from these approaches and identify best practices.

## Thematic approach

In a thesis, the main body of the literature review chapter is often organised thematically, where the relevant literature linked to a theme of the topic of the study is covered in turn. A chapter organised by themes starts by providing an overview of the issue(s) or themes before discussing each in turn. Subsequent paragraphs then break each theme down into comprehensible sub-themes, depending on the expanse of the topic. Each theme discussed in the literature review chapter needs to be relevant to the specific problem being investigated, i.e., the themes need to address the research question of the thesis. The thematic approach is the most common and useful one for structuring literature reviews in most fields. The aim is to produce a synthesis of the previous significant research findings that directly relate to the research problem under investigation.

For each theme or sub-theme, group the studies according to their common denominators, which may be commonalities, similarities, contrasts, significant agreements or disagreements, contradictions, consensus or divergence, or inconsistencies in theory and findings. To group writers with similar opinions, use linking words or phrases such as 'similarly', 'in addition', 'besides', 'also', and 'again'. If there is a disagreement of opinion, you can indicate this by using the following linking words: 'however', 'conversely', 'nevertheless', and so on. Note areas in which scholars considerably disagree or have divided opinions and explain them. As this explanation might not be self-evident, you will need to probe deeper by examining the research design to explain whether the inconsistencies could be due to the authors' diverse methodological approaches and theories. Inconsistencies also occur when similar research yields contradictory results, or where researchers reached conclusions that were not consistent with their evidence.

Each paragraph focuses on a specific theme or sub-theme and explains how that theme is approached in the literature. The themes contain as many paragraphs as needed to discuss all their points. Cite two or more sources per paragraph and avoid long strings of references for a single point. Emphasise the literature that is especially important to your research question.

---

## Example: Thematic approach

This literature review focuses on barriers to medical treatment. The key themes include the side effects of drugs, knowledge of medications, cultural attitudes and beliefs, and economic access to care. This review focuses on health beliefs, social support, and self-efficacy, and their influence on medication adherence. [sub-themes]

### Health beliefs [sub-theme 1]

Empirical evidence on the relationship between health beliefs and medication adherence have been inconclusive. [topic sentence] One of the earliest studies by Xin Gao (2000) revealed no significant differences between health beliefs and medication. These findings agreed with a more recent study conducted by Nutor et al. (2020), who came up with similar findings after adjusting for age, knowledge of transmission, and district locality. A study conducted on adherence in a different health aspect, i.e. pulmonary tuberculosis, by Safri, Sukartini, and Ulfiana (2010) found no significant relationship between patients' health beliefs and medication adherence. [similarities]

On the other hand, a recent study reported a positive, statistically significant correlation between belief in the disease's seriousness and antiretroviral medication adherence (Demartoto & Adriani (2016). Xin Gao (2000) and Demartoto and Adriani (2016) evaluated studies using the same methodological approach and used similar study participants (HIV patients). They measured similar variables (severity of disease and ART adherence) using the same research design (analytical design) but found different results. [inconsistency] However, their approach to data analysis could have caused this inconsistency. While both used a single dichotomous outcome variable (medication adherence), Xin Gao (2000) carried out a multiple regression analysis with more than one independent variable, while Demartoto et al. (2016) used logistic regression analysis with one independent variable. [explanation of inconsistency]

### Social support [sub-theme 2]

Numerous studies have demonstrated an association between perceived social support and medication adherence. For example, in a review of 50 articles,

*(Continued)*

social support was consistently associated with greater medication adherence (Scheurer, Choudhry, Swanton, Matlin, & Shrank, 2012).

### Self-efficacy [sub-theme 3]

A systematic review of 20 years of empirical research on treatment beliefs, perceived barriers, and social support in treatment adherence consistently recognised the importance of self-efficacy in adherence (Holmes, Hughes, & Morrison, 2014). The authors identified self-efficacy as the most prominent and significant determinant of adherence. Another study found that self-efficacy mediated the associations of social support after adjusting for demographic and comorbidity covariates, demonstrating the vital role of self-efficacy in medication adherence.

## Gaps in knowledge

Highlight the gaps in knowledge and clarify what your study adds to the literature. In other words, justify your research by showing how it helps to fill one or more of the gaps identified in your critical review of the literature and how it extends previous knowledge or contributes to the advancement of the topic under inquiry. These gaps are areas that have been overlooked or inadequately addressed by previous studies.

## Writing the theoretical framework

When it comes to writing the theoretical framework, you will already have explored the theories and models on the topic, and evaluated, compared, and selected the most relevant studies for your research question. In addition, by undertaking the critical review of the literature, you will have determined how other researchers defined and drew connections between the key concepts. When writing the theoretical framework, discuss how you drew on existing theories and methods to build a theoretical framework for your own study. Where the evidence is inconclusive, explain one or two competing theories that can be used to resolve or further explain the problem. The rest of this section will explain how to write a theoretical framework.

The framework begins by stating the research problem or gap in knowledge that you identified in the literature review. It is followed by a theory statement. Next, introduce how the theory or model works or functions and how it fits into your research problem. Finally, provide an overview of the other theories or models related to the topic, if any, and explain why they present a better option of similar theories or illustrate the differences in concepts. Demonstrating your theory's usefulness and superiority over other conventional theories convinces the examiner that you are aware that other theories exist and that you have selected the theory that best fits your reseach question.

---

### Example: Writing a theoretical framework in the literature review chapter

This study investigates the patient's self-efficacy or belief that they can achieve their goals of adhering to medication despite their difficulties. [research problem] It uses Bandura's social cognitive theory. For example, according to Bandura's Social Cognitive Theory, self-efficacy has a vital role in medication adherence. [theory statement] The theory is based on social psychology and explains how the presence of others influences thoughts, feelings, and behaviours. This explanation could refer to the internalised social norms humans are influenced by, even when they are alone (Allport, 1985). [how the theory functions]

Many other social and cognitive psychological theories or models can also explain medication adherence. Some that have offered possible underlying social drivers of behaviour or mechanisms for explaining adherence behaviour to chronic medications are the Health Belief Model (Ellickson et al., 2003), the Theory of Reasoned Action (Sayeed et al., 2005), and Social Cognitive Theory (Barkin, et al., 2002). However, these theories are all guided by behavioural risk or prevention efforts and have a relatively limited focus on impacting behavioural change. For example, the Health Belief Model solely focuses on cognitive factors impacting an individual's assessment and belief in health-promoting behaviour. Social Cognitive Theory focuses on the social environment that impacts behaviour. The Theory of Reasoned Action attempts to combine the two theories into one theory to address individual attitudes and group norms that influence health behaviour. One important mechanism underlying these patterns involves identity-based motivation, which includes the perceived efficacy of health-promoting activities. The model's concepts are motivation to perform the behaviour and the behavioural skills necessary to perform the behaviour (Matovu et al., 2020). [alternative theories or models]

---

## Concluding the literature review chapter

The conclusion of the literature review is a statement about the state of knowledge on the topic. It reminds the reader of the most significant themes and how you drew on existing theories and methods to build a theoretical framework for your research. The concluding paragraphs of the literature review identify the knowledge gap and state how the thesis will contribute to knowledge in the field of study. It closes with a link to the next chapter, which is the methodology chapter.

The conclusion should be around 3–5 pages in length. Never include in-text citations or introduce new information in your conclusion. The literature review chapter should make up 15–25% of the suggested length for the thesis.

---

### Example: Writing a conclusion to the literature review

The purpose of this chapter was to present a review of studies conducted within the past ten years on motivation as they relate to medication adherence. [purpose] The literature review was organised thematically. [organisation] Bandura's Social Cognition Theory guided the literature review to explain the factors that motivate behavioural changes. The factors that came up most prominently from the critical review of the literature were health beliefs, social support, and self-efficacy. Most studies consistently identify self-efficacy as a more important factor in medication adherence. In addition, the studies demonstrate the critical role of self-efficacy as a mediating influence between the association of medication adherence and various factors, such as social support. [summary] However, these studies have been mainly analytical and could not infer the effect of causality, which calls for multifaceted interventions. [knowledge gap] Therefore, this research extends existing knowledge further by designing and conducting an experimental study that tests the effectiveness of self-efficacy in promoting medication adherence. [contribution to knowledge] We discuss this experimental design in the following methodology chapter. [link to the next chapter]

---

## Common pitfalls of the literature review chapter

The following points are some of the most common mistakes students make when writing a literature review:

- Distorting information in the review and misrepresentating the authors' views or findings.
- Limiting references to those supporting the student's thesis and playing down controversies and conflicting results.
- Reporting the sources as an annotated bibliography instead of reporting by themes or issues that connect sources.

- Describing what others have published in the form of summaries without critically evaluating the cited papers.
- Failing to cite the current papers or studies and citing irrelevant, trivial, or outdated references.
- Failing to include the sources cited in the text in the reference list or including references that have not been cited in the text.
- Including comments such as 'no studies were found' without thoroughly exhausting the literature review on the subject or related subjects.
- Failing to explain how the theories or models apply to the research question or problem of study.
- The chapter lacks organisation and coherence, and has no clear structure or focus.

---

## Example: Literature review chapter: Motivation and ART medication adherence

### Introduction

Many HIV/AIDS patients do not take their medication as instructed, leading to ARV non-adherence Successful treatment of HIV/AIDS involves a complicated, optimal, long-term routine, and medication adherence requires sustained motivation. The purpose of this chapter is to present a review of studies conducted within the past ten years on motivation as related to medication adherence (only peer-reviewed articles and journals are presented). The main body of the literature review is organised thematically, i.e., it discusses self-efficacy, social support, and health beliefs related to HIV/AIDS medication adherence. We argue that self-efficacy is the most powerful motivating factor for behavioural change and present extensive empirical evidence to support this claim. Details of these themes are discussed in the main body of the chapter.

This literature review focuses on barriers to medical treatment. The key themes include the side effects of drugs, knowledge of medications, cultural attitudes and beliefs, and economic access to care. This review focuses on health beliefs, social support, and self-efficacy, and their influence on medication adherence.

### Health beliefs

Empirical evidence on the relationship between health beliefs and medication adherence have been inconclusive. One of the earliest studies by Xin Gao (2000) revealed no significant differences between health beliefs and medication. These findings agreed with a more recent study conducted by Nutor et al. (2020), who came up with similar findings after adjusting for age, knowledge

*(Continued)*

---

of transmission, and district locality. A study conducted on adherence in a different health aspect, i.e. pulmonary tuberculosis, by Safri, Sukartini, and Ulfiana (2010) found no significant relationship between patients' health beliefs and medication adherence.

On the other hand, a recent study reported a positive, statistically significant correlation between belief in the disease's seriousness and antiretroviral medication adherence (Demartoto & Adriani (2016). Xin Gao (2000) and Demartoto and Adriani (2016) evaluated studies using the same methodological approach and used similar study participants (HIV patients). They measured similar variables (severity of disease and ART adherence) using the same research design (analytical design) but found different results. However, their approach to data analysis could have caused this inconsistency. While both used a single dichotomous outcome variable (medication adherence), Xin Gao (2000) carried out a multiple regression analysis with more than one independent variable, while Demartoto et al. (2016) used logistic regression analysis with one independent variable.

## Social support

Numerous studies have demonstrated an association between perceived social support and medication adherence. For example, in a review of 50 articles, social support was consistently associated with greater medication adherence (Scheurer, Choudhry, Swanton, Matlin, & Shrank, 2012).

## Self-efficacy

A systematic review of 20 years of empirical research on treatment beliefs, perceived barriers, and social support in treatment adherence consistently recognised the importance of self-efficacy in adherence (Holmes, Hughes, & Morrison, 2014). The authors identified self-efficacy as the most prominent and significant determinant of adherence. Another study found that self-efficacy mediated the associations of social support after adjusting for demographic and comorbidity covariates, demonstrating the vital role of self-efficacy in medication adherence.

## The theoretical framework

This study investigates the patient's self-efficacy or belief that they can achieve their goals of adhering to medication despite their difficulties. It uses Bandura's Social Cognitive Theory. For example, according to Bandura's Social Cognitive Theory, self-efficacy has a vital role in medication adherence. The theory is based on social psychology and explains how the presence of others influences thoughts, feelings, and behaviours. This explanation could refer to the internalised social norms humans are influenced by, even when alone (Allport, 1985).

Many other social and cognitive psychological theories or models can also explain medication adherence. Some that have offered possible underlying social drivers of behaviour or mechanisms for explaining adherence behaviour to chronic medications are the Health Belief Model (Ellickson et al., 2003), the Theory of Reasoned Action (Sayeed et al., 2005), and Social Cognitive Theory (Barkin, et al., 2002). However, these theories are all guided by behavioural risk or prevention efforts and have a relatively limited focus on impacting behavioural change. For example, the Health Belief Model solely focuses on cognitive factors impacting an individual's assessment and belief in health-promoting behaviour. Social Cognitive Theory focuses on the social environment that impacts behaviour. The Theory of Reasoned Action attempts to combine the two theories into one theory to address individual attitudes and group norms that influence health behaviour. One important mechanism underlying these patterns involves identity-based motivation, which includes the perceived efficacy of health-promoting activities. The model's concepts are motivation to perform the behaviour and the behavioural skills necessary to perform the behaviour (Matovu et al., 2020).

## Conclusion

The purpose of this chapter was to present a review of studies conducted within the past ten years on motivation as they relate to medication adherence. The literature review body was organised thematically. Bandura's Social Cognition Theory guided the literature review to explain the factors that motivate behavioural changes. The factors that came up most prominently from the critical review of the literature were health beliefs, social support, and self-efficacy. Most studies consistently identify self-efficacy as a more important factor in medication adherence. In addition, the studies demonstrate the critical role of self-efficacy as a mediating influence between the association of medication adherence and various factors, such as social support. However, these studies have been mainly analytical could not infer the effect of causality, which calls for multifaceted interventions. Therefore, this research extends existing knowledge further by designing and conducting an experimental study that tests the effectiveness of self-efficacy in promoting medication adherence. We discuss this experimental design in the following methodology chapter.

---

### Exercise: Literature review chapter

#### Instructions

Discuss to what extent the examiner's comments apply to this text, supporting your argument with examples of words, phrases, or sentences from the text. (Refer to the section on Pedagogical features — 'Discussion-based exercises' — in the Introduction of this book for more details on completing this exercise.)

*(Continued)*

**Text: Barriers related to antiretroviral (ARV) medication adherence among persons living with HIV/AIDS**

## Introduction

This literature review examines antiretroviral (ARV) medication adherence among people living with HIV/AIDS. It focuses on peer-reviewed articles and research journals from Sub-Saharan Africa that explore factors impacting adherence, such as self-efficacy, perceived benefits, and barriers.

## The problem

Studies on non-adherence have mainly focused on patient-related factors like inconvenient dosing frequency, dietary restrictions, pill burden, side effects, patient-healthcare provider relationships, and social support. However, a gap exists in research on the behavioural and motivational aspects that influence adherence.

## Social demographics

Studies examining demographic factors like age, gender, and marital status have yielded inconclusive results regarding their association with adherence. While some studies found no significant link (Talam et al., 2008), others reported lower adherence to ARV therapy among older adults compared to younger ones (Sasaki et al., 2012). Additionally, lower education and poor literacy have been shown to negatively impact patients' ability to adhere. A field study in Zambia found women to be three times more likely to adhere to medication than men (adjusted odds ratio [AOR] 3.3 and 5.0, respectively). Furthermore, research suggests a connection between being single and non-adherence (Talam et al., 2008; Uzochukwu et al., 2009).

## Barriers

Antiretroviral medications can cause both minor and severe side effects. Qualitative studies suggest a link between side effects and decreased adherence (Barnett et al., 2013; Nsimba, Irunde, & Comoro, 2010). However, a quantitative study in South Africa found no significant correlation between the severity of symptoms and adherence, suggesting that some patients may be able to tolerate side effects and continue taking their medication as prescribed (Bhengu et al., 2011).

## Social support networks

Qualitative research suggests that family members provide social support by reminding patients to take medication, refill prescriptions, attend appointments, and offer essential material assistance (food, clothing, finances) (Barnett et al., 2013; Knodel et al., 2010; Nsimba et al., 2010). Studies show that patients with help remembering medication schedules have higher adherence rates (≥95%) compared to those without support. However, quantitative studies report no significant difference in adherence between individuals with and without social support. Interestingly, other research suggests that family communication is a strong predictor of adherence (Knodel et al., 2010).

## Gaps in knowledge

Evidence on the link between social demographics, social support, side effects, and adherence remains inconclusive. Prior studies, mostly qualitative or facility-based, relied on self-reporting and pharmacy refills with minimal use of pill counts at the household level. Notably, this data came from a local Comprehensive Care Clinic (CCC) in a community known for strong social networks. Despite intensive HIV/AIDS interventions, adherence remained low at only 48%.

This highlights the need for more household-based studies that combine self-reporting with pill counts. Additionally, most existing research is descriptive and qualitative, lacking quantitative data. Studies on demographics and side effects also have shortcomings, with demographics offering inconclusive results and side effect studies failing to consider the cumulative burden of various side effects.

My study addresses this gap by utilising an analytical household-based design. It employs pill counts alongside social support (independent variable), perceptions (intervening variables), and demographic factors (exogenous variable) to assess adherence (outcome variable). This approach aims to inform the development of culturally sensitive, localised, practical, and effective interventions to improve ARV adherence.

For better outcomes, multifaceted, long-term, and flexible approaches that target specific barriers to adherence are likely to be most successful. These approaches should address medication adherence barriers at all levels while reinforcing positive adherence behaviours.

*(Continued)*

## Conceptual framework

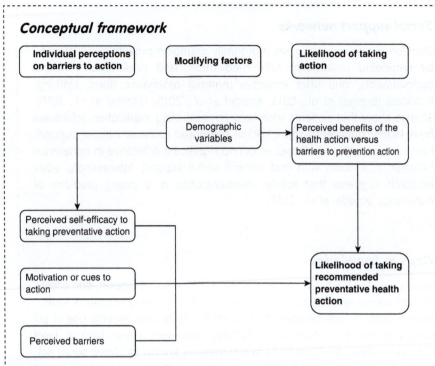

**Figure 5.1**   Modified Health Belief model (Davey, 2004)

## Examiner's comments

- The candidate demonstrates a clear understanding of and familiarity with the relevant literature.
- The candidate identified the gaps in knowledge, had a thorough knowledge of the field, and familiarity with the relevant original literature sources.
- The literature review is concise and presents a well-argued critical perspective on the material.
- The literature was critically reviewed, interpreted, analysed, summarised, and logically structured.
- The literature review was written like a bibliography with no critical, analytic approach or differences of opinion.
- The candidate presents a clear account of the conceptual approach enabling the reader to understand the theoretical framework.
- The conceptual framework was based on literature research, which enhanced the study's scientific quality. Key studies in the field of inquiry were ignored.
- The literature review has some statements with missing citations.

- The literature covered non-essential literature and irrelevant digressions. The literature review had incorrect, incomplete, inaccurate publication dates and inconsistent bibliography and citations.
- The candidate did not demonstrate how the findings contribute to or advance the literature and indicate further research.

# Further reading

Matheson, L., Lacey, F. M., & Jesson, J. (2011). *Doing Your Literature Review: Traditional and Systematic Techniques*. London: Sage.

This book guides the writer through the production of traditional and systematic literature reviews, explains their differences, advantages and disadvantages, and the skills needed to write them. It gives practical advice on reading and organising the relevant literature and critically assessing the reviewed field. Chapter 6, on 'Writing up your review', is particularly helpful as it offers different strategies for writing the literature review so as to avoid making it a simple descriptive list.

Petchko, K. (2018b). Situating a study: The literature review. In *How to Write about Economics and Public Policy*. Oxford: Elsevier.

This chapter shows how authors organise their literature reviews to make statements about the state of current knowledge, and to present their arguments and theoretical positions. It ends by detailing the common problems students may have when reviewing academic literature.

Winchester, C. L., & Salji, M. (2016). Writing a literature review. *Journal of Clinical Urology*, 9(5), 308–312. https://doi.org/10.1177/2051415816650133

This article presents a range of skills needed to write a literature review. These skills include demonstrating a critical appraisal of the current knowledge, evaluating and summarising the literature, explaining similarities or discrepancies, and highlighting knowledge gaps. It also details how to structure the review with an introduction, subsections, and a summary table.

Woodrow, L. (2019). Choosing a topic. In *Doing a Master's Dissertation in TESOL and Applied Linguistics*. London: Routledge.

The chapter provides practical tips for writing the literature review. These tips include doing a good literature search, citing relevant sources, and how to be organised in your approach.

# 6

# Writing the Methodology Chapter

The methodology chapter in the thesis comes immediately after the literature review chapter. It describes the steps taken to address the knowledge gaps identified in the literature review chapter. It presents the research design and methods (qualitative, quantitative, and mixed methods) undertaken to investigate the research topic and includes discussion of ethical considerations and the limitations of the methodology.

This chapter discusses how to write the research design and the methods used in the research, including quantitative, qualitative, or mixed methods, the rationale or justification for choosing these methods, the specific criteria used to select study participants or subjects, their number, and the sampling strategy used. The chapter describes and explains the advantages and disadvantages of the research tools or instruments chosen to collect the data and their ability to produce reliable, valid, or credible transferable dependable results, including the procedure for collecting the data. Finally, the approach for data analysis and a brief discussion on the ethical considerations and limitations posed by the research methodology is presented.

Some universities recommend removing any detailed sections on data analysis from the method section and incorporating it into the results chapter. Institutions specify the writing requirements and academic style for writing this chapter; however, social and natural sciences often follow the American Psychological Association (APA) style.

## Purpose of the methodology chapter

The methodology chapter is the yardstick for the thesis's scientific rigour. Findings from this chapter create the foundation for the overarching argument in the thesis. The methodology chapter demonstrates comprehension and justification of appropriate methodological techniques and an awareness of their limitations. Finally, it explains 'how' the study was conducted, including the events before, during, and after collecting the data.

The methodology chapter is written in the past tense; thus, when writing the thesis, revisit verb tenses in the proposal and change them from future to past tense. It should be concise and provide the reader with only the background information that helps them to understand why the method was selected. Assume the readers possess a basic understanding of the methods; therefore, do not write a 'how-to guide' about a particular method or go into details about the specific methodological procedures. The focus should be on applying the method, not its mechanics, unless it is an unconventional methodological approach.

The chapter has an introductory paragraph, the main body of the chapter and a concluding paragraph.

## Introducing the methodology chapter

The introductory paragraph in the methodology chapter contains a short introduction or preamble restating or reiterating the thesis statement. It also introduces the type of design adopted to answer the research question and the method used (i.e., quantitative, qualitative, mixed methods) in one or two sentences. The last sentence in the paragraph briefly transitions to the first paragraph of the main body of the chapter text.

---

### Example: Writing an introductory paragraph

Sustained motivation is a requirement for successfully treating HIV/AIDS. [restated thesis statement] Therefore, we conducted an experimental trial to investigate the effectiveness of Motivational Interviewing (MI) in increasing self-efficacy and, consequently, ARV medication adherence. [purpose and justification for the methodological approach] Details of the MI approach are discussed in the main sections of the chapter.

---

## The main body of the methodology chapter

The main body of the methodology chapter illustrates how to present research designs and the associated quantitative, qualitative, and mixed methods (the three major approaches to research in the social sciences). Details include writing about sample size and sampling, data collection, approaches to data analysis, ethical considerations, and the limitations of the methodology.

## Research designs and research methods

This section explains how to present the research design and methods used in the thesis and the rationale for using the methods. It is accompanied by examples. There is a difference between research design and the research method. **Research design** is the overall structure, detailing how the chosen method will be applied to answer the research question. **Research methods** are the tools, procedures, and approaches used to gather and analyse the data required to answer the research question(s). The *research problem or question* determines the *type of study* undertaken, whether quantitative, qualitative, or mixed methods. Research methods conform to the type of question(s), the type of study you are conducting, and the best research design to answer the research question.

A well-defined research design dictates the methods of data collection and analysis. Examples of some research designs include action research design, case study design, causal design, cohort design, cross-sectional design, descriptive design, *experimental design*, exploratory design, longitudinal design, mixed methods design, and observational design.

You do not need to present a textbook description of the research design in this section, but you do need to explain the rationale for selecting the specific research design. Examiners specifically check whether the research design and methods are appropriate for the research question. In addition, they need to see how the design and methods are applied and situated in the current study, the appropriateness of the design and methods, and a justification of their selection. Therefore, you must justify why you selected the design — a step that is often forgotten when writing theses. If you use more than one research design, involving multiple research methods, you should explain how they were used together. The following example suggests how methods can be combined in a study.

### Example: Combining designs

The first stage of the study might involve a clinical trial that looks at a drug's efficacy. The second stage might then test the effectiveness of the drug, using a randomised experimental design. A final stage might be an observational design that answers specific questions about the patient's perception of the medication.

# Quantitative research methods

**Quantitative research** is a systematic investigation of phenomena that gathers quantifiable data information using sampling methods, surveys, questionnaires, etc., and performs statistical, mathematical, or computational techniques. There are three main types of quantitative research design: descriptive, correlational, and experimental research. Experimental research can be subdivided into quasi-experimental design and true experimental design.

## Descriptive quantitative research designs

Descriptive quantitative research designs are also referred to as 'observational studies' because the researcher's role is strictly that of an observer. Observational research refers to non-experimental designs where behaviour is methodically observed and recorded. This type of research describes a variable(s) that captures specific characteristics of an individual, group, setting, event, programme, treatment, or unusual observation. It is appropriate for measuring and determining associations between variables but does not establish causal relationships. Types of descriptive studies include case studies (case reports or case series), cross-sectional studies, prospective studies, and case–control or retrospective studies. These designs examine a sample and make a statement or inference about the population from which the sample was drawn.

## Case study design

A case report or case study involves collecting data from only one research subject, whereas a case series involves collecting data from more than one research group or subject.

---

### Example: A case report or case study

A 90-year-old man visited the outpatient department with a recent history of unexplained weight loss. He had also previous presented with episodes of sexually transmitted diseases – gonorrhoea and syphilis. He was single, had no permanent partner, and had an active heterosexual sex life. Although the pre-test counselling indicated that he had never injected drugs, received a blood transfusion, or had sex with men, we felt we should do an HIV test, despite his age.

---

## Cross-sectional study design

Cross-sectional studies are used to study relatively frequent conditions of long duration, such as, in a health context, non-fatal, chronic conditions. For example, the design is unsuitable for studying rare or fatal diseases, or diseases of a short duration. Only one set of observations is collected for each unit in the study at a specific time. It assesses the presence or absence of exposure and disease in the individual. In a cross-sectional study, the researcher analyses variables from a study sample to determine the non-causal relationships. The design measures prevalence, not the incidence of disease; it cannot be used to test for the statistical association as it lacks a comparison group. However, it can be used to formulate a hypothesis. Examples of cross-sectional designs include household or community surveys.

## Example: A cross-sectional study

We assessed self-reported HIV medication adherence among HIV patients attending an HIV clinic between June and August 2010. Structured patient interviews were conducted among 300 consecutively selected patients. We used a Medication Adherence Questionnaire (PMAQ) to assess medication adherence to antiretroviral regimens in the past week. We then assessed the proportion of patients with an adherence level of $\geq 95\%$.

## Prospective study designs

A prospective study is a type of longitudinal study which identifies factors or exposure variables at the beginning of the study, and then examines how these factors relate to the outcome of interest during the study period. These studies can take place over a long period of time, with the aim of discovering how these factors affect the rates of a particular outcome.

A cohort study is a longitudinal study that samples a cohort (a group of people with a shared characteristic) and follows them at specific time intervals. Cohort designs assess individuals with a *known risk factor* or exposure against others who do not share the risk factor or exposure, and look for a difference in the risk (or incidence) of a disease over time. The design shows whether the probability of disease is higher in those who are exposed to a risk factor than in those who are not exposed. In additon, the measure of relative risk ratio is reported.

## Example: A prospective cohort study

We conducted a prospective cohort study to determine the risk of developing melanoma, a form of skin cancer, in people living with HIV/AIDS. We followed a cohort of HIV/AIDS patients to establish whether the risk of developing melanoma was different for people with a diagnosis of AIDS. The study participants were 300 patients enrolled in HIV clinics aged over 18 years and confirmed HIV positive, which permitted a quantitative assessment of HIV/AIDS and melanoma. One group consisted of an immunodeficiency group with CD4+ T cell counts of less than 200/uL (a person with a diagnosis of AIDS), and the other group were HIV/AIDS patients with CD4 lymphocyte count of greater than 200/uL (a person without a diagnosis of AIDS). The study was conducted between January 2010 to November 2012. Statistical analyses were performed using SPSS Version 20. We reported measures of relative risk (RR), namely the Incidence Rate Ratio (IRR).

## Case–control or retrospective study designs

A case–control study, also called a retrospective study, compares cases or subjects with a particular attribute to cases that lack that attribute (the control group). The case–control study is a type of observational study where participants are selected for the study based on whether they have an outcome of interest (the cases) or have no outcome of interest (the controls). Case–control designs compare a group that has a condition or disease and a control group that does not have the condition or disease to establish whether the probability of exposure is higher in those with the disease. The study measures the strength of the association between exposure and an outcome using the odds ratio (OR).

## Example: A case-control study

The study's objective was to establish the risk of acquiring HIV by men sleeping with men (MSM). Participants were recruited from the HIV testing centre from February 2010 through to March 2012. Consecutive sampling was used to include all men attending the HIV clinic. Inclusion criteria for cases and controls were men aged over 18 years who had received HIV test results and had signed an informed consent form once the study's purpose had been explained to them. Cases were men who reported having sex with other men diagnosed with HIV. Controls were males who reported having sex with other men and received a negative test result. Sexual orientation, partnership status,

HIV testing history (month and year of the last test), and other risk behaviours in the last six month were assessed. For example, these behaviours included condom use with different partners (always, rarely, never), number of sex partners, type of sex (anal/oral), whether sex was safe or unsafe, and the person's history of sexually transmitted infections (STI). Unadjusted Odds Ratios (ORs) were used to detect differences between the cases and the controls.

## Correlational research designs

Correlational research is like descriptive research because it does not attempt to influence the variables. The difference between them is that a correlational study seeks to test for the presence of statistical associations between the variables. It establishes whether a significant relationship exists between two variables and the extent and direction of this relationship, i.e., whether it has a positive or negative direction or a zero correlation. Note that correlational research cannot be used to establish causality. Instead, statistics calculate measures of association.

### Example: A correlational research design

This study was a correlational research study. The research question was, 'Is there a relationship between disease severity and medication adherence among people living with HIV/AIDs?' Data were collected from 90 patients in three stages of HIV/AIDS attending an HIV/AIDS clinic. These severity stages were based on CDC clinical categories A (asymptomatic), B (moderately ill) and C (most severely ill patients). We examined the data for medical adherence versus severity of disease using the SPSS version 21 statistical computing package to generate odds ratios and 95% confidence.

## Experimental research designs

Quasi-experimental or true experimental studies involve manipulating the study factor (exposure). In both designs, study participants are subjected to a treatment or condition, and the outcome is measured. In addition, the researchers test whether differences in the outcome are related to the treatment.

## Quasi-experimental research design

**Quasi-experimental research designs** evaluate the effectiveness of an intervention, comparing outcomes for participants who received the intervention (the treatment group) and those who did not (the control group); outcomes are compared at the end of the experiment. The 'quasi' element indicates that the participants are not randomly assigned to treatment or control groups. Instead, participants may choose their group or are assigned to the groups by the researchers. One group is given the treatment. The control group receives a standard treatment. Furthermore, because a randomised control is lacking in quasi-experiments, and it is not possible to isolate different variables, there may be several 'rival hypotheses' competing with the experimental manipulation to explain for observed results. Thus, it is best to statistically control for as many co-founders as possible during the analysis.

## Example: A quasi-experimental design

We conducted a quasi-experimental trial to investigate the effectiveness of Motivational Interviewing (MI) in increasing self-efficacy. We used the Strengths Self-Efficacy Scale (SSES) questionnaire, which had been found to have a solid internal consistency ($\alpha = .95$), to measure self-efficacy. Patients attending an HIV/AIDs were assigned to receive standard counselling (the control group). Others were assigned to the MI (the intervention group) using stratified sampling techniques by sex. Motivational Interviewing (MI), which is a counselling method that enhances a patient's motivation to change (Rollnick et al., 2008), was used for four months. A post-test of similar difficulty was administered to both groups. The differences between the treatment and control groups were analysed to see if the MI counselling technique significantly affected self-efficacy scores. The null hypothesis was that there would be no significant difference in medication adherence between the two groups. Analysis of variance (ANOVA) was used to assess the intervention effect. The effect size showing differences between the two groups was measured using Cohen's d.

## True experimental study design

The true experimental design utilises the scientific approach that specifies procedures that allow researchers to test a hypothesis and causal relationships among variables. A scientific experiment uses a completely randomised design, where each study participant is randomly assigned to a group (a randomised controlled trial or RCT). All the critical factors that might affect the phenomenon of interest are entirely controlled. Randomisation can be done by throwing dice or tossing coins, or using computer software to generate an unpredictable sequence. In a blind RCT, the participants do not know if they are assigned to the treatment or the control group. Whereas in a double-blind RCT, both the participants and the researchers do not know who is assigned to the treatment or control groups. Double-blind RCTs reduce the risk of biased influences on the outcomes of the study by participants and researchers

---

## Example: A true experimental design

We conducted an experimental trial to investigate the effectiveness of Motivational Interviewing (MI) in increasing self-efficacy and, subsequently, medication adherence. We used the Strengths Self-Efficacy Scale (SSES) questionnaire, which had been found to have a solid internal consistency ($\alpha = .95$), to measure self-efficacy. This study was a randomised trial to investigate the effectiveness of utilising Motivational Interviewing, a counselling method that enhances a patient's motivation to change (Rollnick et al., 2008). Patients attending an HIV/AIDs clinic were randomily assigned to the intervention and control arms on a basis of 1:1 using computer software. They recieved counselling for six months.

All participants received standard counselling, which is provided to all AIDS patients. In addition, participants in the intervention arm received additional support sessions utilising Motivational Interviewing. The null hypothesis was that there would be no significant difference in medication adherence between the two groups. A two-factor, mixed-design analysis of variance (ANOVA) was used to assess the intervention effect. The effect size showing differences between the two groups was measured using Cohen's d.

---

## The study population, sample size, and sampling design

### Study population

In a research setting, human beings are referred to as participants and non-humans as subjects. This section of the methodology chapter details the participants or subjects (informants, organisations, events, documents, programmes) in your research study. It explains the partici-pants' appropriateness for the investigation of the phenomenon or problem, and why some participants/subjects were included or excluded from the study. You also need to describe why and how a particular unit of analysis was selected. Cases are primary units of analysis or the pri-mary entities analysed in a study (i.e., who or what is being studied).

### Sample size

This section explains how the sample size was calculated to ensure the study yielded reliable scientific information. Note that larger sample sizes yield greater precision, and, thus, greater power for a given study design to detect an effect of a given size. You need to specify the method used to calculate the sample size in detail so that another researcher can check the calculations if desired. The desired treatment effect to be detected by the experiment should be realistic. The minimum acceptable statistical power is typically 80%, although a 90–95% power is preferable (particularly in studies with extensive or nationally representative samples). You also need to state whether the final sample differed from the intended or calculated sample. Base interpretations of the study outcomes on the final sample and not the intended sample.

## Sampling design

Quantitative research is based on probability sampling (which is based on mathematical formula) to select a representative number of participants from a specific population to generalise the population results. This section of the methodology chapter describes how the sample was selected (using a probability or non-probability sampling technique) and the specific procedures used, such as random, stratified, and purposive sampling. Therefore, you need to know about the various types of sampling design to select the most appropriate sampling technique for your study. You also need to explain why the method and criteria for selecting the sample were appropriate and demonstrate that the sample is free of sampling bias. Finally, you must address any potential sources of bias, such as ensuring that you have an adequate number of participants or subjects (sample size) and unbiased sampling techniques.

---

### Example: Writing about the study population, sample size, and sampling design

We conducted an experimental trial to investigate the effectiveness of Motivational Interviewing (MI) in increasing self-efficacy using an intervention and control group. The study participants came from a list of patients attending the Comprehensive Care Clinic (CCC). All were aged over 18 years and were not severely sick.

To calculate the sample size, we used guidelines provided by Cohen (1988) to interpret the magnitude of a correlation and estimate the power. These are, specifically, r = 0.10, r = 0.30, and r = 0.50, which are considered small, medium, and large in magnitude, respectively. Using these guidelines, we proposed a 90% power to detect an effect of r = .30, or a 30% difference between the control and intervention group, with a significance level of .05, coming up with a sample size of 76. We assigned the 38 males and 38 females randomly to either the intervention or control arm of the study. Our final sample satisfied these requirements.

## Measurements and instrumentation

## Measurements

Measurement is the foundation of any scientific investigation, and studies begin with measuring variables or hypotheses from the theoretical framework. This section of the methodology chapter explains how variables are measured or operationalised to answer the research question. It explains how you measure the variables that define the constructs in the theoretical framework. The level of measurement determines the type of statistical analysis used. Some variables do not lend themselves easily to measurement or observation. For example, it is not easy to measure attitudes, beliefs, and perceptions; thus, you need to explain how you operationalised the concept.

---

### Example: Writing the measurement section

Variables measured in this study were medication adherence (dependent) and self-efficacy (independent), medical literacy and other social demographic variables. We used the pill count method to assess if the medication was taken as prescribed. Patients brought the medication bottle dispensed during the previous visit. We calculated the number of pills taken by subtracting the number of pills remaining in the container from the total number of pills dispensed. We then calculated the drug adherence rate by dividing the number of pills taken by the number of days since the last dispense. Finally, we used this information to calculate Drug Adherence Rates (DAR) using the recommended cut-off value for patient adherence to ARV medication of ≥95% in HIV (Apisarnthanarak & Mundy, 2010; WHO, 2002).

Measuring perceptions of self-efficacy was based on Likert scales developed by Likert in 1932. These scales measure a person's attitude or belief by asking them to respond to a series of statements about a particular topic. We used the Adherence Self-Efficacy Scale for persons with HIV developed by Johnson et al. (2007), which assesses confidence to carry out important behaviours related to treatment adherence. In Johnson's scale, participants respond on a 10-point Likert scale (0 = cannot do at all to 10 = completely certain can do). We adapted these statements, but our scales ranged from 0 = cannot do at all to 5 = entirely certain can do. Other variables measured were medical literacy (can read instructions in English: yes=1 and no=0) and social demographic variables: age (complete number of years), sex (male = 1, female = 2), and education level (from none to tertiary).

---

## Instrumentation

This section of the methodology chapter briefly describes all the instruments (e.g., tests, measures, surveys, observations, interviews, questionnaires) used in the study for data collection and justifies their use. Copies of instruments are placed in appendices and are referred to in this section.

It is always advisable to use already developed instruments which are standardised and widely recognised. However, note that a data collection tool that achieves high reliability in a particular setting might not have that same level of reliability in another setting, representing a different population. For example, if you conducted quantitative research and relied on instruments (such as personality tests) that other researchers have developed and validated, you should reference them; if the instrument is copyrighted, you should demonstrate that permission to use it was granted. Therefore, if you use a developed tool or instrument or a widely recognised scale, you need to be able to report its appropriateness for use with your study participants; for example, is the instrument suitable for the age and culture of your research participants? Instruments can include open-ended questions or observational checklists with clearly defined categories. Data are usually recorded in structured questionnaires with pre-coded and close-ended questions that have predetermined answers (e.g., questions requiring yes/no answers) in quantitative studies.

## Reliability and validity of instruments

**Reliability** is the extent to which a questionnaire, test, observation, or measurement procedure produces the same results on repeated trials and the stability or consistency of scores over time or across observers. Statistically, a measurement lacking precision or reliability is subject to much random error. For reliability, you need to chose a standardised instrument, adapt it to local conditions, and then train observers. **Validity** (accuracy) is the extent to which the instrument measures what it purports to measure, especially content validity, which relates to the degree to which the instrument thoroughly assesses or measures a construct (e.g., attitude). If a measurement lacks accuracy or validity, it suffers from systematic error. For example, validity is a challenge in reports or responses based on memory, or self-reports, such as information on medical history or individual practices, which are subjective, and there is no available gold standard.

Other types of validity include internal validity, the degree of confidence that the causal relationship being tested is trustworthy and not influenced by other factors or variables, and external validity, which refers to the extent to which results from a study can be applied (generalised) to other situations, groups, or events.

## Testing reliability or validity

Testing reliability or validity can be set up in a formal pre-study, which can be reported as a sub-study, or a pilot study, where information is not generally reported.

First, describe the pilot study used to validate the instrument's effectiveness and whether the instrument was self-designed or already developed. Second, indicate how the pilot study was reflected in the research design, development of the instrument, data collection procedures, and sample characteristics, including discussions on how the methodology was improved. A measure has high reliability if it produces similar results under consistent conditions. Finally, report the Alpha coefficient (i.e., Cronbach's Alpha). Generally, an Alpha coefficient of 0.9 is considered to be excellent reliability. Reliability of less than 0.6 is considered weak, and a range between 0.7 and 0.8 is considered to be acceptable reliability. The closer the reliability or Alpha coefficient is to 1, the higher the degree of internal consistency of reliability.

---

### Example: Reporting the instrument's reliability

To test this instrument's reliability in our study, we conducted a pilot study on 10% of the respondents (40 patients) at the health facility. The questionnaire was administered to find out whether the items accurately addressed the research questions and to determine whether the research questions were well defined and clearly understood, and how long it took to complete the questionnaire. All the errors were amended and re-piloted until no further changes were necessary.

We used the Adherence Self-Efficacy Scale for persons with HIV, developed by Johnson et al. (2007), which assesses confidence to carry out important behaviours related to treatment adherence. The instrument has nine items for integrating treatment into daily life factors. These items include keeping the patients away from what they want to do, such as the fatigue caused by HIV, physical discomfort or pain related to HIV, emotional distress caused by HIV, and health problems. Also, reducing the need to see a doctor by doing different tasks and activities to manage HIV, and doing things other than just taking medication to reduce how much the illness affects their everyday lives and to control the side effects of medications.

*(Continued)*

---

Cronbach's Alpha, $\alpha$ (or coefficient alpha), measures reliability or internal consistency, was developed by Lee Cronbach in 1951, and states that a Cronbach's Alpha of 0.90 is an excellent rate of internal consistency. Our study had an acceptable Alpha of 0.75, indicating sufficient internal consistency.

## Data collection procedures

The procedure for data collection relates to the central question. Accordingly, examiners attach importance to competence in research techniques and procedures. This section of the methodology chapter describes the procedures of contacting the research participants, obtaining their cooperation, including instructions to participants or distributing materials, and how the data was recorded. The procedures used include how, when, and where the instruments were administered, such as in the field, classroom, or laboratory. If the study was done in stages, you need to produce a timeline for each stage's completion.

Procedures include informal or semi-structured interviews, physical measurements, close-ended and open-ended questions, which can be coded later, and an observational checklist with clearly defined categories.

### Example: Writing about the data collection procedure

We ensured the credibility and validity of the study by using nurses as interviewers because they had the experience of discussing HIV/AIDS. Therefore, we started by training four nurse counsellors on Motivational Interviewing using the Motivational Interviewing Target Scheme (MITS). This instrument assesses Motivational Interviewing (MI) competency that explicitly integrates traditional clinical methods with practical communication skills (Kurtz, Silverman, Benson, & Draper, 2003; Oberink, Boom, Van Dijk, & Visser, 2017; Zill et al., 2014). The training was conducted over three hour-long sessions, which included refresher sessions, spread over one month. We started data collection after training the nurses. Patients were randomly assigned to each of the four nurses. The nurses informed respondents about the special counselling sessions, which would take at least 30 minutes, without disclosing the expected outcome. After being assured of their confidentiality, the patients provided informed consent. After that, interviews took place privately in a single interview session.

The initial information collected from the patient formed the baseline. In this initial contact, the participants responded to self-efficacy statements listed in the instrument, medication literacy questions, and social demographic background information. Four monthly counselling sessions followed the baseline interview, with the final session being a repeat of the baseline session or the end line survey.

The counselling sessions were different for the control and the intervention group. The MI interviews were video-recorded. Nurses handed over the video recordings of the consultations with patients in each session, and the recordings were stored on a secure server. At the end of the sessions, an assessment was carried out by four assessors, who viewed and listened to all the recordings and took notes. Subsequently, they scored options that best described the holistic impression of the observed behaviour in each of the four sessions.

## Approach used in quantitative data analysis

Although students are diligent about describing how they collect their data, few describe how they process it. However, that information is just as important. Having more data than expected is common, so the overall research question helps the researcher to decide what to focus on without jeopardising the integrity of the research.

In quantitative studies, the data collected are analysed statistically, and the examiner needs to know what statistical tests were used and why. You need to state the approach you used for coding the data, the specific analytical techniques you adopted, and the statistical methods employed, including controlling for confounding variables. The analysis is linked to the research design and methods; therefore, the statistics or tests should be appropriate for the research design. Each research design uses different statistics (as demonstrated in the section on 'Quantitative research methods').

Justify the choice of statistics used to address the hypotheses and research questions or tests. In other words, state why it was the best analytical approach to use. Avoid describing a particular technique from a statistics text; instead, present a short, reasoned statement of why the specific approach was the most appropriate. In addition, describe the quantitative variables you analysed, including their grouping or categorisation. For example, group continuous data (e.g., weight) using cutpoints to specify the range of values in each category. Specify how you dealt with missing data and outliers outside the norm. These descriptions should be detailed enough for the reader to replicate the analysis.

## Example: Writing about the approach to quantitative data analysis

We performed data analysis using the Statistical Package for the Social Sciences (SPSS, version 21) to enter, check and clean data to determine the effect of MI on self-efficacy. First, we examined the ranges of responses for each variable through frequency distributions. In addition, we used SPSS to estimate missing data for possible oversight upon entry, normality, and outliers. We addressed missing data through listwise deletion, which excluded variables that had missing data. However, no cases were excluded from analysis due to missing data in our study. Next, we performed normality checks on these variables using the skewness criterion of −2 to +2 and the kurtosis criterion of −7 to +7 described by West et al. (1995). In our study, variables were normally distributed. Next, we calculated the total subscale scores for self-efficacy. Finally, we determined the final MI score for each participant ranging from 0 (no MI consistency) to 4 (a very high degree of MI consistency). This approach is consistent with the use of communication rating scales in which the final score is the mean of all assessed consultations (Kurtz, Silverman, Benson, & Draper, 2003; Oberink, Boom, Van Dijk, & Visser, 2017; Zill et al., 2014).

We used an independent sample t-test and paired sample t-test to analyse the pre-post test scores for the control and experimental groups. A two-factor, mixed-design analysis of variance (ANOVA) was used to assess the intervention effect. The effect size showing differences between the two groups was measured using Cohen's d.

## Statement on the assumptions, limitations, and delimitations of the study

The final section of the main body of the methodology chapter is a statement on the assumptions, limitations, and delimitations of the study. No method is perfect, and things seldom happen precisely as planned. It is also impossible for the researcher to know that participants have been honest in their responses, for example, or answered to the best of their ability. Sometimes participants say what they think the researcher wants to hear. Thus, the study will still have some natural limitations and the researcher will be compelled to make certain assumptions. Discuss the limitations of the methodology, and acknowledge any assumptions you have made as well as any information that you think might have potentially affected the number or characteristics of the participants.

*Delimitations* are limitations on the research that the researcher has imposed deliberately, such as restricting the number or type of participants (male, female, ethnicity, age). Such delimitations make the study's results generalisable to only these groups. On the other hand, *limitations* refer to restrictions in the study over which the researcher has no control, for example, non-responses, sampling issues, and logistics. Therefore, it is also recommended that when writing this section of the methodology chapter, you should focus on only those limitations that might have affected your findings.

## Potential sources of bias

Potential sources of bias include the following:

- The final sample might have skewed the results, i.e., it was not representative of the study participants.
- A low response rate could have resulted in a smaller sample than the one calculated, or the student ended with one sub-group being over-represented or under-represented.
- The instrumentation did not work as intended, or something was wrong with the instrument itself, or perhaps in the way it was used.
- The methodology used elsewhere did not seem to work as intended among the study participants; e.g., cultural bias distorted the findings.
- There was something wrong with the entire research design; the research design was not suitable for the research questions.
- There were validity issues.

---

### Example: Writing about assumptions, delimitations, and limitations

The findings of this study might have some limitations. The study's significant delimitation was the research design pre-test/post-test. Although we randomly assigned participants to the treatment or control, the participants in the experimental study might have changed or improved their behaviour simply because they sensed that they were being evaluated or studied (this is known as the Hawthorne effect). On the other hand, those in the control group might have learned from the experimental group and changed their behaviour. A key limitation of the study was the assumption that participants answered the questions honestly and to the best of their ability during the interviews. However, we controlled for most confounding variables in the analysis.

---

The section on assumptions, delimitations, and limitations should be a minimum of three to four paragraphs.

## Qualitative research methods

Although this book focuses on quantitative methods, **qualitative research** methods also need to be covered. Qualitative research is descriptive; there are no well-established and widely accepted general rules or principles for measurement.

This section highlights some critical differences between quantitative and qualitative research. It discusses the three fundamental research approaches in qualitative research: **grounded theory**, **ethnography**, and **phenomenology**.

Qualitative research methods enable the study of social and cultural phenomena. They commonly revolve around open-ended survey questions and highly descriptive answers that are difficult to quantify and express through numbers. Nevertheless, qualitative research methods offer a valuable way to collect more complex information, explore people's thoughts and behaviour, formulate predictions, and explain quantitative results.

In qualitative research, there is no sample size calculation. Rather, qualitative research emphasises the richness of information. The researcher needs to explain the rationale for the selection of participants and to describe how they interviewed them. The researcher collects data to the point of saturation, which is the point at which no new information is gained. Qualitative research is descriptive; there are no well-established and widely accepted general rules or principles for measurement.

When discussing the data collection procedure in qualitative research, the researcher needs to explain the approach and briefly discuss the data-gathering procedures used. Researchers can use textual data, such as reports, diaries, general or technical documentation, or any text-based materials, including photographs, images, signage, etc. Focus groups discussions (FGDs) or community meetings are a common source of data; these are recorded and fully transcribed for analysis. Other sources of analysis can be the direct observations of the researcher in the field, recorded as notes, interviews, and participatory methods, which engage community stakeholders through initiatives like focus group discussions.

On the issues of reliability or validity, qualitative methods are often organised so as to provide a check on each other. For example, in research where several qualitative methods have been adopted, triangulation is used to establish consistency. Triangulation is the use of multiple methods or data sources to enhance the credibility of your research study (Patton, 1999). Therefore, the researcher needs to explain how they triangulated their methodology. For example, research assistants participated in focus groups to provide an independent assessment of the findings, or direct observation of a subject's behaviour to check questions' responses.

Trustworthiness in qualitative studies involves establishing the credibility of the findings by showing that the research was conducted in a precise, consistent, and exhaustive manner through recording, transcribing interviews verbatim, providing an audit trail or log, and disclosing the methods of analysis in sufficient detail to enable other researchers to repeat the process. Applying concepts like trustworthiness improves the confidence that others have in the findings.

The approach used in data analysis can be based on content or themes, and the researcher needs to justify why their chosen approach was the most appropriate method for the research question. For example, content analysis, which looks at the relative frequencies of words, phrases, or concepts within a piece of qualitative data (i.e., text), can be used to interpret meanings and relationships. On the other hand, thematic analysis explains how the data were coded and arranged into meaningful categories (themes). It describes what the researcher was looking for in each theme, i.e., similarities and differences or relationships or connections, and how they organised their presentation of the findings and the discussions around the main themes. If the researcher used multiple case-study approaches (of people or organisations), they need to explain how they relate the themes within each case study to the research question. If the researcher used software such as NVivo in their analysis, they need to explain precisely how it was used; saying 'NVivo will be used' is inadequate. Thus, the researcher needs to explain their method of data analysis fully.

Extensive documentation, such as the code list used in analysing qualitative data, is placed in the appendix.

## Example: An approach to qualitative analysis

We used the English translation in the data analysis in this study. A coding dictionary was developed that focused on motivation, behavioural skills,

*(Continued)*

adherence, and emerging issues (e.g., self-stigma). Research team members independently generated a set of codes based on these themes by conducting a line-by-line content analysis. This coding was used to help understand the participants' perspectives and analyse their combined experiences. Coding was conducted both manually and using computer-assisted qualitative data analysis software. We entered data into a qualitative data management program ATLAS.ti (scientific software).

## Examples of qualitative research methods

Three of the main qualitative research methods are: (a) grounded theory, which is an inductive approach where hypotheses and theories emerge from or are grounded in data; (b) ethnography, which is an approach that relies on collecting data in the natural environment, i.e., how individuals' behaviour is influenced or mediated by the culture in which they live or the setting in which it occurs; and (c) phenomenology, which focuses on individuals' interpretation of their experiences and how they express them, i.e., individuals' personal experiences of phenomena.

### Example: Writing a grounded theory study

We conducted a qualitative study using in-depth, semi-structured interviews to explore facilitators and barriers to healthcare access for people living with HIV. The respondents were recruited from a public HIV treatment facility that offered comprehensive HIV care, including case management, counselling, nursing support, and an on-site pharmacy.

The patients were people living with HIV who were over 18 years, had attended at least one case management intake visit, spoke the official or national languages (Swahili or English) and had given informed consent. Fifty patients were recruited consecutively from a weekly list of HIV clinic attendees, ensuring a representative distribution by age and gender.

The respondents were divided into two groups: 25 patients who missed their first appointment following their case management intake visit without cancellation or rescheduling (**non-compliant**), and 25 patients who attended their first appointment following their case management intake (**compliant**).

The initial semi-structured interview guide was based on the Theory of Planned Behaviour (Ajzen, 1991, 2010, 2011), exploring perceived behavioural control beliefs (regarding factors that facilitate or hinder behaviour). The participants were also asked what interventions they would suggest to increase access to care and reduce missed appointments.

The patient interview guide was piloted to test the interview duration and feedback on the appropriateness of questions and prompts. These in-person interviews, which lasted approximately one hour, were audio-recorded and transcribed verbatim. We used Cohen's Kappa for two raters to index inter-rater reliability of 1.00, with a benchmark goal of more than 0.70. We constructed a code list based on themes from the Theory of Planned Behaviour (Ajzen, 1991) and conducted the initial coding in ATLAS.ti Version 7 (Berlin, Germany) to generate new codes as needed.

We used the constant comparative approach for analysis, which is consistent with Grounded Theory (Glaser, 1965; Glaser & Strauss, 2017). Axial coding sorted these codes into themes consistent with the theory of Planned Behaviour: attitudes, subjective norms, perceived behavioural control, and intentions.

Codes that did not fit into the theory's constructs were grouped into independent themes. These additional themes included: structural barriers to access to healthcare, such as transportation, lack of insurance, financial hardship, bureaucracy, waiting times at the clinic, and attitude of the staff. These themes were examined for co-occurrence between patients who complied and those who were non-compliant at their initial medical visit. We then used selective coding to understand how differences in themes between the subgroups — compliant versus non-compliant — might have impacted initial access to healthcare.

## Example: Writing an ethnographic study

We explored how some HIV-positive individuals living in challenging circumstances can achieve successful adherence. Our study involved HIV-positive individuals attending an HIV clinic that provides comprehensive care using an interdisciplinary healthcare team of physicians, nurses, pharmacists, social workers, psychologists and dietitians. The patients were seen every four weeks after initiating ARV medication and then every three to four months. In addition, we used focused ethnography to interview HIV-positive individuals to learn why, despite their difficult circumstances, they could achieve consistent ARV medication adherence.

*(Continued)*

We recruited 41 HIV-positive individuals who lived in a slum area through purposeful sampling during subsequent routine clinic visits, ensuring gender representation. The participants were ARV medication adherent individuals who had maintained virologic suppression (VL ≤50 copies/mL), an indicator of treatment success, for the previous 12 consecutive months.

After explaining the research and the participant agreeing to participate, we obtained written informed consent and scheduled an interview. We conducted all interviews in a private room at the HIV clinic using unstructured one-on-one interviews. The main questions asked were: 'Do you take your medication all the time?' and 'How do you achieve that?'. Other questions included the experience of taking ARV medication (e.g., 'How are you coping with your HIV medication?'), and general ARV medication adherence questions (e.g., 'Why do you think people might miss taking their HIV medication?') The interviews, which were audio-recorded and transcribed verbatim, lasted approximately one hour.

Our goal was to identify systematically, code, and categorise patterns using qualitative content analysis (Hsieh & Shannon, 2005; Mayan, (2016). We used Spradley's domain analysis to identify themes in the data. The data were managed using the qualitative data management software NVivo 8.

## Example: Writing a phenomenological study

The objective of this phenomenological study was to explore the experience of patients living with HIV. We used van Manen's (1990) phenomenological framework, which reflects and interprets the patients' experiences. The framework provides an in-depth insight into the human experience.

Respondents over 18 years were recruited from the HIV clinic of the hospital through purposive sampling by clinicians, case managers and nurses. The selection ensured inclusion by age, tribe, and religion. Prospective respondents were contacted directly. The consent to participate in the study was obtained after explaining the purpose of the study. The participants were 10 females and 10 males living with HIV. The respondents were mentally sound, could express themselves in the official and national language and were willing to participate in the study.

Data were collected between August and December 2020. The interviews were conducted individually at the nurses' office through informal open-ended interviews where participants could share their stories using a non-directive opening question. This question was: 'What are your experiences of living with

HIV/AIDS?' HIV prompts were developed to assist participants who may have had difficulty responding to this broad question. The prompts included probing questions, such as 'Can you give an example?', 'Can you explain further?'. The interviews were open-ended, allowing the participants to elaborate on their experiences in their chosen manner. The interviewers were trained in interview techniques such as active listening, including reflection of content and emotion, to be better prepared for the data collection process. There was no pilot testing since we used an open-ended interview process without an established questionnaire. All interviews were audio-recorded and transcribed verbatim. Interviews varied in length from 30 to 60 minutes.

Each transcript was read line by line, and statements that reflected the research question were identified to generate a catalogue of codes used to describe what the respondents were saying. Transcriptions from audio-taped interviews were analysed using van Manen's three-pronged phenomenological thematic analysis approach across all transcripts, identifying common or repetitive themes. Analysis continued until we arrived at deep, rich, related, and abstract themes.

# Mixed research methods

**Mixed methods** research is mainly used in the behavioural, health, and social sciences, especially in multidisciplinary studies and complex social research. Mixed methods involve collecting and analysing qualitative and quantitative data to answer research questions within a single investigation. Mixed methods are suitable where the quantitative or qualitative approaches are inadequate for understanding a research problem or question. Mixing methods leads to a better and more complete understanding of the issues and views of study participants, as it integrates the strengths of both qualitative and quantitative approaches, helping to gain a complete picture that one cannot get from a stand-alone quantitative or qualitative study. Combining the methods also enables the researcher to generalise the results. It draws on the comparative strength of large sample sizes in quantitative research, which mitigates the relative weakness of qualitative research, which usually has a smaller sample size and is thus not generalisable. Furthermore, converging qualitative and quantitative research methods (triangulation) strengthens the validity of the conclusions. Using different data collection on the same subject makes the results more credible.

Mixed methods are an excellent choice for integrating two questions in one research study. For example, how do HIV/AIDS patients' perceptions of AIDS (qualitative) relate to ARV adherence levels (quantitative)?

There are three types of basic mixed methods designs: sequential exploratory, sequential explanatory, and convergent study designs. The differences between these designs relate to (a) the aim of the research, (b) the timing of the data collection, and (c) the importance given to each data type. These three designs form the foundation for advanced designs, such as experimental, participatory/social justice, case study, and other multi-stage designs (Creswell, 2015).

## Sequential exploratory study design

Exploratory studies begin with a qualitative data collection and analysis phase on which a subsequent quantitative phase can build. For example, the researcher uses qualitative techniques to explore an initial question and to develop a hypothesis. Next, the researcher uses quantitative data to test or confirm the qualitative findings. The findings of these two phases are then integrated, but priority is often given to the qualitative aspect of the study.

---

### Example: Writing a sequential exploratory research design

We used a sequential exploratory design to explore the difficulties that women living with HIV face regarding treatment to identify common or repetitive themes. We used a phenomenological approach in the first phase. Findings from the qualitative data analysis informed and shaped the survey questionnaire that we used to collect quantitative data in the study's second phase.

---

## Sequential explanatory study design

The explanatory design begins with a quantitative data collection and analysis phase, which informs the follow-up qualitative data collection and analysis phase. This design is often used where the qualitative results are used to explain and interpret the findings of a quantitative study. In other words, qualitative data help to explain and contextualise the quantitative findings.

## Example: Writing a sequential explanatory research design

We used a sequential explanatory design to investigate perceptions of ART medication adherence among HIV-infected individuals (quantitative). First, we collected and analysed ARV adherence data, drawing preliminary conclusions about the level of adherence. We then collected qualitative information on perceptions in the study's second phase to help explain the low levels of adherence.

## Convergent study design

In the convergent design, quantitative and qualitative data collection are done simultaneously, and are followed by an integrated analysis. In a convergent parallel design, the researcher simultaneously collects quantitative and qualitative data and analyses them separately. The researcher can also integrate data at the analytic and interpretation levels by presenting and discussing different quantitative and qualitative analysis results. The other way of integrating data is to present the data visually in a table or figure.

## Example: Writing a convergent research design

We mixed the research methodologies in a convergent design research study that answered the question: 'What is the relationship between the level of ARV adherence and the perceptions of HIV/AIDS treatment in adults living with HIV/AIDs?' We collected and analysed data on ARV adherence and participants' perceptions of HIV/AIDS treatment and living with HIV/AIDS simultaneously. On the qualitative side, we analysed the participants' perception of ARVs, and on the quantitative side, we analysed the level of adherence. After completing the analysis, we compared the results and tied our findings together.

## Ethical considerations

This section of the methodology chapter outlines the ethical considerations of the study. It details how to deal with ethical issues and conflicts of interest, and ensuring compliance with the Institutional

Review Board (IRB) requirements. In other words, the purpose of the research and the nature of the research questions need to align with those approved by the relevant ethical committee before commencing data collection.

Ethical issues are guided by 'normal' practice within the discipline. Some disciplinary fields suggest a minimal discussion of these issues in this section, while others expect a thorough account of all the ethical issues involved in the study. Therefore, supervisors and students need to be cognisant of these debates and decide what ethical issues to include when writing up their thesis or dissertation.

Ethics is central in all scientific studies and is closely linked to research integrity. Universities require compliance with ethical procedures and submission of an ethics form before any research involving human subjects is undertaken. Ethical considerations can be presented in the introduction or methodology chapter of your thesis, or as a separate section in its own right. Ethical consideration is not simply saying, 'I followed the ethical guidelines'. Instead, the researcher needs to identify the issues that are specific to their research question and explain how they handled them. Some of the key areas to be addressed in the ethics section of the thesis are outlined below. Although the researcher might need to get permission to conduct the research – for example, from parents, headteachers, and heads of units, informed – consent must be obtained from the individual participants, unless they are minors or from disadvantaged groups.

## Institutional Review Board

The Institutional Review Board (IRB) protects participants involved in research. For example, if the study involves human subjects, compliance with the IRB is necessary. Thus, before implementing a new study, the researcher must apply to the IRB at the research institution or from any outside institutions if the research is conducted at multiple sites. The application is accompanied by a study protocol and documents such as letters, consent forms, and questionnaires. In addition, the organisation(s) in which your research is conducted may have other ethical guidelines and procedures, with which you need to comply.

## Informed consent

Informed consent is usually required in research studies where participants are exposed to minimal or more significant risk. Participants should know what they are being asked to do and the risks before agreeing to participate. The consenting procedure requires that participants are informed of the following: (i) that they are participating in research; (ii) how/why they were selected or invited to participate; (iii) what their involvement in the research entails; (iv) the procedures involved in the study, including potential benefits from the research (both to the participant and to society); (v) issues regarding compensation in the event of a study-related injury or complication; and (vi) they are provided with contact details of the researcher or a member of the research team in case they have further questions, and (vii) they are free to withdraw their consent at any time without having to explain their wish to withdraw. Finally, no incentives will be given in exchange for participating in the study, beyond a minimal or token gesture for the time they commit to the study. Participants are not offered compensation.

## Consent

After explaining the above issues and asking the participant if they have understood and agreed to participate, request that they sign a consent form that includes their demographic details, such as name, address, and occupation. Most studies require a general study consent form; others may require one or more release forms for permission to obtain access to tissue samples, medical records, or diagnostic films. Consent forms require you to explain what the research entails and how any ethical issues raised will be dealt with. For example, you might need to explain the challenges of getting signed consent and how you ensured the informants understood the nature of the research in which they were participating. A copy of the informed consent form that you asked participants to sign is provided in the appendices of the thesis, along with the letters of permission to conduct the research, an invitation to participate, instructions to participants, and ethical release forms.

## Voluntary nature of the research

There is a need to emphasise the voluntary nature of the research study and the participants' right to withdraw without giving any reason, even after signing the consent form. In addition, participants can request that their data be withdrawn from the study. Thus, you need to have a system of linking pseudonyms to the personal information of participants to enable you to remove these details should the participant withdraw. These links must remain confidential and must be kept separately from the data.

## Anonymity and confidentiality

Making the data 'anonymous' means removing the participants' identities, including any information that might identify them. Anonymity also involves organisations, units, and groups, such as their geographical information or type of organisation. Note, however, that in some instances, participants may be keen for their voices to be acknowledged and are comfortable having their identity made known alongside their contribution to the research.

'Confidentiality' relates to protecting the data that you have collected, explicitly private feelings, stories, or information. Remind all researchers on the team that all documents relating to the study contain confidential information and discussions about participant information, and they should guarantee participant privacy. The physical security of all study materials, including tracking information, questionnaires, medical record data, and blood and tissue samples, should be meticulously handled in the manner described in the study consent forms.

## Potential risks and discomforts

Consider issues that might cause harm and address the acceptable levels of harm. Explain how the investigation is deemed to have minimised risks to the participants. Emphasise that the probability and extent of harm or discomfort anticipated in the research will not be more than ordinarily encountered in daily life or during routine physical or psychological examinations, medical tests, or routine medical procedures.

## Care of vulnerable groups

Care is specifically needed in research involving young children, vulnerable people, or those who are sick or recently bereaved. Consider who may be vulnerable in specific contexts, for example, students, employees, dependents, prisoners, or people with traits that could be subject to prejudice. Participants should be protected from harm in every scenario.

If you have had no contact with human informants or gathered no personal information about people, you might not need to discuss ethical considerations in your thesis (Agwor & Adesina, 2018).

---

### Example: Writing about ethical considerations

We used the institution's consent form, which explained the purpose and benefits of the study. We explained to the participants that the study was voluntary, and those who voluntarily agreed to participate in the study would sign a consent form. Information collected from participants was kept in a password-protected network file in the computer, accessed only by the

---

principal investigator. The respondents were also assured of confidentiality, that their names will not appear in the form, and their information will not be disclosed to anyone else. Furthermore, research assistants were trained on the tool and the ethical aspects of the study.

## Concluding the methodology chapter

Finally, in the concluding section of your methodology chapter, summarise the key points of the chapter and insert a bridge to the results chapter. The conclusion of the methodology chapter includes a summary of the research methods, the underpinning approach, and what you see are the key limitations in the research design (you will revisit the same areas in the discussion chapter).

Begin the paragraph by reminding the reader of the research question and providing an overview of the methods used, indicating whether the study was quantitative, qualitative, or a mixed methods design, and whether the research design used was descriptive, correlational, or experimental. Next, describe the rationale for the subject or participant selection and sampling procedure, providing an overview of the data measurements, instrumentation, and collection methods used. Then state the approach for analysing the results. Finish with any ethical considerations and the potential limitations of the methodology and how you addressed these concerns.

### Example: Writing a concluding paragraph of the methodology chapter

This study aimed to establish the effectiveness of a patient-focused approach using the Motivation Interviewing (MI). This counselling method enhances a patient's motivation to change. In an experimental study design, we investigated the effectiveness of MI in increasing self-efficacy and, consequently, behaviour changes related to ARV medication adherence. We used standard instruments to measure self-efficacy, motivation consistency, and adherence. The reliability of these instruments was 0.7, which is considered acceptable. A sample t-test and paired sample t-test were used to analyse the pre-post test scores for the control and experimental group. We observed all the ethical issues regarding participant confidentiality and the handling of participants'

*(Continued)*

data. The critical limitation of the method was that participants might have improved their performance regardless of counselling. In addition, the results were facility-based and could not be generalised to the broader community. The following chapter provides the results of the study.

The methodology chapter should be about 20–25% of the thesis or 10–25 pages long.

# Common pitfalls of the methodology chapter

The following points are some of the main mistakes students make when writing the methodology chapter:

- Confusing the sampling of participants with the procedures used to collect data from the participants.
- Stating the procedure as *doing* a method instead of *applying* a method to the study.
- Providing irrelevant background information that does not explain why a particular method was chosen or how the data were gathered, obtained, and analysed.
- Providing very detailed information about textbook methodological approaches, despite the assumption that readers possess a basic understanding of how to investigate the research problem.
- Using unconventional methodological approaches without describing them adequately or expounding why this approach was chosen and how it enhanced the overall research process.

## Example: Methodology chapter: Motivation and ART medication adherence

### Introduction

Sustained motivation is a requirement for successfully treating HIV/AIDS. Therefore, we conducted an experimental trial to investigate the effectiveness of Motivational Interviewing (MI) in increasing self-efficacy and, consequently, ARV medication adherence. Details of the MI approach are discussed in the body sections of the chapter.

### Research design

We conducted an experimental trial to investigate the effectiveness of Motivational Interviewing (MI) in increasing self-efficacy and, subsequently, medication adherence. We used the Strengths Self-Efficacy Scale (SSES) questionnaire, which had been found to have a solid internal consistency ($\alpha = .95$), to measure self-efficacy. This study was a randomised trial to investigate the effectiveness of utilising Motivational Interviewing, a counselling method that enhances a patient's motivation to change (Rollnick et al., 2008). Patients attending an HIV/AIDs clinic were randomised 1:1 to the intervention and control arms using computer software and were followed for six months.

All participants received standard counselling, which is provided to all AIDS patients. In addition, participants in the intervention arm received additional support sessions utilising Motivational Interviewing. The null hypothesis was that there would be no significant difference in medication adherence between the two groups. A two-factor, mixed-design analysis of variance (ANOVA) was used to assess the intervention effect. The effect size showing differences between the two groups was measured using Cohen's d.

## The study population, sample size, and sampling

We conducted an experimental trial to investigate the effectiveness of Motivational Interviewing (MI) in increasing self-efficacy using an intervention and control group. The study participants came from a list of patients attending the Comprehensive Care Clinic (CCC). All were aged over 18 years and were not severely sick.

To calculate the sample size, we used guidelines provided by Cohen (1988) to interpret the magnitude of a correlation and estimate the power. These are, specifically, $r = 0.10$, $r = 0.30$, and $r = 0.50$, which are considered small, medium, and large in magnitude, respectively. Using these guidelines, we proposed a 90% power to detect an effect of $r = .30$, or a 30% difference between the control and intervention group, with a significance level of .05, coming up with a sample size of 76. We assigned the 38 males and 38 females randomly to either the intervention or control arm of the study. Our final sample satisfied these requirements.

## Measurements

Variables measured in this study were medication adherence (dependent) and self-efficacy (independent), medical literacy and other social demographic variables. We used the pill count method to assess if the medication was taken as prescribed. Patients brought the medication bottle dispensed during the previous visit. We calculated the number of pills taken by subtracting the number of pills remaining in the container from the total number of pills dispensed. We then calculated the drug adherence rate by dividing the number of pills taken by the number of days since the last dispense. Finally, we used this

*(Continued)*

information to calculate Drug Adherence Rates (DAR) using the recommended cut-off value for patient adherence to ARV medication of ≥95% in HIV (Apisarnthanarak & Mundy, 2010; WHO, 2002).

Measuring perceptions of self-efficacy was based on Likert scales developed by Likert in 1932. These scales measure a person's attitude or belief by asking them to respond to a series of statements about a particular topic. We used the Adherence Self-Efficacy Scale for persons with HIV developed by Johnson et al. (2007), which assesses confidence to carry out important behaviours related to treatment adherence. In Johnson's scale, participants respond on a 10-point Likert scale (0 = cannot do at all to 10 = completely certain can do). We adapted these statements, but our scales ranged from 0 = cannot do at all to 5 = entirely certain can do. Other variables measured were medical literacy (can read instructions in English: yes = 1 and no = 0) and social demographic variables: age (complete number of years), sex (male = 1, female = 2), and education level (from none to tertiary).

## The instrument's reliability

To test this instrument's reliability in our study, we conducted a pilot study on 10% of the respondents (40 patients) at the health facility. The questionnaire was administered to find out whether the items accurately addressed the research questions and to determine whether the research questions were well defined and clearly understood, and how long it took to complete the questionnaire. All the errors were amended and re-piloted until no further changes were necessary.

We used the Adherence Self-Efficacy Scale for persons with HIV, developed by Johnson et al. (2007), which assesses confidence to carry out important behaviours related to treatment adherence. The instrument has nine items for integrating treatment into daily life factors. These items include keeping the patients away from what they want to do, such as the fatigue caused by HIV, physical discomfort or pain related to HIV, emotional distress caused by HIV, and health problems. Also, reducing the need to see a doctor by doing different tasks and activities to manage HIV, and doing things other than just taking medication to reduce how much the illness affects their everyday lives and to control the side effects of medications.

Cronbach's Alpha, α (or coefficient alpha), measures reliability or internal consistency, was developed by Lee Cronbach in 1951, and states that a Cronbach's Alpha of 0.90 is an excellent rate of internal consistency. Our study had an acceptable Alpha of 0.75, indicating sufficient internal consistency.

## Data collection procedure

We ensured the credibility and validity of the study by using nurses as interviewers because they had the experience of discussing HIV/AIDS. Therefore, we started by training four nurse counsellors on Motivational Interviewing using the Motivational Interviewing Target Scheme (MITS). This instrument assesses Motivational Interviewing (MI) competency that explicitly integrates traditional clinical methods with practical communication skills (Kurtz, Silverman, Benson, & Draper, 2003; Oberink, Boom, Van Dijk, & Visser, 2017; Zill et al., 2014). The training was in three hour-long sessions, which included refresher sessions, spread over one month. We started data collection after training the nurses. Patients were randomly assigned to each of the four nurses. The nurses informed respondents about the special counselling sessions, which would take at least 30 minutes, without disclosing the expected outcome. After being assured of their confidentiality, the patients provided informed consent. After that, interviews took place privately in a single interview session.

The initial information collected from the patient formed the baseline. In this initial contact, the participants responded to self-efficacy statements listed in the instrument, medication literacy questions, and social demographic background information. Four monthly counselling sessions followed the baseline interview, with the final session being a repeat of the baseline session or the end line survey.

The counselling sessions were different for the control and the intervention group. The MI interviews were video-recorded. Nurses handed over the video recordings of the consultations with patients in each session, and the recordings were stored on a secure server. At the end of the sessions, an assessment was carried out by four assessors, who viewed and listened to all the recordings and took notes. Subsequently, they scored options that best described the holistic impression of the observed behaviour in each of the four sessions.

## Approach to quantitative data analysis

We performed data analysis using the Statistical Package for the Social Sciences (SPSS, version 21) to enter, check and clean data to determine the effect of MI on self-efficacy. First, we examined the ranges of responses for each variable through frequency distributions. In addition, we used SPSS to estimate missing data for possible oversight upon entry, normality, and outliers. We addressed missing data through listwise deletion, which excluded variables that had missing data. However, no cases were excluded from analysis due to missing data in our study. Next, we performed normality checks on these variables using the skewness criterion of $-2$ to $+2$ and the kurtosis criterion of $-7$ to $+7$ described by West et al. (1995). In our study, variables were normally distributed. Next, we calculated the total subscale scores for self-efficacy. Finally, we determined the final MI score for each participant ranging from 0 (no MI consistency) to 4 (a very high degree of MI consistency). This approach is consistent with the use of communication rating

*(Continued)*

scales in which the final score is the mean of all assessed consultations (Kurtz, Silverman, Benson, & Draper, 2003; Oberink, Boom, Van Dijk, & Visser, 2017; Zill et al., 2014).

We used an independent sample t-test and paired sample t-test to analyse the pre-post test scores for the control and experimental groups. A two-factor, mixed-design analysis of variance (ANOVA) was used to assess the intervention effect. The effect size showing differences between the two groups was measured using Cohen's d.

## Limitations and assumptions

The findings of this study might have some limitations. The study's significant delimitation was the research design pre-test/post-test. Although we randomly assigned participants to the treatment or control, the participants in the experimental study might have changed or improved their behaviour simply because they sensed that they were being evaluated or studied (this is known as the Hawthorne effect). On the other hand, those in the control group might have learned from the experimental group and changed their behaviour. A key limitation of the study was the assumption that participants answered the questions honestly and to the best of their ability during the interviews. However, we controlled for most confounding variables in the analysis.

## Ethical considerations

We used the institution's consent form, which explained the purpose and benefits of the study. We explained to the participants that the study was voluntary, and those who voluntarily agreed to participate in the study would sign a consent form. Information collected from participants was kept in a password-protected network file in the computer, accessed only by the principal investigator. The respondents were also assured of confidentiality, that their names will not appear in the form, and their information will not be disclosed to anyone else. Furthermore, research assistants were trained on the tool and the ethical aspects of the study.

## Conclusion

This study aimed to establish the effectiveness of a patient-focused approach using the Motivation Interviewing (MI). This counselling method enhances a patient's motivation to change. In an experimental study design, we investigated the effectiveness of MI in increasing self-efficacy and, consequently, behaviour changes related to ARV medication adherence. We used standard instruments to measure self-efficacy, motivation consistency, and adherence. The reliability of these instruments was 0.7, which is considered acceptable. A sample t-test and paired sample t-test were used to analyse the pre-post test scores for the control and experimental group. We observed all the ethical issues regarding participant confidentiality and the handling of participants' data. The critical limitation of the method was that participants might have improved their performance regardless of counselling. In addition, the results were facility-based and could not be generalised to the broader community. The following chapter provides the results of the study.

# Exercise: Methodology chapter

## Instructions

Discuss to what extent the examiner's comments apply to this text, supporting your argument with examples of words, phrases, or sentences from the text. (Refer to the section on Pedagogical features — 'Discussion-based exercises' — in the Introduction of this book for more details on completing this exercise.)

## Text: Barriers associated with adherence to antiretroviral (ARV) drugs among persons living with HIV/AIDS

### Study design

A cross-sectional analytical design was used in this study because the study's objective was to look at associations of various barriers with ARV adherence. Thus, social support was the independent variable, perceptions and demographic characteristics were intervening variables, and adherence to ARVs was the dependent or outcome variable.

### Study participants

The study participants comprised 320 adults living with HIV/AIDS who confirmed HIV positive through an HIV test and had been on ARV drugs for at least six months before the data collection date. The study excluded seriously ill patients.

The Fischer et al.'s formula (Z2 pq/d2) (Jung SH. 2014) was used to calculate the sample size with a risk and degree of variability (p) of 0.65, level of confidence (Z) of 1.96, and level of precision (d) of 0.05. In addition, a non-response rate of 5% was added. The stratified random sampling method was used from the list of 417 men and 833 women registered as people living with HIV/AIDS to sample 105 men and 215 women. The community health workers (CHWs) assisted in identifying the household where the respondents lived. The collection of information in the household represented real-life settings.

*(Continued)*

## Measurement of variables

The variables measured were derived from the Health Belief Model, which guided the research. Adherence to ARV was measured using self-report and pill count at the household. These two methods are accepted to be the most widely used adherence measure in clinical care and resource-limited settings (Chalker et al., 2010). Respondents reported whether they had missed taking the drug in the past seven days and the number of drugs missed. The pill count method involved checking the number and date the pills were prescribed from the container and counting medication doses in the pill container. We used the quantity of ARV drugs prescribed minus pills counted and used duration in days was used to calculate doses taken. Adherence level was calculated by dividing the number of doses taken by the total doses supposed to be taken within that duration and multiplied by 100. These were categorised as ≥95% or <95%. Using the pill count provided more accurate results, although it was cumbersome to use at the household level for routine purposes. However, scientific studies proved more accurate for assessing the various relationships than the self-report, which is commonly used because it is simple, cheap, and accessible. Limitations of self-reports include the length of the interview, the subjectivity of patient statements, overestimation of adherence, social desirability, or recall bias (Uzochukwu et al., (2009). To measure perceptions, i.e., cue to action (social support), barriers, benefits, and self-efficacy, a five (5) point Likert scale was used to measure perception. Respondents were asked to explain their perceptions using statements. The scale included: strongly agree = 5, agree = 4, disagree = 3, strongly disagree = 2 and no opinion = 1. Total scores were calculated for each variable.

Side effects were measured by asking the respondents if they had experienced side effects and the type of side effects experienced within the previous seven days by yes and no questions. For this study, medicine-related side effects were categorised according to patient or ARV user and biomedical perspectives.

Social demographic characteristics were limited to age (age was measured as exact age in years), marital status (single, married, divorced or widowed), sex (either male or female), and level of education (measured using none, primary, secondary and tertiary). Knowledge of ARV use included the name of the ARV being taken and its use (dosages, frequency, intervals, and observation of any restrictions).

## Methodology

My study used an analytical design using pill counts at the household level with social support (the independent variable), perceptions (as intervening variables), demographic variables as (exogenous variable), and adherence as the (outcome variable).

The study aims to develop results that inform the development of culturally sensitive, localised, practical, and useful interventions to improve ARV adherence.

I used the Patient Medicine Adherence Questionnaire (PMAQ) for data collection, a reliable, valid assessment tool grounded in the Health Belief Model. The PMAQ covers perceived barriers, attitudes, and perceived safety of the medicines. A 5-point Likert scale was used to measure perception, and a composite variable of social support was constructed from the Likert scale. The composite variables were used to test for relationships using a chi-square test for associations and binary logistic regression to assess factors explaining dose adherence.

## Data collection tool

Data were collected using an interviewer-administered, structured pre-coded questionnaire with closed questions adapted from the Patient Medicine Adherence Questionnaire (PMAQ). A reliable, valid assessment tool grounded in the Health Belief Model (Duong M, Piroth L, Grappin M, et al. 2001).

My tool covered perceived cues to action (social support types and sources), barriers, benefits, self-efficacy, knowledge of the ARV medicines, social demographic factors, and ARV drug side effects. The data collection tool was pretested on 10% of study participants. These participants were not included in the study to ensure the data's reliability. The pretesting sought to establish the time taken to administer the tool, ambivalent or sensitive questions, the proper use of language, and the relevance of questions. The changes and recommendations from the pretesting exercise were incorporated into the final tool.

## Ethical considerations

The Institutional Ethical Review Committee of Ministry of Health obtained authorisation to conduct the study. Informed consent was obtained from each participant before filling out the questionnaire. The consent form explained the study's purpose and the benefits to the respondents. The respondents were guaranteed that participation was voluntary, and those who voluntarily accepted to participate in the study signed or thumbed the consent form. The respondents were assured of the confidentiality of their information, and their names were anonymised. Information collected from participants was kept in a password-protected network file on the computer, accessible only to the principal researcher.

## Data analysis procedure

An Excel spreadsheet was used for data entry and cleaning the data, while the SPSS (version 19) statistical software program was used to analyse the data.

*(Continued)*

The dependent variable was ARV adherence. The cue to action (social support) was the independent variable, and the intervening variables were social demographics, perception of barriers, self-efficacy, and perception of benefits. The number of side effects (a barrier) was added up for each to calculate the burden of side effects. The composite variable for social support was constructed from the Likert scale scores. Continuous variables included side effects, age, and adherence. Using chi-square and binary logistic regression analysis, continuous variables were categorised into dichotomous variables to test for relationships. Chi-square tests ($p < 0.05$ was considered significant) were used to test the association between categorised variables. Descriptive statistics were used to compare continuous variables' means and standard deviation. In contrast, the ANOVA test was used to test the difference between the means of sub-categories of data.

Correlations were assessed using Pearson's correlation for continuous data normally distributed and Spearman's rank for skewed or ordinal data. A correlation coefficient (r) was used to describe the strength of the supposed linear association of continuous variables. Variables were fitted in a binary logistic regression model to investigate the relative importance of the type of independent variable that showed some association between the dependent variable and any confounding variables.

## Examiner's comments

- An audit trail of this research design lends itself suitably to resolving the problem at hand.
- The candidate does not show how the hypothesis or the research question is researchable, or how the research design is appropriate for addressing the problem.
- The candidate is conversant and adequately understands the scientific research method's practicalities.
- The candidate did not specify the choice of the particular method used, including a reasoned consideration of the analytic techniques that the chosen methods require.
- The candidate justifies the methods chosen, with an appropriate rationale in each case, and why she/he rejected other potential alternative methods.
- The candidate does not explain how the methodological approach is appropriate or justified, including acknowledging its strengths and possible limitations.
- The candidate did not specify how they arrived at the sample size.
- The candidate did not detail the ethical issues and did not describe the study's limitations.
- Although the standard approach was used, the candidate did not explain or justify it.

- The candidate has mastered a diversity of procedures, and displays competence in various techniques.
- The candidate intelligently employed a wide range of current techniques and used a range of experimental techniques with great effectiveness.

## Further reading

Bazeley, P. (2012). Integrative analysis strategies for mixed data sources. *American Behavioral Scientist*, *56*(6), 814–828. https://doi.org/10.1177/0002764 211426330

This paper identifies strategies and techniques for integrating data in analysis to build strong conclusions. It includes illustrations from various mixed methods studies.

Bryman, A. (2006). Integrating quantitative and qualitative research: How is it done? *Qualitative Research*, *6*(1), 97–113. https://doi.org/10.1177/1468794106058877

This article offers guidance on how to integrate and combine quantitative and qualitative research in practice from a content analysis of 232 social science articles.

Bui, Y. N. (2019). *How to Write a Master's Thesis*. Los Angeles, CA: Sage. https://uk.sagepub.com/en-gb/eur/how-to-write-a-masters-thesis/book250120

This book presents a highly detailed but somewhat prescriptive framework for approaching data analysis focused chiefly on presenting quantitative data.

Creswell, J. W. (2015). *A Concise Introduction to Mixed Methods Research*. Thousand Oaks, CA: Sage.

This book gives an overview of mixed methods research and the essential steps in planning and designing a mixed methods study in the social, behavioural, and health sciences. It is practical for use in workshops, seminars, global webinars, and as a supplementary text in undergraduate and graduate classes; it is ideal for beginners or more advanced researchers.

Faryadi, Q. (2012). How to write your PhD proposal: A step-by-step guide. *American International Journal of Contemporary Research*, *2*(4).

This article points to the rigour of an investigation of a scientific methodology, such as validity, reliability, and unbiased conclusion. It also provides a complete roadmap on how to write an internationally recognised PhD proposal.

Loseke, D. R. (2020). *Methodological Thinking: Basic Principles of Social Research Design* (2nd edition). London: Sage.

The author provides an overview of the basic principles of social research, including the foundations of research (data, concepts, theory). It explains the importance of measurement (conceptualisation and operationalisation), data generation techniques (experiments, surveys, interviews, observation, document analysis), and sampling.

Lunenburg, F., & Irby, B. (2014). Writing the literature review chapter. In *Writing a Successful Thesis or Dissertation: Tips and Strategies for Students in the Social and Behavioral Sciences* (pp. 137–164). Thousand Oaks, CA: Sage/ Corwin Press.

This chapter discusses the various approaches to qualitative data analysis. It pays special attention to quasi-statistical techniques (e.g., discourse and content analysis). Besides, it discusses thematic coding and the grounded theory approach.

Nishishiba, M., Jones, M., & Kraner, M. (2017). *Research Methods and Statistics for Public and Nonprofit Administrators: A Practical Guide*. London: Sage.

This guide is comprehensive and prepares readers to apply research methods and data analysis. The authors incorporate original case examples to demonstrate concepts in which research methods are applied. In addition, chapter 14 of the book briefly covers analysing and presenting results for both qualitative and quantitative data.

Norris, J. M., Plonsky, L., Ross, S. J., & Schoonen, R. (2015). Guidelines for reporting quantitative methods and results in primary research. *Language Learning*, 65(2). https://doi.org/10.1111/lang.12104

This article provides basic expectations for reporting primary quantitative research, focusing on the Method and Results sections. It considers the logic, rationale, and actions underlying both study designs and how data are analysed.

Patten, M. L., & Newhart, M. (2018). Introduction to validity. In *Understanding Research Methods: An Overview of the Essentials* (10th edition). London: Routledge. https://doi.org/10.4324/9781315213033

This chapter describes the theory of validity and specific threats. It provides a helpful scheme for assessing the quality of research conclusions and a framework for judging the quality of evaluations. It gives examples of various validity and specific threats and deals with possible threats to validity for any inference or conclusion.

Robson, C. (2011). *Real World Research* (3rd edition). New York: Wiley.

This book is strong on flexible designs, qualitative methods, and building arguments. It provides a clear route map of the various steps needed to carry out applied research. It presents different social science disciplines (quantitative and qualitative, and their combination in mixed methods designs). It provides strategies for analysing and interpreting data; analysing and interpreting data is refreshingly practical, mainly when using a flexible design.

# 7

# Writing the Results Chapter

This chapter explains ways to present quantitative statistical data, qualitative findings, and mixed methods data from the data collected and analysed in the methodology chapter. It explains how to present descriptive reporting statistics, correlations, and regressions in quantitative methods. It also demonstrates how to summarise results in non-textual formats in quantitative and qualitative research and to report sequential exploratory, sequential explanatory, and convergent research designs in mixed methods approaches.

## Purpose of the results chapter

The results chapter discusses the product or outcome of the analytic process and should be thought of as a 'stand-alone' chapter that a reader can understand on its own, without reference to other chapters. It answers the central and specific research questions outlined in the introduction chapter. However, it only highlights data relevant to the study hypothesis or research question, as outlined in the introduction, and not all the data collected.

The results chapter lays the foundation for the argument in the discussion chapter by presenting evidence that backs up the claims made in the discussion chapter. The results are based on the research design in the methodology chapter, which connects to the conceptual framework set out in the literature review. The results chapter demonstrates how the results help to answer the research questions, or reject or accept hypotheses. It can also acknowledge unexpected results that did not answer the research question. You should spend a short time describing these divergent findings.

Present the most appropriate approach to your analysis, demonstrating that rigorous, robust evidence produced valid results – only present statistical analysis without interpretation, inference, or evaluation. When reporting the findings/results, the main issue is whether to show them separately (i.e., separating the analysis from the interpretation) or to weave analysis and interpretation together. For example, results are separated from the discussion in quantitative research, where hypotheses are determined beforehand. On the other hand, when organising qualitative data consisting of text, classify them using concepts and categories and discuss them together in the same chapter. Appendices can be included if the findings are extensive so that readers can refer to these for more detailed information if they desire. Note that in a qualitative study, the data reported are called findings.

Do not focus mainly on describing negative results or findings that do not support the study's underlying assumptions, but instead highlight them in the discussion section and explain why negative results emerged from the study. It is assumed that the readers understand statistics; therefore, do not explain how or why the test is used unless it is unusual.

An excellent way to begin the results chapter is by reporting descriptive statistics for each variable measured. These descriptions include central tendency measures. In many cases, descriptive statistics might be sufficient if the quantitative analysis plays only a small role in the overall methodology, for example, when reporting the results of a small questionnaire conducted within a more extensive qualitative study. The next step is to go beyond descriptive statistics and report additional statistical tests, such as correlations and regressions.

The results chapter comprises an introductory paragraph, followed by the main body of the chapter, which contains various sections, and ends with the concluding paragraphs. The chapter is written in the past tense because the data gathering has been completed.

## Introducing the results chapter

The results chapter starts with an introductory paragraph that gives the context for understanding the results. In other words, begin with a 'Preamble' or 'Introduction' that restates the research problem, the purpose statement, or hypotheses, and provide a brief overview of the research design and data collection techniques described in the methodology chapter, followed by an overview of the chapter's structure.

---

### Example: Writing an introductory paragraph

The study aimed to develop an effective adherence-enhancing intervention to increase self-efficacy and, consequently, behaviour changes related to medication adherence using Motivational Interviewing (MI). [purpose statement] We hypothesised that there was no significant difference in medication adherence in the group of patients using Motivational Interviewing, a patient-focused approach and those using conventional counselling approaches

Bandura's theory of self-efficacy guided the experimental study where patients were randomly assigned to the intervention and control groups. [theory and method] We began reporting descriptive statistics for each variable and then moved on to additional statistical tests, such as correlations and regressions.

---

## The main body of the results chapter

The main body of the results chapter summarises the key findings, arranged in a logical sequence that generally follows that used in the methodology chapter. The amount and types of data dictate the length of the chapter.

The chapter's structure depends on the study's general conventions, i.e., whether it is a quantitative, qualitative, or mixed methods research design. However, regardless of the convention, an appropriate structure has subheadings based on hypotheses, objectives, research questions, or themes (corresponding to the literature review chapter). An alternative structure is to organise the results by stages of the study (if applicable).

## Reporting quantitative results

Quantitative results can be broadly categorised as descriptive and inferential statistics. Descriptive statistics summarise characteristics about the data numerically (e.g., mean, standard deviation) or graphically (e.g., tables, figures, and photographs). Inferential statistics make predictions ('inferences') from data that can be generalised to a broad population means (e.g., hypothesis tests, correlation analysis, and regression analysis).

### Reporting descriptive statistics

The results can be summarised numerically using measures of central tendency (e.g., mean, median, mode) and measures of dispersion (e.g., standard deviation, variance, range). Results can also be summarised using non-textual elements such as tables, figures (including diagrams and graphs), and photographs or other images.

## Numerical elements – mean and standard deviation

When reporting means, start by describing the type of analysis conducted, and why this analysis was used. Next, describe the mean as the measure of central tendency and the standard deviation as the measure of dispersion in words that people unfamiliar with statistics or scientific language can understand. Italicise all statistical symbols (sample statistics), such as $M$, $SD$, $t$, $p$, and in most cases present them in parentheses ($N = 377$, $M = 40.52$, $SD = 10.87$).

Note! Standard deviation (SD) measures the variability or dispersion of data from the mean. Standard error of the mean (SEM) measures how far the sample is likely to be from the true population mean. SEM is always smaller than the SD.

Some simple results are best stated in a single sentence, with data summarised parenthetically, for example, 'the medication adherence at the baseline was 50%'.

## Non-textual elements – tables and figures

Tables and/or figures are used to communicate information that is not evident from the text alone, highlighting and emphasising the most relevant results. Thus, they serve as illustrations to supplement rather than duplicate the material in the text. For example, figures depict relationships between one thing and another, changes over time, or how one variable compares with another, and demonstrate trends, correlations, or relations between two (or more) variables.

### Creating tables and figures

Tables and figures are most easily constructed using a word processor's table function or a spreadsheet program such as Excel. Therefore, it is important to remember to eliminate gridlines or boxes that are commonly invoked by word processors from the printed version. The format of the table (e.g., title, numbering, and borders) is determined by the style manual recommended by your institution (e.g., American Psychological Association (APA), Modern Language Association (MLA)). The caption or title is inserted above a table and is placed below a figure. Acknowledge the source of any table or figure reproduced or modified from another author or work, such as photographs or a figure you have adapted for your own purpose.

Black and white figures are usually preferred for ease in photocopying or faxing. Intermediate calculations and non-textual elements can be placed in the appendices unless your institution advises otherwise.

### Numbering tables and figures

Tables and figures are numbered independently, in the sequence in which you have referred to them in the text, starting with Table 1 and Figure 1. Tables and figures can be numbered using a decimal system, for example, Table 4.1, Table 4.2, or Figure 4.1, Figure 4.2. Use the same font and type size for all table and figure numbers and headings. Always follow your university's guidelines. Each table or figure must include a brief description of the presented results and other necessary information in a legend. The positioning of the legend in figures is *below* the figure, but at the *top* for tables.

All tables and figures must be listed in the 'List of Tables' or the 'List of Figures'. The number, heading or caption, and page number of each table or figure in the thesis text must be identical to the number, heading or caption, and page number used in the List of Tables and List of Figures. Finally, all tables and figures must fit into the exact margin requirements as the text. On the page, oversized tables or figures can be placed sideways (in landscape orientation).

Depending on the university, tables and figures can be put on separate pages from the main text, such as at the end of a chapter in number sequence, in the order mentioned in the text. Several small tables or figures can be presented on a single page. If your university does not provide guidelines for placement, then place each table or figure close to where it was referred to in the main text to aid comprehension and avoid interrupting the flow of the text.

### Presenting tables and figures

Begin the section by stating the purpose of the table or figure, stressing the key results presented in them that answer the research question(s). Then, discuss the data at length, emphasising keywords or phrases and sentences that draw the reader's attention, highlighting the relationship or trends, significant differences, similarities, and correlations in the table or figure without repeating the data. Tables and figures are illustrations to supplement rather than duplicate the material in a text. In other words, refer to each table or figure individually and in sequence, clearly indicating the key results and singling out new knowledge generated by the study (i.e., the significant findings). Ensure the legend conveys all the necessary information and use table notes to explain the table or figure. Table notes should be present as part of the table and are placed below the table. Avoid sentences that convey no information other than directing the reader to the table or figure, such as 'Table 1 shows the summary results for male and female responses'. Table 7.1 demonstrates the layout of a table taken from our exemplar study of Motivational Interviewing and ARV medication adherence.

**Table 7.1** Baseline data for the study sample of patients attending a Comprehensive Care Clinic (CCC) in September 2020

| Factors | Baseline data | | Std. Error Mean |
| | Control group | Intervention group | |
| | N=148 | N=152 | |
| --- | --- | --- | --- |
| Medication literacy | 2.79±1.11 | 2.80±.93 | .076 |
| Health belief | 3.30±1.02 | 3.57±.84 | .074 |
| Social support | 2.47±1.03 | 2.73±.1.9 | .084 |
| **Self-efficacy** | **2.61±.61** | **2.78±.5** | **.040** |
| Age in years | 39.2±11.6 | 40.62±9.6 | .943 |
| Gender (%) | 48.3 | 51.3 | |
| Medication adherence (mean) | 77.3±14.6 | 80.6±14.2 | |
| Medication adherence (≥95%) | 5.3% | 5% | |

Individual Likert mean scores for medication literacy, health belief, social support, and self-efficacy ranged from 1 to 5. Age was assessed in complete years. Except for self-efficacy, there was no significant difference in the perception in health belief, social support, age, sex, and medication adherence at the baseline.

## Non-textual elements – reporting figures

Frequency histogram

Frequency histograms or frequency distributions show how the measurements are distributed along an axis of the measured variable. Frequency (the Y-axis) can be *absolute* (i.e., the number of counts) or *relative* (i.e., percent). They are important in describing populations (e.g., size and age distributions).

## Example: Reporting a histogram (text)

Figure 7.1 represents the distribution of self-efficacy as assessed through a Likert scale ranging from 0 to 5 of 300 patients living with HIV. Patients with a ranking of over four on the Likert scales were considered to have high self-efficacy. Therefore, only 40% can be classified as having high self-efficacy.

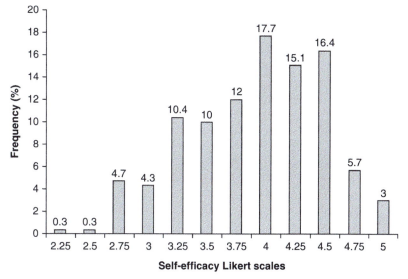

**Figure 7.1**   An example of a histogram

Notice several things about this example: the Y-axis includes a clear indication ('%'), which is the measured variable; the X-axis has been divided into categories to visualise the variable distribution; the sample size is indicated, either in the legend or, in this case, in the graph title; and the Y-axis includes numbers to allow easy determination of bar values.

Bar graph

Bar graphs are used to compare the value of a single variable, such as a mean among several groups. The *measured* variable is labelled on the Y-axis, where, in most cases, units are given. The *categorical* variable (factor) is labelled on the X-axis, and each category is designated. Always insert error bars (SD or SEM) or other measures associated with the mean, such as confidence intervals, or a caption indicating the test and the significance level used. Statistical differences can be indicated by drawing a line over the bars.

## Example: Reporting a bar graph (text)

Figure 7.2 shows the distribution of various motivating factors (social support, health beliefs, self-efficacy) and medication adherence assessed through a Likert scale ranging from 0 to 5 of 300 patients living with HIV. The results indicate that health beliefs were the highest motivating factor in medication adherence.

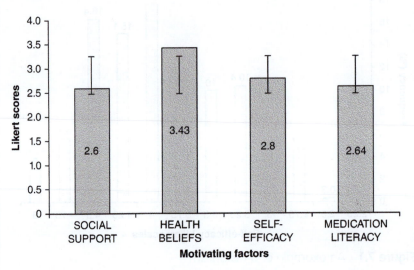

**Figure 7.2**  Motivating factors for medication adherence of HIV patients attending a Comprehensive Care Clinic in September 2020

### Scatter plot

A scatter plot (scatter chart, scatter graph) represents values for two different numeric variables using dots on the horizontal and vertical axis. The position of each dot indicates values for an individual data point. Scatter plots are used to observe relationships between variables. If variables are correlated, the points will fall along a line or curve. A positive correlation indicates that when one variable increases, the other also increases. A negative correlation indicates that when one variable increases, the other decreases, while no correlation indicates no apparent relationship between the variables.

## Example: Reporting a scatter plot

Figure 7.3 indicates no correlation or apparent relationship between the self-efficacy and medication adherence.

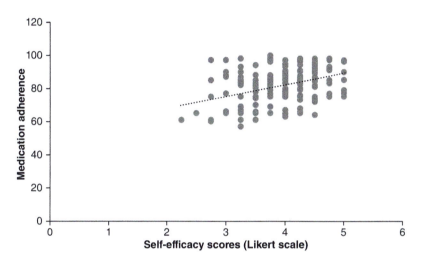

**Figure 7.3**   An example of a scatter plot: Medication adherence and self-efficacy in HIV patients in a Comprehensive Care Clinic August 2021

An X, Y line scatter plot

An X, Y line scatter plot is a series of related values that depict a change in Y as a function of X. These X, Y coordinate plots show the sample's score of *two* variables, indicating whether the two variables change in *value together consistently.*

Note that the dependent variable is placed on the Y-axis and the independent variable on the X-axis. However, if there is no explicit independent variable, the variables are interdependent. An *X, Y plot shows the relationship between them* (rather than the effect of one on the other), and it does not matter which variable is on which axis.

Connect dots if each point in the series is obtained from the *same source* and depends on the previous values. Do not connect dots when the measurements were made *independently* to show a trend. The trend can be modelled by calculating the best-fit line or curve by regression analysis.

## Example: Reporting an X, Y line scatter plot

Figure 7.4 is an example of a trend modelled by calculating the best-fit line or curve by regression analysis. The figure shows the relationship between copies/mL (a test that measures the number of HIV copies in a millilitre of blood) and medication adherence. The results indicate that the individuals who were 100% adherent to their medications were significantly more likely to have an 'undetectable viral load' (<50 copies/mL), which is a key goal of antiretroviral therapy (ART).

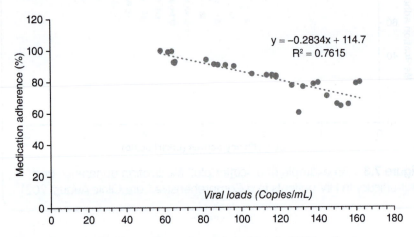

**Figure 7.4**   Medication adherence and viral load of HIV patients attending a Comprehensive Care Clinic (Viral load = copies/mL; Medication adherence = %)

## Non-textual elements – using photographs, images, posters

Photographs, images, and posters can be used as a type of figure to display descriptive statistics, but they need to have sufficient resolution for standard photocopying. A photograph from another source requires attribution in the caption, which conveys all the necessary information. For posters or projected images, citation is required either in a caption below the image or as an entry in the references.

The rule of thumb on using photographs and images as figures is to size the photos to fill about one-half of a page or to use a full page for compound photos. Black and white images are often preferred for ease in photo-copying or faxing, unless it is a poster presentation, when colour is permissable.

## Reporting inferential statistics

While descriptive statistics describe data, inferential statistics are used to make predictions ('inferences') from data that can be generalised to a broad population. Examples of inferential statistics include non-parametric tests, chi-square, t-test, ANOVA, correlation analysis, logistic regression analysis, linear regression analysis, and multiple regression analysis. These statistics can be derived using computer software such as SPSS and SAS.

Always describe the type of analysis conducted and why this analysis was used when reporting all the statistical tests used.

## Non-parametric tests

Parametric statistical tests are used for data that are approximately normal. If the data are not normally distributed, use a non-parametric test. These tests report the *median and range* and not standard deviations. The statistics $U$ and $Z$ (derived from statistical packages such as SPSS or SAS) are capitalised and italicised. Use the Mann-Whitney $U$ test to compare two independent samples/groups when the dependent variable is either ordinal or continuous but not normally distributed.

---

### Example: Reporting a U test

The $U$ test indicated that medication literacy was higher in HIV patients who were in the Motivational Interviewing intervention group (median = 5) when compared to patients who were receiving conventional medication counselling (median = 4), $U = 67.6$, $p = .034$, $r = .37$.

---

Use the Wilcoxon signed-rank test, a non-parametric statistical hypothesis test, to compare two related, matched samples or repeated measurements on a single sample. This test establishes whether your population means differ (i.e., it is a paired difference test).

---

## Example: Reporting Wilcoxon signed-ranks test (two related samples)

Wilcoxon signed-ranks test indicated that ARV medication was more accepted by females (median = 0.85) than in males (median = 0.65), $Z = 4.21$, $p < .001$, $r = .76$.

---

## Chi-square test

The chi-square (the Pearson chi-square test and Fisher's exact test) is commonly used for testing a hypothesis and is the standard test used for nominal (categorical) data. Chi-square statistics are reported with degrees of freedom and sample size in parentheses. For example, $\chi2 = 10.81$ $df = 3$, $p = 0.01$) – $p$-value and odds ratio are reported for a 2 × 2 table). Note! Round Pearson chi-square values to two decimal places.

Present as much information as possible about differences or relationships when reporting the difference between two conditions. For example, state how they were different, i.e., the size, the direction of differences (greater, larger, smaller), and the magnitude of differences (% difference, how many times). Fisher's exact test is used if the sample size is small (less than 10 cases in any cell).

---

## Example: Reporting a chi-square test

We conducted a cross-sectional analytical study to establish the association between medication adherence and self-efficacy among people living with HIV/AIDs. We found a statistically significant association between medication adherence and self-efficacy ($\chi^2 = 10.81$, $df = 3$, $p = 0.01$). High self-efficacy was associated with better medication adherence (odds ratio [OR] = 1.95, 95% confidence interval [CI] = 1.41–2.37.

---

Use McNemar's test, a paired version of the chi-square test for paired samples. These measurements constitute 'paired data' since each 'before' measure is related to the 'after' measure from the same subject. Therefore, reporting the results of a McNemar's test is the same as the chi-square test.

---

## Example: Reporting a McNemar's test

This study aimed to explore the impact of Motivational Interviewing (MI) on medication adherence. We compared the adherent levels before and after the Motivational Interviewing intervention. Medication adherence levels changed from 23.7% to 27.3% in the control group, i.e., a change of about 4%, while in the intervention group, the change was 37%, i.e., from 31.7% to 68.3%. These differences were statistically significant ($\chi^2$ = 31.345, $df$ = 1, $p$ = < 0.001).

---

## Independent sample t-test

Student test (or t-test) is the most used technique for testing a hypothesis of differences between sample means when reporting independent samples. Presentation of t-test data begins by describing the type of analysis conducted, why this analysis was used, and the statistical test used, followed by stating whether there was a significant difference between condition means. T-tests are reported the same way as the chi-square test, but only the degrees of freedom are in parentheses: $t$ (degrees of freedom) = the t statistic, $p$ = p-value, for example, $t$ (33) = 37.35, $p$ < .001. The t-statistic is rounded to two decimal places, and all p-values represent two-tailed tests. Independent sample t-tests use the pooled variance approach. The pooled variance is a weighted average of the independent sample variances. A typical way of reporting significance tests is: '___ was found to be statistically significant' or '___ did not reach statistical significance'.

---

## Example: Reporting t-tests

We used an independent sample t-test to compare the mean Likert scores for self-efficacy of the intervention (MI) and control groups. The aim was to test whether there were differences between these groups using an independent t-test for continuous variables. The independent sample t-tests indicated a significant difference in the self-esteem scores between the intervention group ($M$ = 4.2, $SD$ = 1.3) and the control group ($M$ = 2.2, $SD$ = 0.84); $t$ (8) = 2.89, $p$ = 0.20, suggesting that Motivational Interviewing affects medication adherence.

---

## ANOVA test

While t-tests are used to compare the means from two different data groups, the ANOVA test compares three or more groups or experiments to determine whether their mean differences are statistically significant ($p < .05$).

The one-way within-subjects ANOVA test compares three or more related groups. In comparison, the one-way between-subjects ANOVA test is used to compare three or more unrelated groups that are independent of one another.

In reporting ANOVA, first indicate the type of analysis conducted, why this analysis was used, and what the analysis tested. Next, report whether there was a significant difference between condition means, the degrees of freedom (df), the F value (F), and the p-value. These values can be derived from the SPSS, SAS, or any other statistical software package.

The p-value in a one-way between-subjects ANOVA shows a significant difference between some experiment conditions, but not where the significant difference occurs between any or all experimental conditions. Thus, a post hoc test is used to determine where the significance exists by comparing each condition with all other conditions to determine which conditions are significantly different from other conditions. The Turkey post hoc test compares each condition to every other condition. Report the Tukey post hoc in language that people can understand, especially those who are unfamiliar with science.

One can depict a comparison of the means of two or more groups in a bar graph containing the means and associated error or SD bars. Include asterisks centered over the error bar to indicate the relative level of the p-value, such as $* = p < 0.05 = ** p < 0.01 = *** p < 0.001$, and $**** = p < 0.0001$. A footnote can also define the p-values corresponding to the number of asterisks or the p-value can be added in the figure legend.

ANOVA results are reported as ($F (2, 135) = 0.18$, $p = .894$, partial $\eta2 = .003$). The first number in parentheses refers to freedom numerator degrees, and the second number corresponds to the denominator (error) degrees of freedom. The partial $\eta2$ refers to the effect size of the test. Note that the self-efficacy level must be high to detect an effect.

## Example: Reporting one-way within-subjects ANOVA

We used a one-way within-subjects ANOVA to compare the effect of self-efficacy (high self-efficacy, medium self-efficacy, and low self-efficacy) conditions on medication adherence. There was a significant effect of self-efficacy on medication adherence at the $p < .05$ level for the three conditions ($F (2, 135) = 0.18$,

$p = .894$, partial $\eta2 = .003$). Post hoc comparisons using the Tukey HSD test showed that the mean score for the high self-efficacy condition ($M = 2.89$, $SD = .81$) was significantly different from the low self-efficacy condition ($M = 1.94$, $SD = 0.87$) and medium self-efficacy condition ($M = 2.35$, $SD = 0.93$). These results suggest that high levels of self-efficacy affect medication adherence. Specifically, our results suggest that the high levels of self-efficacy result in increased adherence.

## Example: Reporting a one-way between-subjects ANOVA

We used three paired samples t-tests to perform post hoc comparisons between self-efficacy, health beliefs, and social support conditions. The first paired samples t-test indicated that there was a significant difference in the scores for self-efficacy ($M = 4.30$, $SD = .87$) and health belief ($M = 2.64$, $SD = .92$) conditions; $t(4) = 23.50$, $p = <.001$. The second paired samples t-test indicated that there was a significant difference in the scores for self-efficacy ($M = 4.30$, $SD = 0.87$) and social support ($M = 2.69$, $SD = 1.02$) conditions; $t(4) = 23.09$, $p = <.001$. The third paired samples t-test indicated no significant difference in the scores for social support ($M = 2.69$, $SD = 1.02$) and health belief ($M = 2.64$, $SD = .92$) conditions. These results suggest that motivation type affects medication adherence. Wilks' Lambda $= 0.10$, $F(2,4) = 13.39$, $p = .042$. Specifically, the results suggest that patients with high self-efficacy adhere more to medication. However, there is no real difference in medication adherence when comparing health beliefs and social support.

## Correlations

A correlation is a statistical calculation that describes the strength and direction of a relationship between two variables. A strong or high correlation indicates that two or more variables are strongly related, and a weak or low correlation indicates that the variables are hardly related. Pearson $r$, also known as linear or product-moment correlation, is the most widely used correlation coefficient. Correlation coefficients range from −1.00 to +1.00. An $r$ is close to +1 if $x$ and $y$ have a strong positive linear correlation with an r-value of +1, indicating a perfect positive fit. Positive values indicate that as values for $x$ increase, $y$ also increases. An $r$ is close to −1 when $x$ and $y$ have a strong negative linear correlation. An r-value of exactly −1 indicates a perfect negative fit. Negative values indicate that as values for $x$ increase, $y$ decreases. An $r$ close to 0 indicates no linear correlation, or the correlation is a weak linear correlation.

Correlations are reported with degrees of freedom ($N$-2), followed by the significance level. If the coefficient correlation is strong, include a scatter plot that summarises the results in a figure. In reporting Pearson's $r$ and scatter plots, first describe what type of analysis was conducted and why it was used, including the analysis tests. A correlation greater than 0.8 is described as strong, whereas those less than 0.5 are described as weak. The correlation results include the degrees of freedom in parentheses, the r-value (the correlation coefficient and a p-value). Note a p-value less than .001 or .0000 is reported as $p < .001$.

---

### Example: Reporting a Pearson correlation

Pearson correlation indicated a significant strong positive association between self-efficacy and medication with adherence ($r$(299) =. 710, <001). The number following $r$ in parentheses corresponds to the degrees of freedom ($df$), tied to the sample size, followed by the correlation coefficient and the p-value.

---

## Logistic regression

Logistic regression is the extension of correlation and determines whether an independent variable can predict a dependent variable. The logistic regression model establishes a relationship between a binary dichotomous dependent variable and a group of predictor or independent variables that can be continuous or categorical. Probability ranges from 0 and 1, and odds range from 0 and positive infinity.

A binary logistic analysis table is generated by statistical analysis software such as SPSS. Therefore, all one needs to do is interpret the results from a table. First, present descriptive statistics in a table, making it apparent that the dependent variable is discrete (0, 1) and not continuous. Logistic regression is a standard statistical procedure; therefore, one does not need to describe it in detail.

Organise the results stating the dependent variable YES is equal to 1 and 0 is equal to NO. Then, a logistic regression result presents coefficient estimates, t-statistics or Wald, and the model chi-square statistic for overall model fit.

There is no need to discuss the magnitude of the coefficients but you need to state the sign (+ or −) and statistical significance. For example, when doing 'risk analysis' to interpret the coefficients with the odds ratio, briefly describe the odds ratio for an unfamiliar audience. Always state the degrees of freedom for the likelihood-ratio (chi-square) tests.

Binary logistic regression is the most utilised regression model. The dependent variable is binary, i.e., it takes only two values, 0 or 1. There must be two or more independent variables, or predictors, for logistic regression. The intervening variables (IVs), or predictors, can be continuous (interval/ratio) or categorical (ordinal/nominal).

Use the following general format to report the results of a logistic regression model: 'Logistic regression was used to determine the relationship between ____ [the predictor variables or intervening variable] and ____ [response/dependent variable].

## Example: Reporting a logistic regression

We performed logistic regression to ascertain the relationship between social support, self-efficacy, health beliefs, and age on the likelihood of medication adherence ($\geq$ 95% adherent = 1) versus non-adherence (< 95% non-adherent = 0). The statistical tests of each regression coefficient were tested using the Wald chi-square statistic. The Wald criterion demonstrated that only self-efficacy significantly contributed to adherence ($p$ = <.04), as shown in Table 7.2. The logistic regression model was statistically significant ($\chi^2(1, N\,300) = 129.28$, $p < .001$). The model explained 35.0% (Nagelkerke R2) of the variance in medication adherence and correctly classified 75.0% of cases.

Social support, health beliefs, and age were not associated with medication adherence, but increasing self-efficacy score was associated with increased medication adherence (OR = 1.27, 95% CI [1.1, 1.4]). These results indicate that patients with high self-efficacy were twice as likely to adhere to medication than low self-efficacy (OR = 2.5, 95% CI [1.3, 4.6]).

**Table 7.2**   Logistic regression analysis of social support health beliefs, medication literacy, age, gender, self-efficacy of 300 PLHAs on ARV medication adherence

| Factors | B | SE | Wald | df | sig | Exp(B) | 95% C.I. for EXP(B) | |
|---------|---|----|----|----|----|--------|--------|--------|
| | | | | | | | Lower | Upper |
| Social support | −.010 | .195 | .002 | 1 | .961 | .991 | .675 | 1.453 |
| Health beliefs | .148 | .244 | .370 | 1 | .543 | 1.160 | .719 | 1.870 |
| Medication literacy | −.216 | .230 | .883 | 1 | .347 | .806 | .513 | 1.264 |

*(Continued)*

**Table 7.2** (Continued)

| Factors | B | SE | Wald | df | sig | Exp(B) | 95% C.I. for EXP(B) | |
|---|---|---|---|---|---|---|---|---|
| | | | | | | | Lower | Upper |
| Age | −.006 | .019 | .091 | 1 | .763 | .994 | .957 | 1.033 |
| Gender | .519 | .402 | 1.666 | 1 | .197 | 1.680 | .764 | 3.694 |
| **Self-efficacy** | **.915** | **.313** | **8.523** | **1** | **.004** | **2.497** | **1.351** | **4.616** |
| Constant | −6.1961 | .835 | 11.402 | 1 | .001 | .002 | | |

## Simple linear regression

Linear regression is used to predict the value of a variable based on the value of another variable. The predicted variable is the dependent variable (or the outcome variable). The independent variable is the predicting variable. Generally, regression allows one to ask, 'What is the best predictor of...?'. For example, one could use linear regression to understand whether medication adherence can be predicted based on self-efficacy.

Linear regression uses a continuous variable as the dependent variable in the model. Like correlation, causation cannot be inferred in a regression. Regression results are best presented in a table (like those generated from SPSS or SAS) with the beta, the t-test, and the corresponding significance level.

## Example: Reporting a simple linear regression analysis

We calculated a simple linear regression to predict the patients' medication adherence (%) based on their self-efficacy (Likert scores). The scatter plot indicated a strong positive linear relationship between the two variables, with a Pearson's correlation coefficient of $r = .96$ and a p-value of $< 0.001$. The slope coefficient for self-efficacy was 19.7, so the medication adherence increases by 19.7% for each extra self-efficacy Likert score. The $R^2$ value was .915, or 91%, which shows that the model containing only self-efficacy can explain the medication adherence variation. The scatter plot of standardised predicted values compared to standardised residuals showed that the data met the homogeneity of variance and linearity assumptions, and the residuals were approximately normally distributed. We found a significant regression equation of $F(1,298) = 19.03$, $p = <.001$.). The regression equation was medication adherence Y = 19.03 + .636, (self-efficacy) $R^2 = .915$.

## Multiple linear regression

Multiple linear regression is the term used for more than one independent variable in the analysis. Multiple regression is the relationship between several independent or predictor variables and a dependent or outcome variable. Many variables are 'plugged in' in multiple regression, and, usually, at least a few will turn out to be significant. The number of observations, however, needs to be high. Most authors recommend that there should be at least 10 to 20 times as many observations (cases, respondents) as variables (e.g., 10 variables need 100–200 cases); otherwise, the estimates of the regression line are unlikely to replicate.

When writing up the results, there are specific statistics that one needs to report: (i) State the proportion of variance that the model can explain, which is depicted by the statistic $R^2$ and ranges between 0 and 1, which can be reported, for example, as $R^2 = .915$. It can also be multiplied by 100 to get the percentage of variance the model explains (e.g., 91.5%); (ii) Report whether the model was a significant predictor of the outcome variable using the results of the ANOVA; (iii) Include information about the predictor variables, $B$ values for both variables, and the significance of the contribution to the model. It is also useful to include the final model.

### Example: Reporting multiple regression

A multiple regression was carried out to investigate whether self-efficacy and social support significantly predict a patient's medication adherence. The regression results indicated that the model explained 91% of the variance and that the model was a significant predictor of medication adherence, $F(1,298) = 19.03$, $p = <.001$. Self-efficacy contributed significantly more to the model ($B = .636$, $p = <.001$) than social support ($B = .336$, $p = <.001$). The final predictive model was medication adherence = 19.03 + (.336 social support) + (.636 self-efficacy).

## A note on effect size

An overview of the effect size is given in this section because it is an area that seems to be less well understood and is often left out in reporting statistics. A lower p-value in statistical significance is interpreted to mean a stronger relationship between two variables. However, statistical significance means rejecting the null hypothesis and does not describe the results of measures of magnitude. Effect size measures the magnitude of relationships quantitatively – the greater the effect size, the stronger the relationship or difference between the two variables.

For example, you can use the effect size in the reporting comparison between two means, t-test and ANOVA results, to see how substantially different they are. The effect size can also be used to establish, for example, the effect of a particular drug on treating HIV to determine whether the drug had a small, medium, or significant effect on viral suppression, and to compare the extent of differences. In addition, you can use the effect size to assess the difference between pre-test and post-test results in a quasi-experimental study to establish how substantially the medication adherence changed due to the Motivational Interviewing approach. Finally, effect sizes can be used to compare the results of studies undertaken in different settings (this is widely used in meta-analysis).

The effect size is calculated using Cohen's $d$ (i.e., effect size), which is derived, for example, by subtracting the control group mean from the experimental group mean and dividing the product by the standard deviation of one of the groups. A Cohen's $d$ of 1 indicates that the two groups differ by one standard deviation, and a Cohen's $d$ of 2 indicates the groups differ by two standard deviations. Standard deviations are equivalent to z-scores (1 standard deviation = 1 z-score). According to Cohen (1988), $d = 0.2$ is regarded as a 'small' effect size, $d = 0.5$ represents a 'medium' effect size, and $d = 0.8$ is a 'large' effect size. These cut-offs indicate that if two groups' means do not differ by 0.2 standard deviations or more, the difference is insignificant, even if the p-value shows the relationship or difference is statistically significant, i.e., $< .001$ (Sawilowsky, 2009; Sullivan & Feinn, 2012).

---

### Example: Reporting effect size

An independent sample t-test was conducted to examine the effectiveness of Motivational Interviewing (MI) on self-efficacy. The results indicate an effect size of $d = .80$, indicating a large effect. Thus, individuals in the experimental MI group ($M = 4.74$, $SD = .69$) had a higher self-efficacy following the intervention than individuals in the control group of conventional counselling ($M = 4.19$, $SD = .70$).

---

## Reporting qualitative findings

This book mainly focuses on quantitative research, but the following sections will briefly illustrate how to present qualitative results in your thesis. As before, the discussion will focus on grounded theory, ethnography, and phenomenology research designs – the three fundamental research approaches in qualitative research. It details the critical issues to consider in presenting qualitative research, mainly using tables and quotations.

A qualitative study typically analyses qualitative data for patterns or themes. It provides rich descriptions of each case, followed by interpretation. The discussion revolves around whether the research question was answered, based on the thematic areas emanating from the research. It is natural to combine qualitative analysis with the interpretation of findings in qualitative research. However, it is essential to indicate the difference between the findings and the meaning or interpretation of these findings.

In a thesis, you arrange the data by emerging, significant themes. These themes form the main sections of the results chapter and the sub-themes form subsections. Report general observations about the data, showing recurring agreements or disagreements, patterns, trends, and individual responses that were particularly significant to the research question. Observations are arguments can be supported with direct quotations. Finally, report the most significant outliers, including any unexpected and exciting results linked to the research question.

Inductive logic does not require arguing that the themes presented were the only themes to emerge. Instead, you must show how the data link to the theme and explain how and why these themes are significant to the research question by referencing them to the theoretical framework, unless you are carrying out a strict version of grounded theory (Langford, 2012).

The following examples illustrate how to report qualitative findings in grounded theory, ethnographic, and phenomenological types of studies.

---

## Example: Reporting findings in a grounded theory study

We conducted a qualitative study using in-depth, semi-structured interviews to explore facilitators and barriers to accessing healthcare for people living with HIV. We conducted qualitative interviews with 40 patients: 20 who never missed appointments (compliant) and 20 who missed more than two of the six scheduled appointments (non-compliant). A stratified analysis of the compliant and non-compliant groups was done to establish shared themes and differences in the themes. These themes were derived from behavioural control, normative beliefs, and the social support Theory of Planned Behaviour (Ajzen, 1991). The themes are described, and representative quotations are presented. We first present common themes between non-compliant and compliant participants, followed by differences between the two groups.

*(Continued)*

## Behavioural control

Both compliant and non-compliant groups expressed a high level of perceived behavioural control, believing that they were able to determine whether they engaged in their care or not. For example, on the one hand, a compliant patient stated, 'I know though I might feel healthy, I should keep coming for my appointments and taking my medication'. On the other hand, the non-compliant patient described control as choosing whether to engage in their care or not. For example, one non-compliant participant said, 'I am 100% in control. However, sometimes I ask myself if it is necessary to make each appointment when I feel well.' Another non-compliant responded, 'I feel mentally unprepared to engage in care'.

## Normative beliefs

Both non-compliant and compliant groups expressed strong normative beliefs, which in this context are the patients' perceptions of others' beliefs regarding HIV infection or the need to engage in care; for example, in response to the question: 'Does worrying about what others think of your HIV keep you from seeking care?' A notable difference in the normative referents between non-compliant and compliant was that half of the compliant group expressed worry about what others in the community would think of their HIV status. This worry acted as a motivation to seek care so that they pretend to appear healthy so as not to be suspected of being HIV positive. On the other hand, the non-compliant were also concerned, but instead, they avoided seeking care because of stigma. For example, one said: 'I saw someone I knew from my village just as I was about to enter the HIV clinic and took off'.

## Social support

Facilitating factors that both groups expressed in seeking care included positive relationships, including shared decision-making with physicians, community-based support groups, and primarily support from family and friends. 'I think the most important thing is for a patient who has HIV not to feel alone because feeling alone can affect your motivation to seek care' (compliant patient). On the other hand, a non-compliant patient is more pessimistic: 'My family disowned me when they found out about my HIV diagnosis. When nobody even cares anyway, why would I?' (non-compliant).

## Discussion

These findings are particularly interesting considering the responses to questions about what others think about a person's HIV status. The results conform to the Theory of Planned Behaviour. Normative beliefs, or what individuals believe about the expectations of others, help inform behavioural intention, which leads to behaviour change (Ajzen I., 1991, 2011, 2014). This study explored whether patient participants were concerned about what others thought of their HIV status. We found that those who expressed worry about others' opinions regarding their HIV status spoke of this worry as a normative belief that led them to seek care. They did not want people to know that they were living with HIV because they looked sick. Although this type of normative belief could be considered negative and a product of stigma, it facilitated engagement in care for several patients.

Patients in both compliant and non-compliant groups had many shared perspectives, including a strong belief in their control over seeking care. Our findings differ from other care studies in that most of our participants, regardless of engagement in care status, expressed high self-efficacy and behavioural control. In contrast, in other studies, low self-efficacy was associated with medication non-adherence (Traeger L et al., 2012; Risher KA et al., 2017).

Our findings raise important considerations of the reasoning behind ARV adherence which provided these participants with the ability to have 'authority' over a critical part of their lives. Unfortunately, the few studies investigating this concept and ARV adherence have been inconclusive. While some evidence suggests no relationship between the internal position of control and ARV adherence (Lynam et al., 2009), other studies show that the self, powerful others, and chance were the best predictors of ARV success (Evans, Ferrando, Rabkin, and Fishman, 2000).

In conclusion, this study provides unique insights into the different perspectives of patients who initially engage in care by attending scheduled appointments and those who do not, and critical distinctions between perceptions of motivations to care. Our data suggest a considerable motivation for participants to successfully manage their medication was their attitudes to life, which mainly involved family and significant others. The main limitation to our findings was that data collection took place in a hospital setting, and reasons for ARV adherence should therefore be explored in a community setting.

## Example: Reporting findings in an ethnographic study

This study explored how some HIV-positive individuals living in challenging circumstances can achieve successful adherence to their medication. The participants discussed their HIV medication regimen, daily adherence to HIV medication, and daily life. The main themes arising from the study include family support, self-worth, self-efficacy, and the support of health providers.

*(Continued)*

## Family support

Almost all the participants spoke about how family connection, support, love, and involvement motivated them to take the medication. For example, one participant said: 'I went into depression and started drinking heavily until I realised how this affected my children and husband, who dearly loved me. As a result, I was encouraged to take the medication. Therefore, motivation came from my children and husband.' Another stated, 'my family provided meaning to my life and was a powerful motivator for lifelong adherence'. These findings show that family support was a common motivating factor for these participants.

## Support from health providers

According to some participants, the health staff and community workers treated them with respect. One participant commented: 'The health providers sincerely care for my well-being and genuinely want to help me and want the best for me.' Another stated: 'The health providers are the family I never had because they focus on the positive, whereas my family focuses on the negative. As a result, they motivated me, and I was confident and determined to be as healthy as possible by consistently heeding their advice to take ARVs.'

In conclusion, participants recognised that they could control their HIV by taking medication and expressed gratitude and appreciation for the meaning of life, mainly involving the family.

# Example: Reporting findings in a phenomenological study

The objective of this phenomenological study was to explore the lived experience of patients living with HIV. Twenty participants (10 males and 10 females) aged 18 to 60 years attending an HIV/AIDs clinic were involved in this study. From the interviews, we identified three thematic categories. These categories were the time of diagnosis, medication fatigue, and the experience of living with HIV.

## Time of diagnosis

Participants in the study had been living with HIV for three to 30 years. Individuals diagnosed in the late 1980s and early 1990s described changes in HIV healthcare, noting that medications have significantly improved with time and were more tolerable. For example, one patient diagnosed in the 1980s shared that his positive diagnosis came with the advice to 'prepare to die', leading him to sell all his belongings. 'After selling all my belongings, my quality of life was adversely affected for several years until I realised the medication seemed to be working and that I needed to live my life to the fullest.' Other individuals, including those diagnosed recently, when medication and understanding have significantly improved, echoed this thought.

## Medication fatigue

Patients had a variety of feelings and attitudes about medication. Some remarked that sometimes they missed a dose due to stress: 'I just get tired of taking the drugs'. Others described taking medication inconsistently: 'I went for a week without taking the medication because I was simply tired of pills, knowing very well that I need to keep taking them'. However, most comments show that almost all participants were compliant.

Some patients with non-detectable viral loads continued with the medication regime to maintain their quality of life.

## Experience of living with HIV

The interviews also captured the overarching experiences of living with HIV, precisely the words or phrases used to describe life after HIV. Common descriptions depicted HIV as a journey, an ongoing process that improves. They seemed to become more aware of and were more attuned to how dealing with stress, diet, exercise, and medication adherence affected their daily lives. Some expressions supporting these sentiments were: 'it is not a death sentence'; 'I have learnt to live with it'; 'it is only part of my life but does not define me'; 'It is an ongoing process that will never end, but it is ok as long as I continue to manage the disease successfully'; and 'It has been a long journey, and I do not believe it will ever be over'.

The depth of findings generated from this research demonstrates the usefulness of the phenomenological perspective in understanding the realities of what it feels like to live with HIV. In addition to the positive personal outcomes for each participant, all individuals provided significant insights into the experience of living with HIV.

## Using tables in qualitative research

Data collected from qualitative methods can also be converted to tables. Nonetheless, using tables in qualitative research is not widely understood and is rarely considered to support data analysis and ensure trustworthiness.

Tables in qualitative research help relay information about research sites and methods, summarise observations, or display data. They also serve as analytical devices to arrange data to facilitate researchers in finding similarities and differences and noticing patterns, including co-occurrences, themes, and trends, which are essential for interpreting qualitative data.

This section provides a brief overview of the sorts of tables commonly used in qualitative research. It is based on an article by Cloutier and Ravasi (2021), who discuss various types of tables and describe their possible uses. These authors provide valuable advice on displaying evidence findings succinctly and convincingly to readers. According to Cloutier and Ravasi, the main types of tables used in qualitative research are:

- **Concept-evidence tables**: Concept-evidence tables help researchers to track the extent to which each component of their emerging theoretical framework is supported by available evidence. In addition, they provide definitive evidence supporting their claims and highlight similarities or differences by gathering and ordering evidence by concept and case.
- **Cross-case comparative tables**: Cross-case comparative tables explore similarities and differences across cases. These tables help to organise and compare cases. In addition, they support an overarching theoretical framework by reflecting similarities across cases or by grouping cases based on intra-group similarities and inter-group differences.
- **Co-occurrence tables**: Co-occurrence tables are particularly useful when the number of cases is high. The intent is to cluster cases based on similar properties or behaviours, to identify other co-occurring properties, and possibly to explain them.
- **Temporally ordered tables**: Temporally ordered tables, or time-ordered tables, help to track events or changes in a unit of analysis (actors, organisations, activities) or a concept over time. By ordering data by time and sequence, researchers can examine what happened when and what might have led to what happened or compare changes in empirical observations over time. For example, the researchers compare units of analysis or concepts across time to document whether they appear at different time points or how they manifest changes over time.
- **Typologically ordered tables**: Typologically ordered tables are used to compare different manifestations or properties of a concept (e.g., different types of processes, practice, strategy, structure, and belief), across a study to highlight similarities and differences in empirical observations.
- **Theoretical summaries**: Theoretical summaries help researchers to 'think through' their interpretations by adding depth to understanding and highlighting relationships between the essential concepts. They emerge from the empirical observation to offer a theoretical explanation, especially in complex models that need to illustrate and simultaneously account for variation across units of analysis. Theoretical summaries replace empirical content (i.e., evidence in raw or processed form) with theoretical content (e.g., labels or explanations).

## Quotations in qualitative research

Direct quotations are the raw data in qualitative research; they reveal the informants' views. However, this provides a dilemma for qualitative researchers. Many scholars find it challenging to decide why, how, or when to quote in qualitative research. For example, when informants' views are the principal evidence in the study, how can the researcher protect their participants' confidentiality while also providing a faithful account of the evidence they have given? When should informants' own words be used and when should the researcher 'speak for them' by paraphrasing? What is the right number of quotations to include in your analysis of your results and findings? Eldh et al. (2020) provide some useful guidelines, as follows:

- Verbatim descriptions of participants' accounts can be edited or condensed.
- Shortening or condensing the quote is acceptable, but state that the quotation(s) are edited or truncated. A text that includes an ellipsis signifies that part of a verbatim utterance has been left out. For example, 'The health providers are the family I never had because they focus on the positive, whereas my family focuses on the negative. [...] they motivated me [...] to be as healthy as possible by consistently heeding their advice to take ARVs'.
- In group or focus group interviews, quotations illustrate the associations between the participants. To highlight this purpose, longer passages from transcripts may be relevant, although one can shorten them to indicate a particular relation or structure.
- From a research ethics perspective, it is important to protect the confidentiality of the participant, for example, by using identifiers that do not reveal identities when you are quoting.

# Reporting mixed methods results

Mixed methods research designs involve integrating qualitative and quantitative data within a single investigation. The three main types of mixed methods designs are sequential exploratory, sequential explanatory, and convergent study designs.

In a sequential exploratory design, the characteristics or findings of the qualitative phase of the study are reported first, followed by the results of the quantitative phase. If there is an overlap between the setting, participants, and instruments, present the details of the common threads together.

In a sequential explanatory design, the elements of the quantitative phase of the study are reported first, followed by those of the qualitative phase. All the same rules and guidance apply in presenting your quantitative results and qualitative data. Describe the setting, participants, and instruments separately if they differ between the quantitative and qualitative data collection.

Organising the results in a convergent design is complicated because data are analysed simultaneously. An overlap is predominant in a convergent mixed methods design where the setting and participants may be the same. For example, to select a sub-sample from the population participating in the quantitative phase for study in the qualitative phase, purposeful sampling is undertaken. The rule of thumb is to write in the order in which data were first examined or the order that provides the best organisational framework. For example, in an extensive quantitative survey where a subset of the population is interviewed qualitatively, the quantitative procedures are presented first. Alternatively, the order of analysis could drive the order of writing. For example, if you analysed the qualitative data while the quantitative data were still being collected, and a theory emerged based on the iterative analysis of qualitative data, then you would use the quantitative data to illustrate the theory.

The results can be structured and described using a weaving pattern where quantitative and qualitative findings are presented together thematically (Bazeley, 2012; Bryman, 2006; Creswell, 2015; Robson, 2011).

## Concluding the results chapter

The result chapter ends with a summary reflecting the results and summarising the overall findings. It highlights the most critical findings in one or two paragraphs in order of significance as per the objectives/hypothesis or significant patterns found. It reminds the reader of the critical patterns coming out of the data and points out essential details that suggest the emergence of key trends throughout the results sections. These include complex or unanticipated findings that could lead to action (i.e., can be pursued feasibly or applied to practice). This conclusion should not include any new information or analysis.

The last sentence of the concluding paragraph makes the transition and presents a hook that ties the results chapter to the discussion chapter.

### Example: Concluding the results chapter

Our results demonstrate the critical role of Motivational Interviewing (MI) in medication adherence. We found that MI significantly influenced social support, self-efficacy, and, consequently, medication adherence. Self-efficacy was the most important predictor of medication adherence. Thus, a person's likelihood of adhering to medication was related to their self-efficacy.

> Findings from the qualitative research confirm the importance of self-efficacy and social support in medication adherence. The qualitative data also suggest that participants are considerably motivated to succeed in taking their medication. In the discussion chapter that follows, we discuss the implications of our results and findings.

The results chapter should preferably be about 20–30% of the thesis.

# Common pitfalls of the results chapter

The following points are some of the common mistakes students make in writing the results chapter.

## Presenting tables and graphs

- Tables or graphs are intended to communicate information to the target audience, but communication is ineffective if the choice of graph design is inappropriate and ineffective in conveying the message. Make sure you use the best format for the message.
- Overloading tables or figures with too much data makes them harder to read and interpret. Redesign the layout or, if necessary, produce more than one table or figure to represent your findings effectively.
- Another mistake is having too many variables or too many categories in a chart, which affects readability. Use a maximum of six categories. Combining the last 7+ categories into a single category called 'Others' is recommended.
- Combining too many visual attributes in one graph overloads the reader's perception, making it difficult to interpret. Keep it simple and avoid using too many colours, fonts, typesizes, etc., that are not easy to compare.
- The data, which are the most critical elements of the graph, do not stand out and all the reader can see are gridlines, labels, or non-data elements. The design should display the data effectively.
- Avoid using overly fancy graphs and figures that do not add value and make the graph challenging to understand. Keep it simple and fit for purpose – use simple charts.
- Scales need to use equally spaced intervals representing periods, and charts must always have a zero baseline.
- Avoid having too many tick marks and labels in graphs that make them difficult to read, or too few to estimate the value data points.
- A common mistake in tables is failing to attribute the table if it is taken from another source. Sources always need to be attributed to avoid any issues with plagiarism.
- Ensure all elements of the table need to be clear and easily understood, including the legend, column titles, and the main body of the table.

## The text

- The data does not help to answer the research questions or does not match what was described in the methodology chapter.
- Repeating data from the tables and figures in the text instead of highlighting the key findings.
- Reporting raw, unprocessed data when they can be summarised as means, percentages, and numbers.
- Using percentages that do not add up.
- The presentation of text does not allow the reader to see whether the hypotheses have been tested or the questions answered.
- Using phrases that are vague or non-specific, such as 'appeared to be greater than other variables...' or 'demonstrates promising trends that...', without supporting data.
- Overusing the word 'significant' instead of limiting its use to only when statistical tests were done.
- Ignoring negative results (i.e., a finding that does not support the study's underlying assumptions), or failing to discuss them in the discussion chapter.
- Discussing or interpreting the results in the results chapter instead of leaving them for the discussion chapter.

---

## Example: Results chapter: Motivation and ART medication adherence

### Introduction

Most adherence efforts that focus on group efforts have not reached adherence levels of ≥95% globally. Therefore, the objective of our study was to test the effectiveness of a patient-focused approach using the Motivation Interviewing (MI) in an experimental study design.

This chapter compares the study variables between the control and intervention groups at the baseline. Next, we analyse behavioural factors associated with medication adherence, followed by ascertaining the relationship between motivation factors (social support, self-efficacy, health beliefs) and age on medication adherence. Then, we compare the effect of self-efficacy (high self-efficacy, medium self-efficacy, and low self-efficacy) conditions and the effectiveness of Motivational Interviewing in improving medication adherence. Finally, we explore facilitators and barriers to accessing healthcare for people living with HIV using a grounded theory approach.

## Comparison of study variables at the baseline

This analysis aimed to establish whether the various factors studied differed between the intervention and control groups at the baseline using a t-test. Except for self-efficacy, we found no differences between the intervention and control group variables at the baseline, as shown in Table 7.1.

**Table 7.1**  Description of the study sample of patients attending a Comprehensive Care Clinic (CCC) in September 2020

| | Baseline data | | |
| --- | --- | --- | --- |
| Factors | Control group | Intervention group | Std. Error Mean |
| | N=148 | N=152 | |
| Medication literacy | 2.79±1.11 | 2.80±.93 | .076 |
| Health belief | 3.30±1.02 | 3.57±.84 | .074 |
| Social support | 2.47±1.03 | 2.73±.1.9 | .084 |
| *Self-efficacy* | *2.61±.61* | *2.78±.5* | *.040* |
| Age in years | 39.2±11.6 | 40.62±9.6 | .943 |
| Gender (%) | 48.3 | 51.3 | |
| Medication adherence (mean) | 77.3±14.6 | 80.6±14.2 | |
| Medication adherence (≥95%) | 5.3% | 5%. | |

We performed logistic regression to ascertain the relationship between social support, self-efficacy, health beliefs, and age on the likelihood of medication adherence (≥ 95% adherent = 1) versus non-adherence (< 95% non-adherent = 0). The statistical tests of each regression coefficient were tested using the Wald chi-square statistic. The Wald criterion demonstrated that only self-efficacy significantly contributed to adherence ($p$ = <.04), as shown in Table 7.2. The logistic regression model was statistically significant ($\chi 2(1, N\ 300) = 129.28, p < .001$). The model explained 35.0% (Nagelkerke R2) of the variance in medication adherence and correctly classified 75.0% of cases.

Social support, health beliefs, and age were not associated with medication adherence, but increasing self-efficacy score was associated with increased medication adherence (OR = 1.27, 95% CI [1.1, 1.4]). These results indicate that patients with high self-efficacy were twice as likely to adhere to medication than low self-efficacy (OR = 2.5, 95% CI [1.3, 4.6]).

*(Continued)*

**Table 7.2** Logistic regression analysis of social support health beliefs, medication literacy, age, gender, self-efficacy of 300 PLHAs on ARV medication adherence

| Factors | B | SE | Wald | df | sig | Exp(B) | 95% C.I. for EXP(B) | |
|---|---|---|---|---|---|---|---|---|
| | | | | | | | Lower | Upper |
| Social support | −.010 | .195 | .002 | 1 | .961 | .991 | .675 | 1.453 |
| Health beliefs | .148 | .244 | .370 | 1 | .543 | 1.160 | .719 | 1.870 |
| Medication literacy | −.216 | .230 | .883 | 1 | .347 | .806 | .513 | 1.264 |
| Age | −.006 | .019 | .091 | 1 | .763 | .994 | .957 | 1.033 |
| Gender | .519 | .402 | 1.666 | 1 | .197 | 1.680 | .764 | 3.694 |
| **Self-efficacy** | **.915** | **.313** | **8.523** | **1** | **.004** | **2.497** | **1.351** | **4.616** |
| Constant | −6.1961 | .835 | 11.402 | 1 | .001 | .002 | | |

## The effect of Motivational Interviewing on behavioural factors

The results given in Table 7.3 indicate a significant increase in all the behavioural factors and medication adherence at the post-test. However, the effect sizes were small (below .5) except for efficacy, with a $d = .8$, indicating a significant effect. Specifically, our results indicate that high levels of self-efficacy result in increased medication adherence.

**Table 7.3** The effect of Motivational Interviewing on behavioural factors of patients attending a Comprehensive Care Clinic (CCC) in September 2020

| Factors | Pre-test N = 148 | Post-test N = 152 | p-value | Effect size |
|---|---|---|---|---|
| Social support | 2.47±1.03 | 2.73±.1.0 | 0.24 | .25 |
| **Self-efficacy** | **3.87±.80** | **4.54±.69** | **.000** | **.8** |
| Health belief | 3.30±1.02 | 3.57±.84 | .013 | .26 |
| Medication literacy | 2.48±.89 | 2.80±.93 | .003 | .36 |

Individual Likert mean scores for medication literacy, health belief, social support, and self-efficacy ranged from 1 to 5. Age was assessed in complete years. Except for self-efficacy, there was no significant difference in the perception in health belief, social support, age, sex, and medication adherence at the baseline.

## The effect of Motivational Interviewing on self-efficacy

An independent sample t-test was conducted to examine the effectiveness of Motivational Interviewing (MI) on self-efficacy. The results indicate an effect size of $d$ = .80, indicating a large effect. Thus, individuals in the experimental MI group ($M$ = 4.74, $SD$ = .69) had a higher self-efficacy following the intervention than individuals in the control group of conventional counselling ($M$ = 4.19, $SD$ = .70).

## The effect of self-efficacy conditions on medication adherence

ANOVA was conducted to compare the effect of motivation type (self-efficacy, health belief, and social support) conditions on medication adherence. We used three paired samples t-tests to perform post hoc comparisons between self-efficacy, health beliefs, and social support conditions. The first paired samples t-test indicated that there was a significant difference in the scores for self-efficacy ($M$ = 4.30, $SD$ = .87) and health belief ($M$ = 2.64, $SD$ = .92) conditions; $t(4)$ = 23.50, $p$ = <.001. The second paired samples t-test indicated that there was a significant difference in the scores for self-efficacy ($M$ = 4.30, $SD$ = 0.87) and social support ($M$ = 2.69, $SD$ = 1.02) conditions; $t(4)$ = 23.09, $p$ = <.001. The third paired samples t-test indicated no significant difference in the scores for social support ($M$ = 2.69, $SD$ = 1.02) and health belief ($M$ = 2.64, $SD$ = .92) conditions. These results suggest that motivation type affects medication adherence. Wilks' Lambda = 0.10, $F(2,4)$ = 13.39, $p$ = .042. Specifically, the results suggest that patients with high self-efficacy adhere more to medication. However, there is no real difference in medication adherence when comparing health beliefs and social support.

We calculated a simple linear regression to predict the patients' medication adherence (%) based on their self-efficacy (Likert scores). The scatter plot indicated a strong positive linear relationship between the two variables, with a Pearson's correlation coefficient of $r$ = .96 and a p-value of < 0.001. The slope coefficient for self-efficacy was 19.7, so the medication adherence increases by 19.7% for each extra self-efficacy Likert score. The $R^2$ value was .915, or 91%, which shows that the model containing only self-efficacy can explain the medication adherence variation. The scatter plot of standardised predicted values compared to standardised residuals showed that the data met the homogeneity of variance and linearity assumptions, and the residuals were approximately normally distributed. We found a significant regression equation of $F(1,298)$ = 19.03, $p$ = <.001.). The regression equation was medication adherence Y = 19.03 + .636, (self-efficacy) $R^2$ = .915.

*(Continued)*

## The effect of Motivational Interviewing on medication adherence

The objective of this study was to assess the effectiveness of Motivational Interviewing in improving medication adherence of persons living with HIV. Our null hypothesis was that there would be no significant difference in medication adherence between patients receiving Motivational Interviewing that uses an individualised, patient-centred approach and those receiving the conventional small group intervention (control group).

McNemar's test, a version of the chi-square test for paired samples, was used for 'paired data' comprising a 'before' measure and a related 'after' measure from the same subject. The test showed a significant increase in patients who reached the recommended levels of $\geq 95\%$ ($\chi 2 = 31.34$, $df = 1$, $p = <.001$, OR = 1.87).

The results indicate that while the medication adherence levels in the control group changed by 4%, those in the intervention MI group rose by 37% from the pre-test. There was a significant increase of patients who reached the recommended levels of $\geq 95\%$ in the MI group (33%) compared to only 4% in the control group. The MI group was eight times more likely to adhere to medication than those using conventional counselling approaches after the four-month follow-up, totalling 400 minutes, with 98% response rates. Thus, MI had a more significant impact on medication adherence than the conventional small group counselling approach.

### Conclusion

Our results demonstrate the critical role of Motivational Interviewing (MI) in medication adherence. We found that MI significantly influenced social support, self-efficacy, and medication adherence. Self-efficacy was the most important predictor of medication adherence. Thus, a person's likelihood of adhering to medication was related to their self-efficacy.

Findings from the qualitative research confirm the importance of self-efficacy and social support in medication adherence. The qualitative data also suggest that participants are considerably motivated to succeed in taking their medication. In the discussion chapter that follows, we discuss the implications of our results and findings.

## Exercise: Results chapter

### Instructions

Discuss to what extent the examiner's comments apply to this text, supporting your argument with examples of words, phrases, or sentences from the text.

(Refer to the section on Pedagogical features — 'Discussion-based exercises' — in the Introduction of this book for more details on completing this exercise.)

## Text: Factors influencing adherence to antiretroviral (ARV) drugs among persons living with HIV/AIDS

### Introduction

This chapter presents the findings of a study whose aim was to establish whether social support from various social networks influences adherence to ARV medication. The chapter is arranged by specific objective. The main body consists of (i) a description of social demographics, (ii) the level of adherence to antiretroviral (ARV), (iii) knowledge of the ARV medication adherence and how it is used, (iv) and perception of social support and ARV medication adherence. Each section starts with a description of the variable and its relationship, association, or correlation with ARV medication adherence. The last section is a logistic regression model applied to estimate which factor(s) are most critical in influencing ARV medication adherence.

### Social demographics

I computed measures of central tendency to summarise the age variable. The mean age ($N = 310$, $M = 42.06$, $SD = 10.08$) ranged from 21 to 66 years. Sixty per cent (60%) were married, 22% were single, 8% were divorced, and 10% were widowed. There were more women (60%) than men. Most participants (66.1%) either had no formal education or had only eight years of primary/basic education, and only 6.3% had tertiary education.

### Antiretroviral adherence

Results indicate that the ARV medication adherence, measured using self-report of 86.6%, was 29% higher than that using the pill count. Only 60% of the respondents had reached the recommended level of $\geq 95\%$ adherence using pill count. Among the 15.4% who had missed the drug, 70% had missed only one drug, whereas the rest had missed more than one drug. Only 40% of the respondents took pills as prescribed, 60% took more or fewer pills, and 36% changed drugs.

Education levels were significantly associated with adherence to ARV medication adherence ($\chi2 = 14.066$, $df = 3$, $p = 0.004$). Pearson's chi-square test indicated a significant relationship between marital status and adherence level ($\chi2 = 10.8$, $df = 3$, $p = 0.01$). Divorcees tended to be more adherent as out of the 27 divorcees, only one fell into the non-adherent category (< 95%). Age, sex, and education were unrelated to ARV medication adherence ($p = \geq 0.05$).

*(Continued)*

## Knowledge of ARV drugs

Two-thirds (65%) of the PLHIV/AIDS knew the names of the drug they were using, how it was supposed to be taken, and the consequences of not following the instructions. The consequences reported were drug resistance (70%), treatment failure (15%), and death (28%). The education level ($\chi2 = 4.0$, $df = 1$, $p = 0.045$) and sex ($\chi2 = 13.067$, $df = 3$, $p = 0.004$) were significantly related to the knowledge of the names of the ARV drugs. Women were more knowledgeable of the names of the drugs than men. Marital status and age were not associated with knowledge of the ARV drug names ($p = \geq 0.05$). The Pearson correlation results indicated a significant positive association between knowledge of the ARV drugs and medication adherence, ($r(113) = .70$, $p = .013$).

## Side effects

Side effects were experienced by 30% of PLHIV/AIDS. They were given as the main reason for changing or stopping the drugs. Among those who experienced side effects, 25% experienced one side effect, 50% had 2–3 side effects, and 25% experienced ≥ four. The main side effects experienced were dizziness (20%), headaches (15%), and skin rashes (10%). Side effects were significantly associated to ARV medication adherence ($\chi2 = 68.412$, $df = 2$, $p = \leq 0.001$).

## Social support and ARV medication adherence

In this section, I look at the source of social support from the social networks (nuclear family, extended family, and other community networks) and the type of support (food, emotional, and material support) using the 5-point Likert scale. The results indicated that the nuclear family was ranked first in providing food support (60%). On the other hand, it is noteworthy that the social networks (church, welfare associations) were ranked second in providing support (20%).

Means of the various support using the Likert scale were nuclear family, 3.9 ± 0.5; social networks, 3.2 ± 0.7; extended family, 2.8 ± 1.2; friends, 2.8 ± 0.8; and community, 1.9 ± .09. Results on the type of support given are emotional support, 1.8 ± 0.2; material support, 1.9 ± 0.2; ARV support, 1.9 ± 0.5; and food support, 1.7 ± 0.3. Half of the respondents rated the support received as adequate. Independent sample t-tests are reported as indicating significant differences between groups, ($t(33) = 37.35$, $p = < .001$).

Social support was highly associated with adherence ($\chi^2 = 8.970$, $df = 1$, $p = 0.002$), with an odds ratio of 2.6 (CI 1.2–3.5). These results indicate that people with a positive perception of social support were more likely to adhere to ARV drugs than those with a negative perception.

A Pearson product-moment correlation coefficient was computed to assess the relationship between social support and medication adherence. The result indicates a positive correlation between the level of social support and medication adherence, $r = .35$, $p = < .001$, with an $R2 = .124$. The variance explained by social support was 15%, which means that 75% of the variance is unexplained.

A one-way between-subjects ANOVA was conducted to compare the effect of family support (IV) on adherence (DV). These results suggest that the nuclear family influenced adherence. In addition, the results indicate a significant relationship between social support and adherence (1, $N = 368$) = 6.38, $p = .011$), with an odds ratio of 6.0. These results indicate that patients with social support were six times more likely to adhere to treatment.

The three social support groups had a significant effect on ARV medication adherence ($p = \leq .05$ level) with [$F$ (2, 12) = 4.94, $p = 0.027$]. Post hoc comparisons using the Tukey HSD test indicated that the mean score for the nuclear family support ($M = 3.9$, $SD = 1.30$) was significantly different from the extended family ($M = 2.8$, $SD = 1.2$) friends, ($M = 2.8$, $SD = 0.8$); and community, ($M = 1.9$, $SD = .09$).

The logistic regression model was applied to estimate the factors associated with ARV medication adherence (social support, side effects, marital status, and education) to find out which is most influential. The dependent variable (ARV medication adherence) is discrete and coded (0, 1) and not continuous; thus, logistic regression was used. The dependent variable that measures the adherence to ARV medication of ≥95% was a yes equal to 1. The statistical tests of each regression coefficient were tested using the Wald chi-square statistic, and Nagelkerke $R^2$ statistics were used to evaluate model performance. The intercept test result of Y = 0.825 was greater than $p = > 0.05$, suggesting that an alternative model without an intercept needed to be applied. Goodness-of-fit test – Hosmer–Lemeshow (H–L) – was thus used. The goodness of fit, which indicates the model's appropriateness and how well it fits the actual outcome, was estimated with the H–L test. My results had a p-value of 0.294, indicating that the model was appropriate (a significant $p = > 0.05$ indicates the model fitted the data satisfactorily).

The Wald criterion demonstrated that marital status ($p = 0.029$) and the burden of side effects ($p = \leq 0.001$) predicted ARV medication adherence significantly. Thus, a person's likelihood of adhering to medication was related to their marital status and side effects. Specifically, divorced persons were 11 times more likely to adhere to medication. Nagelkerke $R^2$ of 0.406 shows that these variables explained 41% of the variation in the ARV medication adherence.

The null model, i.e., the model with no explanatory variables, showed ARV medication adherence (dependent variable) in the equation accurately classified 55% of the respondents. However, when the explanatory variables were

*(Continued)*

added to the model, the accurate classification increased to 58%, indicating only a slight improvement. Omnibus tests of model coefficients, which provide information on whether the block of explanatory variables contributed significantly to model fit, had a p-value of 0.06, showing that the model significantly influenced the null model. The statistical significance of individual regression coefficients was tested using the Wald chi-square statistic, which demonstrated that only family influence made a significant contribution ($p = 0.021$).

Measures of the log-likelihood, which are tentative indicators of the range in which the explanatory variables' actual influence on the dependent variable lay, showed that the explanatory variables explained only 5–7% of the dependent variable's variation (Cox & Snell $R^2$ and Nagelkerke $R^2$ respectively).

## Examiner's comments

- The candidate reported the data following the reporting format and adhering to the research design. They described the assumptions, sensitivity, and reliability of the tests used, along with the potential sources of measurement error and bias.
- The analyses were linked to the hypotheses and research question(s) and the aim of the study.
- The candidate demonstrated why each analysis was conducted, how the analysis was done, and what the analysis said.
- The candidate demonstrates the ability to interpret the research results.

# Further reading

Burton, N., Brundrett, M., & Jones, M. (2018). *Doing your Education Research Project*. London: Sage.

This book is a valuable guide for teachers and practitioners new to research. It guides the reader through the entire research process, from clarifying the context and conceptual background to presenting and analysing the evidence gathered.

Cloutier, C., & Ravasi, D. (2021). Using tables to enhance trustworthiness in qualitative research. *Strategic Organization*, *19*(1). https://doi.org/10.1177/14 76127020979329

This article discusses how to use tables to ensure (and reassure) trustworthiness in qualitative research. It presents some of the tables that are most frequently used by qualitative researchers, explains their uses, discusses how they enhance trustworthiness, and provides illustrative examples to inspire readers to use tables in their research.

Cronk, B. C., (2019). *How to Use SPSS Statistics: A Step-by-step Guide to Analysis and Interpretation* (11th edition). Abingdon: Routledge.

Written for novice computer users, this book provides a step-by-step guide to using SPSS statistics. It begins with the basics and moves on to the major statistical techniques, such as descriptive statistics, prediction, association, parametric inferential statistics, and non-parametric inferential statistics.

Eldh, A. C., Årestedt, L., & Berterö, C. (2020). Quotations in qualitative studies: Reflections on constituents, custom, and purpose. *International Journal of Qualitative Methods*, *10*(2), 229–248. https://doi.org/10.1177/1609 406920969268

This paper provides diverse guidance in the presentation of quotations. It includes an overview of the scientific reasoning for including quotations in qualitative studies.

Few, S. (2012). Differing roles of tables and graphs. In *Show Me the Numbers: Designing Tables and Graphs to Enlighten* (2nd edition). El Dorado Hills, CA: Analytics Press.

This book is a useful guide to presenting quantitative data. It looks at the purpose of tables and graphs, and examines other design issues. This chapter introduces tables and graphs and gives simple guidelines for selecting which one to use for a particular purpose. It explains how to design high-quality graphics that help to present patterns, outliers, and relationships.

Langford, R. (2012). Qualitative research methods, by Monique Hennink, Inge Hutter and Ajay Bailey. *Critical Public Health*, *22*(1), 111–112. https://doi.org/ 10.1080/09581596.2011.565689

This article shows you how to plan, conduct, and analyse qualitative research and select appropriate methods to publish the findings. It demonstrates how to link research design to data analysis. It offers guidance on writing qualitative research, including how to respond to critiques of qualitative methods. It is supported by online resources, including a checklist and reflective questions.

Reynolds, G. (2014). *Presentation Zen Design: A Simple Visual Approach to Presenting in Today's World* (2nd edition). Berkeley, CA: New Riders.

This book highlights many of the key points of successful presentations. It has a bibliography of suggested reading and links to websites referred to in the presentations.

Sawilowsky, S. S. (2009). New effect size rules of thumb. *Journal of Modern Applied Statistical Methods*, *8*(2), 597–599. https://doi.org/10.22237/ jmasm/1257035100

This article provides recommendations that expand Cohen's (1988) rules of thumb for interpreting effect sizes to include very small, very large, and substantial effect sizes.

Sullivan, G. M., & Feinn, R. (2012). Using effect size—or why the p value is not enough. *Journal of Graduate Medical Education, 4*(3), 279–282. https://doi.org/10.4300/jgme-d-12-00156.1

This article emphasises the importance of reporting effect sizes instead of merely reporting the statistical significance of the results. The results are described in terms of magnitude measures, for example, whether treatment affects people and how much it affects them. The authors argue that a research inquiry's primary product is one or more measures of effect size, not p-values.

# 8

# Writing the Discussion Chapter

This chapter demonstrates how to summarise the significance of the results and how they support the core argument or claim of your thesis. It demonstrates how to present your interpretation of the results, considering the gaps in knowledge of previous studies, and how to generalise your results to other contexts. It also discusses how to write about the limitations in your study.

## Purpose of the discussion chapter

The primary purpose of a discussion chapter is to answer the 'so what?' question and spell out why the study contributes to knowledge on a topic. The chapter builds on arguments and claims based on the research findings, and describes, interprets, and critically examines findings, situating them in previous knowledge and generalising them to other contexts. It demonstrates the researcher's ability to make sense of data and to create connections between theoretical discussions, research questions, methods, and conclusions. It also reveals the study's limitations and shortcomings, which may identify new gaps in the literature and justify further research studies – an important aspect of the thesis. The discussion chapter is the most critical part of the thesis and the most complex and challenging to write. The difficulties often stem from recognising that the discussion chapter should not repeat the results chapter, but not knowing how to frame it differently.

The discussion chapter explains how you interpret results, discusses previous research and theory, describes the implications and limitations of the study, and suggests topics for future research. It also summarises the main findings and arguments in the conclusion. The chapter must not contain new data or results, but only offer an interpretation of the results. It should assess the study's limitations and shortcomings, and how these might have impacted results or findings, and state the study's contribution to knowledge. The chapter ends with a concluding paragraph and a sentence linking it to the conclusion chapter.

In qualitative research, results are usually presented and interpreted together. Although there is no statistical analysis of data in qualitative research, there is still a need to interpret the findings in a separate discussion chapter. The discussion revolves around the thematic areas emanating from the research. You need to highlight any unexpected and exciting results, linking them to the research question.

Most qualitative research is associated with an inductive, hypothesis-generating design, where hypotheses, propositions, or theories are developed once the data has been collected. Findings are based on the data. Reference is made to previous studies, and comparisons are drawn on how the study is different. The idea is not to test the theory used in the thesis, but rather to argue its plausibility. Connect the claims to the data and express them as testable theoretical propositions or as a basis from which to derive testable hypotheses. The claim is only valid for a given situation. In qualitative research, the sample is relatively small; thus, it is likely to limit how much you can generalise the findings beyond the research setting.

The examination committee studies the discussion chapter meticulously because it signals the candidate's ability to make sense of data. As a result, many universities award the most marks to the discussion chapter. Nonetheless, most students rush through this chapter because they believe they have reached the end of their writing efforts after conducting their research, analysing their findings, and writing up their results. Therefore, they feel frustrated when their work is shot down by their supervisors or the oral defence (viva) panel or committee, who challenge their interpretation and disagree with their argument. Unfortunately, this is the norm in thesis preparation. Theses and dissertations require several attempts at writing.

The discussion chapter begins with an introductory paragraph, which is followed by the main body of the chapter, and ends with a concluding paragraph.

## Introducing the discussion chapter

The discussion chapter begins with a convincing one-paragraph summary of the critical study findings, using 'layperson' language with little or no statistical jargon, and a summary of the chapter's structure. Briefly introduce the thesis and the literature reviewed, indicating your voice relative to that of other researchers, and the gaps in knowledge that made a space for the work's relevance.

---

### Example: Writing an introductory paragraph

The objective of our study was to establish the effectiveness of Motivational Interviewing (MI) on motivation factors (such as social support and health beliefs) and medication adherence of people living with HIV. Our results demonstrate that Motivational Interviewing plays a critical role in improving self-efficacy and medication adherence. Furthermore, self-efficacy emerged as the strongest predictor of medication adherence compared to other motivational factors. Qualitative findings also confirm the importance of self-efficacy and social support in medication adherence.

The remainder of this chapter will discuss: the effect of Motivational Interviewing on self-efficacy, the effect of Motivational Interviewing on medication adherence, and facilitators and barriers to accessing healthcare for people living with HIV.

---

## The main body of the discussion chapter

Organise the main body of the discussion chapter in the same way you presented the results chapter and in the same sequence. The main body of the discussion chapter consists of various subsections, comprising: (i) a summary of the findings; (ii) an interpretation of the findings; (iii) the context of the findings and generalisations to other contexts; and (iv) the limitations of the study.

### Summarising the results or findings

This section summarises the significance of the results and how the results support the core argument or claim of the thesis or dissertation. Revert to the research question(s) or hypothesis and discuss how the findings shed light on the question and, if you used the hypothesis, the extent to which the findings support the hypothesis. Present a synthesis of the data to help the reader understand how a data set or a preceding conceptual analysis helps to answer the thesis's fundamental questions or support the hypothesis. In this part of the thesis, you fully develop the main argument by discussing the research question, highlighting unexpected and exciting results, and linking them to the research question. You can follow the results with a short explanation of the findings. For example, pointing out any unusual correlation between two variables in the results section, speculating why this correlation exists, and offering a hypothesis about what may be happening helps the reader to understand each finding.

---

## Example: Reporting a summary of results and findings

Although the intervention group started with significantly higher self-efficacy, there were no significant differences between the rest of the motivational factors in the intervention and control group variables at the baseline (this factor was controlled for at post-test). Our results indicated that although there was a moderate significant increase in all the post-test behavioural factors, only self-efficacy had a significant effect ($d = .8$). Motivational Interviewing (MI) was very effective in improving self-efficacy and medication adherence. Individuals in the experimental MI group had a higher self-efficacy and medication adherence than those in the conventional counselling group. Findings generated from the qualitative research data, which was undertaken to explain the quantitative results, confirm that participants recognised that they had the confidence to adhere to the complicated regime of taking their medication with the support of their family and significant others.

---

### Interpreting the findings

This section explains the results or the meaning or interpretation of the findings. Use bridging sentences to remind the reader of the results you are discussing. For example, 'in the previous section, key results indicated that___'. Discuss whether the results were as expected or supported the hypothesis, contextualising the findings within previous research and theory, and explain unexpected results, considering possible alternative explanations and arguments.

Explain what the data mean and formulate one or more claims that respond to the research question(s) and an overarching argument that cuts across the specific questions and hypotheses. In other words, explain why your study contributes to knowledge. The discussion should provide evidence to support your arguments about the research.

## Example: Reporting the meaning or interpretation of the findings

Our findings establish the critical role of Motivational Interviewing (MI) on self-efficacy and medication adherence. These results thus confirm the statement of the IBM model that well-informed, well-motivated, socially supported patients who possess adequate skills can perform the complicated patterns needed for an adherence-related behaviour regimen.

These results were valid, reliable, and trustworthy. However, a mix of factors could have resulted in the delivery of quality counselling. First, the principal investigator who closely supervised the study was a senior medical practitioner, which might have impacted the commitment of the counselling nurses. Second, the study was conducted in a hospital setting, which might have influenced compliance and minimised the attrition rate of research participants. Finally, the nurses conducting the interviews already had expertise and knowledge of the sorts of problems faced by HIV/AIDS patients. However, they needed to be provided with high-quality, intensive Motivational Interviewing training before the study and supervision while undertaking data collection. In addition, we used accurate measures of adherence, such as a medication event monitoring system (MEMS) and pill counts.

Thus, we claim that Motivational Interviewing is a powerful change agent in person-to-person interactions. This thesis revises how health education has been deployed by insisting that a patient-centred approach is preferable to other traditional group interventions. As a result, MI is more effective than the conventional counselling approaches that use small group interventions. However, we also note that small group counselling services can lead to more effective time management for staff and patients with similar concerns.

## Placing the findings into context

Place the argument into a broader context by returning to the literature review chapter where you identified gaps in knowledge. Discuss how your argument addresses these gaps and how it builds on challenges or supports other literature, meaning that although important, your work is not the only one in the topic area. Thus, it must fit the existing literature and situate the argument into a broader context because the research question was motivated by knowledge gaps in the literature.

Revert to the literature review and draw comparisons on how the study is different from these other studies. Evaluate whether the results or findings agree with different authors' varying opinions or views on similar topics. Highlight similarities and differences or inconsistencies (where other researchers' conclusions were not consistent with yours). Explain the reasons for these similarities or why your research yielded different results.

Findings can differ in a variety of ways, for example, the geographical context, study population – such as socio-economic or demographic characteristics – assessment instruments and sampling and procedural issues, research design, methods used, or variables and confounding variables. You can locate information on the differences by visiting the methodology sections of the articles cited in your thesis and look for explanations there.

If the literature you have cited in the literature review chapter cannot be used in the discussion chapter, consider it to be irrelevant and remove it from the literature chapter. If, on the other hand, you discover relevant literature when discussing your research findings, include it in the literature review chapter. Otherwise, no new literature should be introduced in the discussion chapter.

---

## Example: Placing the findings into context

We compared our results with studies on other health issues, such as alcohol use, exercise, and drug addiction, to put our study into perspective because we could not find studies conducted explicitly on Motivational Interviewing (MI) and HIV/AIDS medication *per se*. Nevertheless, our decision or assumption to refer to these studies is supported by a body of theory and research suggesting that MI may be effective for many fundamental life problems (Arkowitz & Mann, 2002).

Our findings suggest that MI strongly and positively affects (effect size of .8) HIV medication adherence, conforming with earlier studies. For example, randomised controlled trials (RCTs) from a meta-analysis by Wampold (2001) showed an effect size between 0.75 and 0.85, similar to our study.

Other studies also showed that relative treatment doses played a role in the outcomes. For example, studies that took an average of under 100 minutes in two treatment sessions had small effect sizes; in contrast, studies that had at least eight sessions (400 minutes) of treatment (similar to our study) had four times the effect sizes (Stanton & Shadish, 1997; Burke, 2003).

MI effectiveness was also demonstrated in a randomised controlled trial measuring viral load and CD4 cell count and alcohol consumption in HIV patients in an 8-session 6-month follow-up intervention based on Motivational Interviewing and cognitive-behavioural skills-building by Parson et al. (2007).

---

In this study, the participants in the intervention group demonstrated significant decreases in viral load and increases in CD4 cell count at the 3-month follow-up, but were not sustained at six months (however, our study did not look at CD4 cell counts). However, there were no significant intervention effects for alcohol use.

Research has also shown that the number of MI counselling sessions impacted sexual behaviour. For example, Chariyeva et al. (2013) found that as the number of sessions increased, participants' sexual risk behaviour decreased. In addition, Polcin et al. (2004) speculated that providing more MI counselling gives the client more time to consider and work through any uncertainty.

## Limitations of the study

This section of the discussion chapter details the limitations of the study method and how they might influence the conclusion. All studies have limitations, and this section is referred to as the 'humility subsection' by some authors. Being aware of your work's limitations is imperative; an overly confident discussion of 'everything is great' is suspect. Furthermore, limitations are not a list of errors but provide a picture of what could not be concluded from the research. Therefore, only discuss the limitations directly relevant to the research question, and evaluate their impact on achieving the research aims.

Potential limitations of the study originate from the methodology chapter, from either the study's design or the challenges arising from implementing the research. Thus, consider the potential limitations of the methodology and then discuss those that may have affected the findings. Design issues involve decisions about sampling, assessment, procedures, and choice of research design, the methodology used (quantitative or qualitative methods), and measurement issues (e.g., the reliability and validity of assessment instruments). For example, the sample might have skewed the results. If the generalisability is poor, it may be because the sample size was too small or the research was limited to a specific group of people. Limitations of statistical analysis discuss power issues, effect size, and the statistical test used. Other limitations could be that the instrumentation did not work as intended or an implicit cultural bias distorted the findings. Alternatively, there may be issues with the overall research design. This necessitates a closer examination of the study's validity. The theoretical framework might have focused on certain aspects of the phenomenon while neglecting others, potentially highlighting areas for future research.

Limitations can also be related to the study questions that should have been included but were left out. For example, the data collection may have relied solely on perceptions but not practice – perceptions do not always match action. You can also state whether the study could have benefitted from using other skills and knowledge.

Noting your work's limitations helps you to suggest follow-up research studies. Weaknesses, loopholes, or limitations of your study help you to define your study's contribution and can be used to recommend how the study can be used to gain further knowledge in the field.

---

## Example: Reporting the limitations of the study

A strength of this study was its randomised controlled research design, which aimed to reduce bias when testing the effectiveness of MI in a health facility setting. However, there are threats to external validity with this type of research. First, the feasibility study presented in this thesis only explored delivery in a referral hospital; therefore, it can only be generalised to such facilities and not to other, smaller facilities. Thus, additional research is required to explore how this type of intervention could be adapted for delivery in a more modest health facility or at the community level. Second, this was a four-month study; therefore, future research should attempt to assess changes in adherence after at least six months to measure the longer-term effects of the intervention.

Although the main strength of this study is a randomised controlled trial, future studies could include the self-selection of participants, which is in line with the spirit of Motivational Interviewing. Self-selection would also be more reflective of a real-world situation. In this case, the participant decides which goal to work on and which method of health coaching to have — thus, the participant takes ownership of their experience in the study.

---

## Concluding the discussion chapter

End the discussion chapter with one or two paragraphs that reinforce the study's overall significance and contribution to knowledge, using your own words without quotations or references to other sources. Discuss findings that indicate further research questions or issues that suggest future research directions; this way, the discussion chapter is connected to the conclusion and recommendation chapter that follows.

Demonstrate your contribution to new knowledge or how your study has extended knowledge, or indicate if a new understanding of the problem can be based on your results.

---

### Example: Concluding the discussion chapter

We have demonstrated that Motivational Interviewing (MI) via person-to-person interaction is more effective than the conventional counselling approach that uses small group intervention. However, we also note that offering small group counselling services to patients with similar concerns might be more cost-effective. There is a need to expand this research by replicating it in other settings, measuring the longer-term effects of the intervention, using self-selection rather than randomisation for recruiting study participants, and including more objective adherence measures, such as viral loads or CD4 counts. These studies would be to discern whether they would yield different results.

---

## Common pitfalls of the discussion chapter

The following points are some of the common mistakes students make when writing the discussion chapter:

- Placing too many technical details in the discussion chapter makes it too long and verbose.
- Repeating the introduction, the literature review, and results in the discussion chapter or restating the results without interpretation or links to other research.
- Failing to differentiate between strong and weak results when drawing conclusions that make strong claims about weak results, or treating numbers that seem to suggest a direction, but are not statistically significant, as if they were significant.
- Straying too far from your data and exaggerating the results.
- Using verbs that imply causation, such as claiming that an independent variable (IV) 'caused' changes in the dependent variable (DV) even when the study was not a 'true experiment', instead of words and phrases such as 'correlated with', 'was associated with', and 'related to'.
- Failing to acknowledge the limitations of your study, or beginning the discussion with too many limitations and unnecessarily negative information that leads readers to wonder what the benefits of the study were.
- Offering no concluding statements or ending the chapter with the study's limitations.

# Example: Discussion chapter: Motivation and ART medication adherence

## Introduction

The objective of our study was to establish the effectiveness of Motivational Interviewing (MI) on motivation factors (such as social support and health beliefs) and medication adherence of people living with HIV. Our results demonstrate that Motivational Interviewing plays a critical role in improving self-efficacy and medication adherence. Furthermore, self-efficacy was the most critical predictor of medication adherence than other motivation factors. Qualitative findings also confirm the importance of self-efficacy and social support in medication adherence.

The main body of this thesis consists of the following subheadings: the effect of Motivational Interviewing on self-efficacy, the effect of Motivational Interviewing on medication adherence, and facilitators and barriers to accessing healthcare for people living with HIV.

## Summary of the results and findings

Although the intervention group started with significantly higher self-efficacy, there were no significant differences between the rest of the motivational factors in the intervention and control group variables at the baseline (this factor was controlled for at post-test). Our results indicated that although there was a moderate significant increase in all the post-test behavioural factors, only self-efficacy had a significant effect (d = .8). Motivational Interviewing (MI) was very effective in improving self-efficacy and medication adherence. Individuals in the experimental MI group had a higher self-efficacy and medication adherence than those in the conventional counselling group. Findings generated from the qualitative research data, which was undertaken to explain the quantitative results, confirm that participants recognised that they had the confidence to adhere to the complicated regime of taking their medication with the support of their family and significant others.

## Meaning or interpretation of the findings

Our findings establish the critical role of Motivational Interviewing (MI) on self-efficacy and medication adherence. These results thus confirm the statement of the IBM model that well-informed, well-motivated, socially supported patients who possess adequate skills can perform the complicated patterns needed for an adherence-related behaviour regimen.

These results were valid, reliable, and trustworthy. However, a mix of factors could have resulted in the delivery of quality counselling. First, the principal investigator who closely supervised the study was a senior medical practitioner, which might have impacted the commitment of the counselling nurses. Second, the study was conducted in a hospital setting, which might have influenced compliance and minimised the attrition rate of the research participants. Finally, the nurses conducting the interviews already had expertise and knowledge of the sorts of problems faced by HIV/AIDS patients. However, they needed to be provided with high-quality, intensive Motivational Interviewing training before the study and supervision while undertaking data collection. In addition, we used accurate measures of adherence, such as a medication event monitoring system (MEMS) and pill counts.

Thus, we claim that Motivational Interviewing is a powerful change agent in person-to-person interactions. This thesis revises how health education has been deployed by insisting that a patient-centred approach is preferable to other traditional group interventions. As a result, MI is more effective than the conventional counselling approaches that use small group intervention. However, we also note that small group counselling services can lead to more effective time management for staff and patients with similar concerns.

## The context of the findings

We compared our results with studies on other health issues, such as alcohol use, exercise, and drug addiction, to put our study into perspective because we could not find studies conducted explicitly on Motivational Interviewing (MI) and HIV/AIDS medication *per se*. Nevertheless, our decision or assumption to refer to these studies is supported by a body of theory and research suggesting that MI may be effective for many fundamental life problems (Arkowitz & Mann, 2002).

Our findings suggest that MI strongly and positively affects (effect size of .8) HIV medication adherence, conforming with earlier studies. For example, randomised controlled trials (RCTs) from a meta-analysis by Wampold (2001) showed an effect size between 0.75 and 0.85, similar to our study.

Other studies also showed that relative treatment doses played a role in the outcomes. For example, studies that took an average of under 100 minutes in two treatment sessions had small effect sizes; in contrast, studies that had at least eight sessions (400 minutes) of treatment (similar to our study) had four times the effect sizes (Stanton & Shadish, 1997; Burke, 2003).

MI effectiveness was also demonstrated in a randomised controlled trial measuring viral load and CD4 cell count and alcohol consumption in HIV patients in an 8-session 6-month follow-up intervention based on Motivational Interviewing and cognitive-behavioural skills-building by Parson et al. (2007).

*(Continued)*

In this study, the participants in the intervention group demonstrated significant decreases in viral load and increases in CD4 cell count at the 3-month follow-up, but were not sustained at six months (however, our study did not look at CD4 cell counts). However, there were no significant intervention effects for alcohol use.

Research has also shown that the number of MI counselling sessions impacted sexual behaviour. For example, Chariyeva et al. (2013) found that as the number of sessions increased, participants' sexual risk behaviour decreased. In addition, Polcin et al. (2004) speculated that providing more MI counselling gives the client more time to consider and work through any uncertainty.

## Limitations of the study

A strength of this study was its randomised controlled research design, which aimed to reduce bias when testing the effectiveness of MI in a health facility setting. However, there are threats to external validity with this type of research. First, the feasibility study presented in this thesis only explored delivery in a referral hospital; therefore, it can only be generalised to such facilities and not to other, smaller facilities. Thus, additional research is required to explore how this type of intervention could be adapted for delivery in a more modest health facility or at the community level. Second, this was a four-month study; therefore, future research should attempt to assess changes in adherence after at least six months to measure the longer-term effects of the intervention.

Although the main strength of this study is a randomised controlled trial, future studies could include the self-selection of participants, which is in line with the spirit of Motivational Interviewing. Self-selection would also be more reflective of a real-world situation. In this case, the participant decides which goal to work on and which method of health coaching to have — thus, the participant takes ownership of their experience in the study.

## Concluding the discussion chapter

We have demonstrated that Motivational Interviewing (MI) via person-to-person interaction is more effective than the conventional counselling approach that uses small group intervention. However, we also note that offering small group counselling services to patients with similar concerns might be more cost-effective. There is a need to expand this research by replicating it in other settings, measuring the longer-term effects of the intervention, using self-selection rather than randomisation for recruiting study participants, and including more objective adherence measures, such as viral loads or CD4 counts. These studies would be to discern whether they would yield different results.

# Exercise: Discussion chapter

## Instructions

Discuss to what extent the examiner's comments apply to this text, supporting your argument with examples of words, phrases, or sentences from the text. (Refer to the section on Pedagogical features — 'Discussion-based exercises' — in the Introduction of this book for more details on completing this exercise.)

## Text: Factors influencing adherence to antiretroviral (ARV) drugs among persons living with HIV/AIDS

### Introduction

Most studies on ARV medication adherence have been facility based and are qualitative and use self-recall to assess the medication. There are inadequate quantitative studies at the household level that have used pill count, which is a more accurate assessment. The Health Belief Model was used to help understand internal and external motivations/cues to action required for adherence. My argument was that self-motivation and significant endorsement of others are driving forces in ARV medication adherence of ≥95%. The results indicate that people living with HIV/AIDS (PLHIV/AIDS), who had social support from the nuclear family, and those with basic education adhered to their ARV medication regimen. Side effects and being single adversely affected ARV medication adherence. The unexpected result of the study was that divorcees tended to be more adherent than married couples. To my knowledge, this is the first study to investigate the role of motivation using a model to guide the research.

I organise the discussion chapter in the same way as the results chapter. I begin the chapter with an overall summary followed by sub sections, each sub section contains a summary, interpretation and context of the finding.

The sub sections are: social demographics, adherence levels, knowledge of ARV drugs, side effect of drugs, social support. I end the chapter with the study's limitations and shortcomings.

### Social demographics

The results demonstrate that the key demographic factors that influenced adherence were marital status and education levels of PLHIV/AIDS. Marital status influenced the likelihood of adhering to medication. Specifically, divorcees were more likely to adhere to medication. Spouses would probably be expected to consult each other as results indicate that the nuclear family played a role in adherence.

*(Continued)*

My research findings that age and sex were associated to ARV medication adherence are consistent with those found in other studies from Kenya, Talam NC et al. (2008). However, the findings are inconsistent with others, showing more adherence of women and younger age groups (Sasaki Y, et al. 2012). The discrepancies relating to age could be because different authors used different cut-off points in categorizing the age groups. My study found that marital status was strongly associated with ARV medication adherence. Other studies indicate that a low level of education and poor literacy affect the patient's ability to adhere (Manyeki RW, 2012; Munthali CS, 2010).

## Adherence to antiretroviral (ARV) medication

Using the pill count, people living with HIV/AIDS in this community did not achieve the recommended adherence ($\geq$ 95%). The reason for this could have been the many barriers described later that affected the intake.

The results confirm those from other, more recent studies from African countries that indicate that $\geq$ 95% adherence has not been achievable. When the respondents' self-report recall data was used, the average adherence rate of 85.6% was higher than those found in other African countries. For example, average adherence rates of 62.6% in Togo by Potchoo et al. (2010), 68% in Kenya by Talam et al. (2008), and 87% found by Mitiku H, et al. (2013) in Ethiopia. The lowest aderence levels of 25% (Uzochukwu B, Onwujekwe O, Onoka A, 2009) were found in Nigeria.

## Knowledge of the ARV drug and how it is used

Though only a few people knew the name of the drug they were taking, Boateng has argued that unawareness of the name of the drugs used should not be an issue, and patients do not necessarily need to know the drug's name as long as they could follow instructions (Boateng D, et al., 2010).

## The drug side effects

Side effects were significantly associated with ARV non-adherence.

Qualitative studies indicate that side effects have been consistently associated with adherence.

Few quantitative studies have been conducted on the relationship between side effects and adherence. My study indicates that the burden of side effects contributed to ARV adherence is contrary to the South African study, which showed no significant relationship between adherence and symptoms concentration. The latter study implies that despite the concentration of side effects, patients could cope and continued being adherent.

## Social support

Family members and social networks played a positive role in ARV medication adherence. Thus, health providers should pay attention to family interaction among patients receiving ART, as family communication can be a significant contributor to ART adherence. The results indicating the considerable lack of support from the extended family indicate a move away from the expected traditional African extended family or kinship who traditionally would have been expected to have a contextual influence in the lives of PLWHAs.

Studies on relationships between social support and adherence in Africa are inadequate. Most of the studies are either descriptive or qualitative. Usually, they describe the type of support, such as accompanying the patient to a hospital for appointments and reminders take your drugs, and get refills, as demonstrated in a Tanzanian study by Nsimba SED et al. (2010).

Quantitative studies conducted in Uganda, Tanzania, and Botswana found no significant differences in adherence between persons with social support and those who did not have support (Hardon A, Davey S, Gerrits T, et al., 2006). This finding conforms to the findings of my study. These studies contrast those from a qualitative study in Kenya carried out in a hospital that showed social support to be a factor in adherence (Sumbi VM, 2010).

Given the recommendation of $\geq$ 95% ARV adherence has universally been found to be unachievable, there might be a need for more studies to demonstrate whether moderate adherence less than 95% can lead to a viral suppression under more potent regimens.

## Study limitation

My study did not assess the cost of treatment which also include transport and laboratory tests. Treatment costs are cited as primary obstacles to optimal adherence by Potchoo et al. (2010) in Togo. The reasons for divorce being a key predictor of adherence was not explored because the study was mostly quantitative. The answer requires a qualitative study.

A significant limitation of my study is that its scope did not include a comprehensive assessment of other PAMQ tools that hinder adherence, including psychological and cognitive aspects. The study also did not capture other dimensions of non-adherence, such as schedule non-adherence, which refers to not following a specific schedule for ARV medication (e.g. '3 times a day' or 'every 6 hours'). It also did not include following special instructions for ARV medication, such as 'take with food' or 'take on an empty stomach' or dietary guideline adherence. Understanding medication is essential because it motivates

*(Continued)*

patients to overcome barriers to adherence; however, I did not explore the knowledge of ARV dosages, frequencies of the dosages, and intervals between those dosages. Most importantly, our study did not include a qualitative research component that would have provided useful information on the above factors, including decision-making concerning ARV adherence at the household level.

## Examiner's comments

- The discussion summary included unnecessary repetition of results.
- The candidate did not relate the interpretation of the main findings to theory (and practice where appropriate).
- The candidate had weaknesses in interpreting, analysing, critically appraising their findings, drawing conclusions, and showing the implications.
- The candidate did not report what they learned while undertaking the research, the limitations of the research design and methodology, or how they might have impacted the findings.
- The candidate did not outline alternative or additional approaches that could have been pursued in the light of knowledge gained.
- The candidate did not include logic in his arguments, and the ideas were poorly linked. He seemed to present a series of listings and had trouble linking them and presenting them coherently and cohesively. The candidates linked the findings to the empirical studies in the literature review.
- The candidate demonstrated knowledge of original sources of the field and understood the main theoretical and methodological issues.
- The candidate provided pointers for future practice and identified issues that require further clarification.
- The candidate did not present a strong case for the findings and tended to underestimate their significance or oversell the significance of his findings.

## Further reading

Golding, C. (2017). Advice for writing a thesis (based on what examiners do). *Open Review of Educational Research*, 4(1), 46–60. https://doi.org/10.1080/23265507.2017.1300862

Golding, C., Sharmini, S., & Lazarovitch, A. (2014). What examiners do: What thesis students should know. *Assessment & Evaluation in Higher Education*, 39(5), 563–576. https://doi.org/10.1080/02602938.2013.859230

These articles demonstrate how examiners assess theses. They show how, as academic readers, examiners favour a thesis with an effective approach that engages with the literature and the findings. They explain that examiners require a sound interpretation of the literature, an important topic, and an appropriate method. Conclusions should make a significant, publishable contribution to the field. After submission, examiners make comments, most of which help to improve the thesis.

Petchko, K. (2018c). Data, methodology, results, and discussion: Models and examples. In *How to Write about Economics and Public Policy*. Oxford: Elsevier.

This chapter explains how to interpret results, discuss previous research and theory, describe your studies' implications and limitations, make suggestions for future research, and summarise the main findings and arguments in a conclusion. The chapter provides detailed suggestions for describing and discussing results in a quantitative or a qualitative study and for writing an effective conclusion. It also offers guidance in using and describing visuals, and in qualifying claims to make them more acceptable to readers.

# 9

# Writing the Conclusion and Recommendations Chapter

This chapter shows how to present the research contribution, indicating what the research achieved and explaining the new understanding of the problem. It also offers ways to present the implications of the research for theory, future research directions, practice, and policy.

## Purpose of the conclusion and recommendations chapter

The conclusion chapter pulls together the arguments developed in all the other chapters. It is comparable to a mini-thesis because it touches on all aspects of the thesis, from the introduction to the conclusion. The conclusion wraps up your thesis, making the argument as concise as possible and bringing out the implications of your work for theory, practice, or future research.

Information from the introduction chapter includes an explanation of whether the research achieved its purpose. The conclusion and recommendations chapter argues how the study arrived at solutions to the research problem suggested in the problem statement. The evidence supporting the arguments is built through the literature review and empirical research, demonstrating that the study was located within the research topic's broader context. The chapter also explains how the central theory or model used (from the methodology chapter) influences the debate on the topic. It emphasises the key results (from the results chapter) and summarises the main discussion points (from the discussion chapter). Most examiners flip from the introduction chapter to the conclusion chapter to understand how the concluding ideas align with those set out in the introduction.

In summation, the conclusion chapter presents specific messages that the reader can remember – the thesis's take-home message. Thus, someone reading nothing but the conclusion chapter will have an overview of the whole thesis.

The chapter's most critical aspect is to draw attention to the study's contribution to the research area – in other words, the 'so what?' of the whole thesis, and what you are adding to the conversation. A PhD requires an original contribution to the research field, while a Master's thesis might require an extension of the current knowledge. Apart from providing information on the study's contribution to the research literature, it may also be important to mention the practical or professional value attached to the research, as might be the case with industry applications, commercial uses, and reform recommendations.

As you write your conclusion chapter, you may have some additional thoughts about your introduction and literature review chapters. Go back to these chapters and fine-tune them so they correspond to the conclusion.

In some universities, the conclusion and recommendations sections form part of the discussion chapter, while in other universities they are treated as a discrete chapter.

The chapter structure begins with an introduction paragraph, continues with the main body of the chapter containing various sections and discussion points, and ends with the concluding paragraph.

## Introducing the conclusion and recommendations chapter

Begin the introduction with a paragraph that gives the reader an overview of the entire thesis. Think of it as an extended abstract in one paragraph. This overview includes restating the thesis statement, the research purpose, the methods, and the main results. If the thesis is structured to test one or more alternative hypotheses, evaluate whether the hypotheses were weakened, strengthened, or modified.

The conclusion chapter should wrap up your argument; therefore, ensure you explain the relevance of your thesis to the field of research and how it contributes to or considerably revises existing scholarly debates. Remember to be firm in your conclusion and to avoid apologetic-sounding phrases, such as 'This thesis attempted to show…'.

## Example: Writing the introduction of the conclusion chapter

The argument in this study was that Motivational Interviewing (MI) is more effective in medication adherence for persons living with HIV/AIDS than the traditional, small group counselling. [thesis statement] Therefore, this study aimed to design approaches targeting health behaviours that can be introduced as part of routine care or counselling sessions provided by healthcare providers. [purpose] We conducted an experimental trial to investigate the effectiveness of Motivational Interviewing in increasing self-efficacy and medication adherence in people living with HIV. The study was guided by the Identity-Based Motivation (IBM) model, which is used as a foundation for various interventions to close gaps in achieving health-promoting activities. Furthermore, our study suggests that Motivational Interviewing is a powerful change agent in person-to-person interaction. [method] MI had a significant influence on social support, self-efficacy, and medication adherence. [results] This study challenges the conventional counselling approaches that use small group counselling. This thesis revises how health education has been used by advancing a patient-centred approach other than small group interventions. [contribution/significance]

# The main body of the chapter

The main body of the conclusion and recommendations chapter presents the conclusions and recommendations of the thesis. It usually consists of the following sections: (i) a review or restatement of the thesis's key points; (ii) an explanation of what the thesis contributes to the body of knowledge; (iii) an explanation of the thesis's original contribution to knowledge; (iv) the implications of the findings for theory, practice and policy; and (v) a statement on the future direction of further research.

## Restatement of the thesis's key points

After introducing the chapter, the next step is to synthesise the main points of the thesis by examining the most important ideas, striking quotations, or key statistics (no more than two). The hint here is to view and synthesise the concluding paragraphs of each chapter. The conclusion represents your closing thoughts on the topic, and it should therefore mainly be your own words.

---

## Example: Restating the key points of the thesis

Using an experimental design, we proved that Motivation Interviewing influenced behaviour changes related to HIV/AIDS medication adherence. Motivational Interviewing (MI) had a strong effect on HIV medication adherence, which conforms with the meta-analysis of randomised controlled trials (RCTs). The significant effect size in our study could be attributed to the length and duration of the MI sessions (400 minutes over four months). Another interpretation was the continuity and compliance of patients across sessions, and the low dropout or attrition rate (less than 5%). Therefore, this type of intervention should be considered for dissemination and integration into HIV clinics providing comprehensive care for HIV-positive persons.

---

## Contributions to the body of knowledge

This section demonstrates how the research has enhanced existing knowledge. The contribution section is essential to those judging the merit of the work because it demonstrates that you have considered how your work adds value. However, due to limitations in their ability to produce academic writing, students find it challenging to argue for their study's contribution to knowledge or to the current literature in the relevant field or discipline, so they usually do not include this section.

The contribution does not have to be some significant advancement in the field; it can simply offer a different angle on a topic, or a different approach to a topic, or investigate a different population to advance knowledge and be of value. Contributing means adding something valuable to the field of inquiry by demonstrating that the research adds to the specific field or by arguing that it is an original contribution to the topic area.

Emphasise your contribution by revisiting the problem statement to explain how the research helped to solve the problem. Refer to the literature review to show how you addressed a knowledge gap or how the results confirm or challenge an existing theory or assumption. Leave the reader with a strong opinion that the research has contributed to knowledge in the field: select the most important contributions and summarise them concisely, situating them in the research's broader context. Avoid repeating what you have already covered in the discussion chapter. You need to convince the examiners that your research contributed to the inquiry.

Higher-level research conclusions show how the findings lead to further knowledge and understanding of the problem examined. Restating the knowledge gaps (unresolved issues) identified from the literature review sets an opening to show the relevance of the research and how it added to the conversation.

In this section, you consider whether you have explained the importance of your work, its implications, and how it links to existing knowledge, how your work informs or influences policymaking, or how to resolve unanswered questions or gaps in knowledge in the field of study. Does it develop better theoretical models, or change the way people do their jobs in a particular field or how people live?

---

## Example: Reporting your contribution to knowledge

This experimental study extends knowledge on medication adherence as current studies were mainly analytical. As health interventions become patient-centred, our study sets precedents for determining favourable responses to specific interventions. We demonstrated that MI is an effective communication process. Using a patient-centred approach, we showed how MI can motivate HIV patients to maintain behavioural changes that promote health and their quality of life. To our knowledge, there is no research on the relationship between HIV medication adherence and Motivational Interviewing as a counselling technique.

---

## Original contribution

At PhD level, you are expected to present an 'original' piece of research, investigating a new area of knowledge and advancing science in that area of inquiry. Making a significant original contribution to knowledge remains the standard against which a PhD dissertation is measured. One way of demonstrating an original contribution to knowledge is if your work opens up a new research area, introduces or applies a new or traditional method, theory, or concept, or provides a novel interpretation or synthesis of published data, theories, or conclusions. The originality can be in the tools, techniques, or procedures used, or in their application in new and untested ways, such as developing a new use for an established procedure or technique (a statistical test, a projective technique), applying existing tools and techniques for a specific purpose, or adopting or discovering a new method or approach to tackling a problem.

Originality can also include the addition of constructs from another theory to an existing theory to explain the problem, or an expansion of the domain of a theory, for example, testing a theory's applicability to a new phenomenon, new population, and new setting.

The other way to show originality is to highlight a 'potentially publishable' article. A PhD submission is equivalent in quantity and quality to at least two papers in peer-refereed journals. If a peer-reviewed journal is interested in publishing a paper on your research, it is an indication of its quality because it meets established academic standards. Therefore, you will get more credit if your work has been accepted for publication in a peer-reviewed journal at the time of your examination.

Another way to show an original contribution is to have your work published as a chapter in a book, as a research monograph, or in conference proceedings. Even if your submission to publication is not accepted, the reviewers' evaluation and comments will help you to sharpen and improve the thesis. Presenting your work in seminars or conferences is another useful way to receive valuable feedback about how peers respond to your work. Thus, producing a publishable article that contributes to the literature is the most crucial information that examiners look for.

## Implications of the findings

This section of the concluding chapter presents the implications of the findings and how they may impact existing theories, develop an understanding of these theories, or be applied to contribute further to knowledge on the research problem. The implications of research findings may also impact on practice and policy, especially in the social sciences, which relate to real-world social interactions. Thus, implications resulting from research mostly fall into two categories: how they impact current theory, and how they impact practice or policy.

## Theoretical implications

If you deliberately set out to test a theory, discuss how your findings support that theory. Discuss whether the findings are consistent with the theory, and explain how the findings extend, or support, or challenge the theory. If your results do not support the theory, speculate about why they do not by using critical thinking skills. Finally, describe how the theory contributes to understanding the problem and its implications.

Note: If your study's purpose is to observe a particular setting and interpret the findings through a specific theoretical lens, the theory is just helping you to observe a specific context. However, if the thesis's purpose was to generate a theory, including a section called 'implications for theory' might not be appropriate because generating theory was the thesis's whole point. In this case, develop an entire chapter that draws on the findings to develop an argument for one or more theoretical proposition.

---

## Example: Reporting a theoretical implication

This thesis was guided by the Identity-Based Motivation (IBM) model. Our results confirmed the statement of the IBM model that well-informed, well-motivated, socially supported patients who possess adequate skills can perform the behaviour patterns necessary to maintain adherence to a complicated medication regimen. Furthermore, the model helped explain how the perception of self-efficacy, a factor affecting patients' medication adherence, facilitated motivation and self-regulation, leading to effective medication adherence efforts.

---

## Implications for practice or policy

Although the primary purpose of a thesis is to contribute to academic discourse, some of the findings will likely have relevance to the 'real world' because the social sciences are grounded in real-world interaction between human beings and society. If your research has implications for practice, explain how the study results provide valuable guidance on solving the problem in terms of practice; for example, how the stakeholders benefit from the study's findings or how the findings support current health practitioners' practice. Expound on which professionals would be interested in using the results and why they would pay attention to what the findings reveal. Explain what might lead to changes in the way professionals do things.

Most theses are relatively small studies; thus, you cannot suggest that your findings can demolish government policy or practice unless the research is ground-breaking – which most Master's or doctoral research is not. However, even if the results might not change policy, they can raise serious questions about policy and suggest possible changes in practice or recommendations to do things differently. If your graduate programme is specifically intended to be relevant for practice, your thesis is incomplete if it does not discuss the implications of your findings for practitioners or a related policy. Thinking through the real-world implications of your research is always a good idea and may be of genuine value for future grant-writing endeavours.

---

### Example: Reporting an implication for practice or policy

Our study has several implications for practice. First, the results from this study suggest that Motivational Interviewing is an effective intervention to increase medication adherence of HIV patients. We therefore recommend integrating it into the practice of healthcare service providers.

This research clearly illustrates that MI effectively improves medication adherence but raises questions of whether in-person health coaching is practicable when applied in real settings. Other training methods, such as online health coaching, maybe more cost-effective than in-person health coaching when applied to the healthcare field; this issue needs further research. Although eight sessions (400 minutes over four months) were shown to be more effective, future research could seek to establish if counselling sessions of shorter duration may be optimal. This type of study would give practitioners the information necessary to choose how to adjust their MI technique.

---

## Recommendations: Future direction of further research

Finally, the main body of the conclusion chapter ends with a discussion of the direction of future research. There will always be some open-ended questions that remain unanswered in all research, which another researcher might pick up where you stopped. The claim for further research on a topic is based on the deficit identified in the limitations section of the discussion chapter. It will have highlighted gaps in knowledge and demonstrated how future research could fill in those gaps or build on existing research by recognising and responding to the limitations. Therefore, you need to go back to the discussion chapter's limitations section to establish a case for further investigation. The limitations sections are reported in three steps: (i) identify/or refer to the limitation in the discussion chapter; (ii) explain how they impact your study; and (iii) propose a direction for future studies.

The research reveals previously unrecognised problems or the need to reconceptualise a problem. These issues might suggest topics that need further study, revised hypotheses, new research questions, new confounding variables that need to be understood, measurement issues, design issues, and concepts that need to be elaborated or refined. The findings may, in addition, have significant implications in terms of research (e.g., theoretical, methodological, or modelling implications) or practice (e.g., implications regarding application to industry, policy, or legislation). The research could also result in policy implications that establish how well a particular policy works, and predictions of what could work better; or it could highlight research-based practice that generates practice knowledge, such as action research. If you have not indicated these issues in the limitations section of the discussion chapter, go back to that section and rewrite it based on the findings.

Another way to think about recommendations for future research is to ask questions such as: 'If I were to write a sequel to this thesis, what might come next?', 'How would I respond to a question asking what I would have done differently?', 'How would I communicate more explicitly, for example, by suggesting improvements to the research or replicating my study in a better way?'

Avoid exaggerating the applicability of your research. It is generally best to frame recommendations for further research as suggestions, because academic research aims not to instruct but to inform, explain, and explore. Moreover, future studies might confirm, build on, or enrich your conclusions.

Provide recommendations for future directions of research, but keep it to no more than two.

---

### Example: Reporting recommendations for future research

Although the MI approach resulted in successful behaviour change, the cost, time effectiveness, applicability, and sustainability in routine practice need further research.

We did not assess the mediating effect of factors such as social support, health beliefs, and self-efficacy on medication adherence. Therefore, the moderating effects of these behaviours can be more thoroughly examined with a larger sample, additional variables, and more complex types of analyses (e.g., path analysis).

---

## Concluding the conclusion and recommendations chapter

In the case of dissertations and theses, end the conclusion and recommendations chapter with one or two paragraphs that sum up your take-home message or leave a memorable impression on the reader, such as a key question, a call to action, an indication towards future research, or a statement about how the problem or your idea remains relevant. The paragraphs should reinforce a thesis statement and establish the overall significance of your study and its contribution to knowledge on the topic. In adding to the body of knowledge, answer the following questions: What and how does your study add to the existing scholarship? What is your new understanding of the research problem? If you were to continue from where you stopped, what would be your next step (e.g., what research or experiments would you do next or how would you extend your current research)? If you were to write a sequel to this thesis, what might come next?

The concluding paragraphs should be in your own words. Do not use quotations or include references to other sources.

---

## Example: Concluding the conclusion and recommendations chapter

Many efforts to improve medication adherence have focused on taking all the medicines as prescribed, in the correct dose and quantity, at the right time, through the correct route, while observing dietary restrictions. These requirements are complex, and despite efforts that have so far focused on offering small group interventions, medication adherence remains a challenge. This study challenges conventional ways of promoting medication adherence among healthcare givers, offering small group interventions. Furthermore, we demonstrated that Motivational Interviewing (MI) in person-to-person interaction is a more powerful change agent than group interventions. This thesis revises how health education has been used by insisting on a patient-centred approach.

Non-adherence will continue to be of concern in the coming years for all health issues which require medication. This research adds to the broader literature on medication adherence, a field that has attracted significant attention in the last few decades. Finally, the study has demonstrated the need to integrate social and health sciences' theories and methodologies as a viable concept for linking social sciences and medicine.

---

The conclusion and recommendations chapter should be about 5% of the thesis.

# Common pitfalls of the conclusion chapter

The following points are some of the common mistakes students make when writing the conclusion chapter:

- The candidate's conclusions do not respond to the study's aim or problem statement.
- The candidate repeats information from the previous chapters or introduces new material that is not in the introduction, context setting, literature, methods, or discussion chapters.
- The candidate has difficulty presenting an overall argument, which holds the thesis's introduction and conclusion chapters firmly together.
- The candidate does not pull together the arguments developed in all the chapters to synthesise them into a cohesive account; thus, they fail to demonstrate how the arguments converge to solve the research problem and contribute new knowledge or extend existing knowledge.
- The candidate fails to differentiate between strong and weak results, making strong claims about weak results, which are not statistically significant, and treating them as significant.
- Most candidates' recommendations lack theoretical contributions and further extend conclusions and recommendations beyond what is supported directly by the findings.
- The candidate 'plagiarises' recommendations from other programmes and strategic plans or studies rather than draw conclusions from their own results.
- The candidate's recommendations are not practical or feasible.
- The candidate's summary is weak and incoherent, reflecting a poorly structured thesis with no common theme or compelling argument.

---

## Example: Conclusion chapter: Motivation and ART medication adherence

### Introduction

The argument in this study was that Motivational Interviewing (MI) is more effective in medication adherence for persons living with HIV/AIDS than the traditional, small group counselling. Therefore, this study aimed to design approaches targeting health behaviours that can be introduced as part of routine care or counselling sessions provided by healthcare providers. We conducted an experimental trial to investigate the effectiveness of Motivational Interviewing in increasing self-efficacy and medication adherence in people living with HIV. The study was guided by the Identity-Based Motivation (IBM)

*(Continued)*

model, which is used as a foundation for various interventions to close gaps in achieving health-promoting activities. Furthermore, our study suggests that Motivational Interviewing is a powerful change agent in person-to-person interaction. MI had a significant influence on social support, self-efficacy, and medication adherence. This study challenges the conventional counselling approaches that use small group counselling. This thesis revises how health education has been used by advancing a patient-centred approach other than small group interventions.

## Restatement of the thesis's key points

Using an experimental design, we proved that Motivation Interviewing influenced behaviour changes related to HIV/AIDS medication adherence. Motivational Interviewing (MI) had a strong effect on HIV medication adherence, which conforms with the meta-analysis of randomised controlled trials (RCTs). The significant effect size in our study could be attributed to the length and duration of the MI sessions (400 minutes over four months). Another interpretation was the continuity and compliance of patients across sessions, and the low dropout or attrition rate (less than 5%). Therefore, this type of intervention should be considered for dissemination and integration into HIV clinics providing comprehensive care for HIV-positive persons.

## Contribution to the body of knowledge

This experimental study extends knowledge on medication adherence as current studies were mainly analytical. As health interventions become patient-centred, our study sets precedents for determining favourable responses to specific interventions. We demonstrated that MI is an effective communication process. Using a patient-centred approach, we showed how MI can motivate HIV patients to maintain behavioural changes that promote health and their quality of life. To our knowledge, there is no research on the relationship between HIV medication adherence and Motivational Interviewing as a counselling technique.

## Implications of the findings

**Theoretical implications**: This thesis was guided by the Identity-Based Motivation (IBM) model. Our results confirmed the statement of the IBM model that well-informed, well-motivated, socially supported patients who possess adequate skills can perform the behavior patterns necessary to maintain adherence to a complicated medication regimen. Furthermore, the model helped explain how the perception of self-efficacy, a factor affecting patients' medication adherence, facilitated motivation and self-regulation, leading to effective medication adherence efforts.

**Implications for practice or policy**: Our study has several implications for practice. First, the results from this study suggest that Motivational Interviewing is an effective intervention to increase medication adherence of HIV patients. We therefore recommend integrating it into the practice of healthcare service providers.

This research clearly illustrates that MI effectively improves medication adherence but raises questions of whether in-person health coaching in a research setting is practicable when applied in real practice. Other training methods, such as online health coaching, maybe more cost-effective than in-person health coaching when applied to the healthcare field; this issue needs further research. Although eight sessions (400 minutes over four months) were shown to be more effective, future research could seek to establish if counselling sessions of shorter duration may be optimal. This type of study would give practitioners the information necessary to choose how to adjust their MI technique.

## Future direction of further research

Although the MI approach resulted in successful behaviour change, the cost, time effectiveness, applicability, and sustainability in routine practice need further research.

We did not assess the mediating effect of factors such as social support, health beliefs, and self-efficacy on medication adherence. Therefore, the moderating effects of these behaviours can be more thoroughly examined with a larger sample, additional variables, and more complex types of analyses (e.g., path analysis).

## Conclusion

Many efforts to improve medication adherence have focused on taking all the medicines as prescribed, in the correct dose and quantity, at the right time, through the correct route, while observing dietary restrictions. These require-ments are complex, and despite efforts that have so far focused on offering small group interventions, medication adherence remains a challenge. This study challenges conventional ways of promoting medication adherence among healthcare givers, offering small group interventions. Furthermore, we demonstrated that Motivational Interviewing (MI) in person-to-person interac-tion is a more powerful change agent than group interventions. This thesis revises how health education has been used by insisting on a patient-centred approach.

Non-adherence will continue to be of concern in the coming years for all health issues which require medication. This research adds to the broader literature

*(Continued)*

on medication adherence, a field that has attracted significant attention in the last few decades. Finally, the study has demonstrated the need to integrate social and health sciences' theories and methodologies as a viable concept for linking social sciences and medicine.

# Exercise: Conclusion chapter

## Instructions

Discuss to what extent the examiner's comments apply to this text, supporting your argument with examples of words, phrases, or sentences from the text. (Refer to the section on Pedagogical features — 'Discussion-based exercises' — in the Introduction of this book for more details on completing this exercise.)

### Text: Motivational factors influencing adherence to antiretroviral (ARV) drugs among persons living with HIV/AIDS

#### Introduction

Levels of antiretroviral (ARV) adherence of ≥ 95% are recommended to suppress HIV viral load and reduce morbidity and mortality rates among people infected with HIV. However, achieving this high adherence level is difficult considering HIV/AIDS is a lifelong condition, and adapting to a long-term treatment plan is demanding. In addition, internal and external motivation and knowledge directly affect ARV medication use, primarily through acquisition or enhancing behavioural skills on factors that enhance the impact of uptake.

External motivation involves social support, which is the help a person receives from family, friends, and social networks that are necessary to enhance antiretroviral adherence. Individual motivation involves self-efficacy issues, which includes patients understanding that their medication is important because it motivates them to overcome adherence barriers. Individual motivation includes self-efficacy issues concerning the individual's belief in their competency to take ARV drugs, given what they perceive to be a complicated routine. Other individual motivations include knowledge of drugs and the benefits of ARVs. Adverse side effects and perceptions of the drug were perceived barriers that resulted in an individual deciding that the benefits are not worth the efforts.

Studies on non-adherence have mainly focused on patient-related factors such as inconvenient dosing frequency, dietary restrictions, pill burden, side effects, patient–healthcare provider relationships, and system care. However, there are hardly any studies focusing on behavioural and motivational aspects. Therefore, I used the Health Belief Model, which helps our understanding of internal and external (significant endorsement of others) motivation or the cue to action that are required for the desired behaviour to occur, to guide the study (Strecher, Champion & Rosenstock, 1997).

My study was a cross-sectional analytical design establishing factors that facilitate or inhibit adherence to ARV medication in People Living with HIV/AIDS (PLHIV/AIDS). Motivation/cue to action was the independent variable, while perceptions of the drug and demographic characteristics were intervening variables, and adherence to ARVs was the dependent or outcome variable.

This chapter presents the conclusions and recommendations (synthesis of empirical findings that answer the research question) on whether motivation influences ARV medication adherence and the overall argument from the chapters. It also includes an explanation as to whether the results can be extended to other situations. Finally, the chapter also extends the understanding of ARV medication adherence and offers recommendation for improving practice and further research.

## Synthesis of empirical findings

The ARV adherence of 60% was way below the recommended level of $\geq$ 95% ARV adherence using pill counts. In addition, the study rejected the hypothesis that individual motivation influences adherence to ARV medication adherence more than external motivation – the results revealed that a peer network and the family support were significantly correlated with medication adherence ($r = .35$, $p = < .001$). In contrast, individual motivation, such as side effects and knowledge of drugs, negatively impacted adherence.

This study's results cannot be generalised to other contexts because they only represented one community with unique social and cultural beliefs and behaviour. Therefore, the study needs to be replicated using a more extensive representation encompassing different geographical and cultural backgrounds and following the subjects for a more extended period. Such a study would generate findings that would be more representative of the population with HIV and AIDS and would have the power to measure the effects of covariates associated with adherence more accurately.

## Contribution to the body knowledge

My study contributes knowledge by enlightening the motivational factors related to ARV adherence inadequately addressed in previous studies. In addition, my analytical, quantitative study using pill counts at the household level complements past studies, mainly qualitative, descriptive, hospital- or facility-based, which used self-reports that tend to overestimate adherence level. In contrast, pill count is a more accurate measure.

*(Continued)*

To my knowledge, this is the first study using the Patient Medicine Adherence Questionnaire (PMAQ), a reliable, valid assessment tool grounded in the Health Belief Model, and the first study to quantify the 'burden of side effects' as a barrier to ARV adherence in Africa.

## Implication for practice

There is a need to improve the county's adherence levels by incorporating adherence issues in the community health strategy, strengthening counselling, education, training, and information interventions. This strategy would address issues that increase ARV adherence, such as education on correct drug use. Education on correct drug use would address how to differentiate ARV drugs from other drugs, and explain the side effects that mostly occur within the first three months of initiation. Follow-up of PLWHA using adherence data sheets at the household level is essential. The important role played by family members and support groups need to be included in future ART adherence programs.

## Future direction and further research

This study's main limitation was that it was quantitative and lacked the qualitative research component to explain the quantitative findings. It left psychological and cognitive variables and non-adherence issues such as schedule non-adherence and decision-making at the household level. I recommend that these issues be addressed in future studies using a theory-based approach. Since $\geq$ 95% might not be achievable, there is a need for studies testing various adherence levels and viral suppression under more potent regimens to develop a standardised definition of adherence and valid objective adherence measures appropriate for both clinical and community settings.

## Examiner's comments

- The final chapter is well argued, summarising the key contributions of the research well, presenting some thoughtful reflections on the research process and future directions for work in this area.
- Both the findings and the recommendations concur with the aim formulated. The recommendations are viable and should be seriously considered by the relevant institution. The findings and recommendations of this research could contribute to the relevant institution at large.
- The research contributed to the extension of knowledge strategies for improving practice. The extension of knowledge in the form of new significance for improvement in practice has therefore been established.
- The thesis is an original work that contributes to knowledge and understanding in the field of study, and contributes to the field, discipline, practice, and shows original and critical thought.
- The thesis is original, has ample scope and significance,

- The summary and conclusions are a meaningful expression of the study's spirit in total and concur with the study's aim.
- The candidate fails to justify or explain arguments and leaves the reader to connect one proposition to another.
- The candidate did not present a strong case for the findings and tended to underestimate their significance or oversell the significance of their findings.
- The candidate has a rational interpretation of the literature, an important topic, and an appropriate method, and the conclusions make a significant contribution.
- The candidate overstated and misrepresented findings or interpretations, and the conclusions went beyond what the findings supported.
- The candidate inserted too many unqualified opinions and presented material irrelevant to the topic or argument developed. The candidate had problems in creating a clear argument.
- The conclusion chapter is very brief and does not reflect each chapter's arguments or contributions, shortcomings, and potential for further work.
- The conclusions make a significant, publishable contribution to the area of inquiry field.
- The candidate inserted too many unqualified personal opinions and introduced irrelevant claims unrelated to the study.

# Further reading

Bottery, M., & Wright, N. (2019). *Writing a Watertight Thesis: A Guide to Successful Structure and Defence*. London: Bloomsbury Academic.

This book demonstrates how to produce such a 'watertight' thesis. It shows the reader how to build a strong structure for the entire work and maintain it throughout the doctoral journey. The book uses a main research question and sub-questions derived from it to structure the thesis. It uses examples from genuine theses as illustrations and numerous exercises.

Bourke, S., & Holbrook, A. P. (2013). Examining PhD and research masters theses. *Assessment and Evaluation in Higher Education*, 38(4), 407–416. https://doi.org/10.1080/02602938.2011.638738

This article investigates the approaches examiners of PhD and research Master's theses take when marking submissions. The paper addresses whether the examiners treat the different chapters of PhD and Master's theses differently. Findings showed that the examiners rated both types of degree similarly, but they focused on contribution to knowledge in PhDs more than in Master's theses. The examiners also made a more holistic assessment of thesis quality at the PhD level.

Craswell, G., & Poore, M. (2011). *Writing for Academic Success: A Postgraduate Guide* (2nd edition). Thousand Oaks, CA: Sage.

This book provides a comprehensive guide to academic writing. It places particular emphasis on a critical appraisal of sources. It covers all aspects of writing, including dealing with writer's block, and addresses the difficulties of handling critical feedback and organising effective time-management strategies. Chapters are rich with detailed, step-by-step explanations and tips on thesis and exam writing, and offers advice on how to get articles published.

Everett, E. L., & Furseth, I. (2013). *Doing Your Master's Dissertation: From Start to Finish*. Sage Study Skills Series. London: Sage.

This book provides examples from real theses and includes useful action plans in each chapter. It offers guidance from dealing with emotional blocks to identifying the strengths and weaknesses of writing and ways to improve it. It presents the social aspects of the writing process, such as choosing and working with an advisor, using social media, and forming workgroups.

Fisher, C. M., & Buglear, C. M. J. (2010). *Researching and Writing a Dissertation: A Guidebook for Business Students* (3rd edition). Harlow: Prentice Hall.

This book uses a practical, skills-based approach. It covers research methods and the process of choosing, planning, researching, and writing the dissertation at the Master's level step-by-step. It includes examples, and skillsets, such as arguing, are developed.

Kretchmer, P. (2021). Twelve steps to writing an effective results section. *San Francisco Edit*. Retrieved 17 May 2023, from https://www.sfedit.net/wp-content/uploads/2021/07/Results.pdf

The article discusses how to present the key results which address the research questions presented in the introduction. It details how to organise your data and summarise your findings in a concise manner. The goal is to write with accuracy, brevity and clarity.

Lajom, J. A., & Magno, C. (2011). Writing your winning thesis. *SSRN Electronic Journal*. https://doi.org/10.2139/ssrn.1429357

This handbook discusses the techniques needed to write a clear and accurate undergraduate thesis proposal, from conceptualising your research questions to writing the manuscript.

Nygaard, L. (2017). *Writing Your Master's Thesis: From A to Zen*. London: Sage.

This book's primary emphasis is on navigating structure, arguments, and theory for deeper critical engagement. It covers understanding the writer's role in communicating research, choosing a research question, and planning an appropriate design. It also includes advice on research ethics, writing (life)style, and working with supervisors. The book teaches you how to contextualise your research and maximise its impact.

Samuels, B., & Garbati, J. (2018). *Mastering Academic Writing* (1st edition). Thousand Oaks, CA: Sage.

This book helps you deal with the potential pitfalls of academic writing through hands-on exercises. The authors enable you to develop and sharpen arguments, organise and interpret source material, and write practical research proposals.

Thompson, P. (2012). Thesis and dissertation writing. In B. Paltridge & S. Starfield (Eds), *The Handbook of English for Specific Purposes*. New York: Wiley.

This chapter focuses on postgraduate writing. The chapter reviews the genre descriptions of introductions, literature reviews, discussion sections, and conclusion chapters.

# 10

# Finalising the Thesis

This chapter suggests ways of finalising the thesis before submitting it for examination. The chapter has a section on writing the fore sections of the thesis, including writing a title and abstract. The focus is on editing for clarity, language, style, referencing, formatting, and structural editing.

## Reviewing your work

Writing the final chapter of a thesis is not the end of a thesis; there are still many weeks of work to do. When you have typed that last full stop in the conclusion and recommendations chapter, you should go through the whole thesis before submitting it to your supervisor for a critique. This way, it becomes easy for your supervisor to give you feedback on a reasonably accurate document. Then you will need to revise your thesis again, taking on board and responding to your supervisor's criticisms, before you have the final, complete thesis to submit for examination.

The comments you receive back from your supervisor will be more valuable to you if you have already reviewed your work than if you submit a document that is full of errors and weaknesses. You will have checked editing details such as grammar, spelling, punctuation, captions to tables and figures, writing style, reference style, and language, ensuring rigour in these elements, from the front page to the references and appendices. When editing a detailed review of your thesis, it is advisable to work on a printed copy rather than the computer screen.

You should be familiar with the mechanisms and protocols that apply to the degree. When conventions are not explicit, refer to highly regarded completed theses from the department. Remember, you have the final responsibility for the thesis and cannot blame your advisors. Therefore, it is crucial to set aside adequate time to make the final corrections.

After the thesis is examined, areas requiring significant amendments are identified in the examiner's report. These are not necessarily criticisms, but are meant to improve the thesis.

# Finalising the preliminary sections

### Title of the thesis

The thesis title should be concise and relatively self-explanatory, and yet adequately describe the contents of the thesis. It should contain the keywords describing the work presented. A good title is crucial because most people skim titles to find out what the thesis is about. Most readers will find your thesis via an electronic database, where search engines will focus on the keywords used in the title or the abstract. Thus, the title should be easy to understand and represent the common theme of the thesis. It should indicate the relationship between the independent and dependent variables.

The title needs to reflect the who, what, and where questions: *what* question you are trying to investigate, *who* the respondents or subjects are, and *where* the research study was conducted. It should not read like a specific objective; for example, avoid phrases like 'An investigation of_____'. The title for a thesis should be less than 20 words.

You will have set out with a title in mind, which may have been changed as you progressed with your research, so start with your earlier title and modify it once the final form of the thesis is known.

---

### Example: Writing a title

The effectiveness of Motivation Interviewing (IM) in improving medication adherence [what], of patients living with HIV/AIDS [who], attending a Comprehensive Care Clinic of a referral hospital in Nairobi, Kenya [where]

---

### The front page of your thesis

Your university will stipulate the information required on, and the style of presentation of, the front page of a thesis. Always follow their guidance. However, the example given below is one that is commonly used by universities.

Full title of your thesis

Your full name

Submitted in [partial] fulfilment of the requirements for _____ [Your existing degrees, e.g., Doctor of Philosophy or Master of Science in ____]

Your Faculty and University

Month and year in which the thesis is submitted

---

## Example: A front page of a thesis

The effectiveness of Motivation Interviewing (IM) in improving medication adherence, of patients living with HIV/AIDS, attending a Comprehensive Care Clinic of a referral hospital in Nairobi, Kenya

Jane Doe

Submitted in partial fulfilment of the requirements for the degree of Master of Science in Public Health

Faculty of Health Sciences, University of Nairobi

June, 2022

---

## Statement of original authorship or committee approval form

Depending on the university, the original authorship or committee approval form might take various formats, but the common one is stated as follows:

> The work contained in this thesis has not been previously submitted to meet requirements for an award at this or any other higher education institution. Furthermore, to the best of my knowledge and belief, the thesis contains no material previously published or written by another person except where due reference is made.

## Abstract

Whereas the title of the thesis only makes a simple statement about the content of the thesis, the abstract elaborates on significant aspects of the thesis. Thus, the abstract is a critical element as it gives the reader an overview of the thesis. Moreover, it might be the only part that those who want a quick overview of the study will read and the only part they might find from electronic searches. Therefore, you must include enough information to make the abstract useful for someone who may reference the work. The abstract summarises the entire thesis in the following sequence:

- The first two sentences in an abstract include either the problem statement or the thesis statement, the purpose of the study, and the central research question(s) or the hypothesis.
- It is followed by a description of the importance or significance of the overall research problem (e.g., who would care if the problem is solved) [from the introduction chapter].
- Present the theoretical foundations, if appropriate, and the gap in knowledge [from the literature review chapter].
- Briefly describe the overall research design, key techniques used, data collection method(s), and analytic data procedures; indicate the sample size and sampling [from the methodology chapter]. If you are using an improved version of an existing method or have developed it, explain the primary reason for developing it or why it is needed, including how it was tested and evaluated or how well it worked.
- Report the most important findings that answer the questions, such as trends, relative change, or differences, and present a brief interpretation of the findings [from the results and discussion chapter(s)].
- Conclude with a statement on the implications for positive social change in one or two findings that capture the heart of the research. Then, describe the implications for research, practice, and policy, and outline any recommendations [from the conclusion and recommendations chapter].

The abstract should be concise, accurate, and readable. Ensure each sentence adds value to the reader's understanding of the research. The abstract is usually about 400 words or a maximum of one typed page. A simple rule of thumb is to imagine that the abstract is the only part of the thesis that will be read, so it has to present all the key information of your research. The abstract should be text only, with no references or citations of other literature, and no tables, figures, or illustrations. Use active voice as much as possible. Once the abstract is complete, confirm that all the information appearing in the abstract emerges in the main body of the thesis.

## Example: Writing an abstract

Medication non-adherence, sometimes called an 'invisible epidemic' is a significant public health problem that involves a complicated, routine, lifelong treatment requiring sustained motivation. [problem statement] Non-adherence leads to clinical disease progression and the development of drug resistance, which has implications for health service delivery in terms of cost and prevention efforts. [significance] This study aimed to design approaches targeting health behaviours that can be introduced as part of routine care or counselling sessions provided by healthcare providers. [purpose] Our study was guided by the Identity-Based Motivation (IBM) model, an individualised, patient-centred approach that has been used as a foundation for various aspiration-achievement gaps. [theoretical foundation]

This study was a randomised experimental design whose objective was to investigate the effectiveness of Motivational Interviewing on medication adherence of 300 persons living with HIV/AIDs attending an HIV/AIDs Comprehensive Care Clinic (CCC). They were allocated randomly 1:1 to the MI group (the intervention group) that uses in-person health coaching or personalised intervention and a conventional small group counselling (the control group). The patients were followed for four months, totalling 400 minutes of contact hours per person, with 98% response rates. [method]

Multiple linear regression results indicated that a person's likelihood of adhering to medication was related to self-efficacy. Our results further demonstrate that MI is a more effective change agent than the conventional counselling approaches that use small group intervention. After the four-month follow-up, the intervention group was eight times more likely to adhere to medication than the control group. [results]

This thesis revises how health education has been used by advancing a patient-centred approach. However, although this approach resulted in successful behaviour change, the cost, time effectiveness, applicability, and sustainability in routine practice need further research. [conclusion]

## Acknowledgements (optional)

This page aims to recognise persons or institutions to whom you are grateful for any special assistance and any grant fund support you may have received that helped you in research and writing. These are the people who contributed to the actual thesis.

## Dedication (optional)

The dedication page recognises persons, organisations, or others who provided extraordinary encouragement during your academic career. Unlike persons mentioned in the acknowledgement, those in the dedication may not have contributed to the work. Most dedications are brief statements of tribute beginning with 'To___', such as 'To my family'.

## Table of contents

The table of contents provides an overview of the thesis structure and the relationships between the issues discussed. Sections and subsections can be listed by headings alone, although a decimal system of numbered sections is easier to follow and thus often recommended. The organisation scheme of the table of contents must match the scheme displayed in the text. The system of indenting used in the table of contents to indicate subdivisions within chapters must also match the subdivision system in the chapters. Finally, the title of each entry must correspond precisely to the title as it appears in the text.

Limiting to three subheadings or numbered heading levels (e.g., Chapter 4.1.2.) is advisable to avoid the text consisting almost exclusively of subheadings that contain no argumentation. For example, no heading should be the same as the title of the thesis. In addition, do not use a full stop after the heading number or the heading text but use dot leaders (...) to connect the last word of each entry to the page numbers. Most word processing packages can create a table of contents with dot leaders from the headings in a document. However, all entries and page numbers must match the text exactly: double-check these details for accuracy.

## Tables and figures or illustrations

Include a list of tables and figures (illustrations) if you have one or more items in these categories. List the number, caption, and page number of every table and figure in the main body of the thesis. The enumeration of tables and figures is based on the chapter number. Therefore, the first digit represents the chapter number, and the second is the number of the table or figure. List items within each category consecutively throughout the chapter; thus the first table in Chapter 4 will be numbered Table 4.1 and the first figure in the chapter will be Figure 4.1. Use a uniform style for all figures (shading, frames, line width, font size, etc.) and tables, although styles of the latter may have to vary according to the information they display. The list of tables and figures should be presented on separate pages.

## Abbreviations and symbols

If you use symbols in your thesis or dissertation, you can either combine them with your abbreviations and title the section 'List of

Abbreviations and Symbols', or set up a separate list of symbols and your definitions.

Use abbreviations consistently throughout the whole document. You should spell out an abbreviation in full, and define it, the first time you use it in the text, especially if it is not commonly known or used. Generally accepted or known abbreviations, such as the 'USA', do not have to be defined. When using many abbreviations, list them in alphabetical order.

Define the symbol the first time you use it in a chapter and present it alphabetically in the 'symbols' subsection of your list of abbreviations and symbols. Ensure that every symbol has a unique meaning, and hence use it only in that specific context.

## Definitions of terms

You need to provide complete scientific definitions and appropriate references if necessary. Define only terms, words, or phrases which have special or unique meanings (operationally) in your study, or that you used in you study. You can define your terms in your own words or use definitions from encyclopaedias, books, magazine and newspaper articles, dictionaries, and other publications, but you must acknowledge your sources. Definitions taken from published materials are called conceptual or theoretical definitions. Definitions should be as brief, clear, and unambiguous as possible.

# Editing for clarity, language and grammar, and style

A thesis-writing process helps you to become an effective writer who focuses on content and clear and persuasive writing. In addition, clear writing helps the examiners follow your train of thought throughout the thesis and understand how each point relates to the overall thesis.

Ensure you adhere to your university's guideline criteria and instructions for a thesis regarding formatting, structural editing, and strict rules about the number of spaces before headings, the method for emphasis of significant headings, and the use of numbering systems. These can be effectively managed by using templates in a word processor.

Do not underestimate the editorial impact of the presentation of your thesis, assuming that only the research counts. Even if your language skills are excellent, you still need to edit your work. When writing your thesis, consider the expected language use in your profession, including the use of voice (active, passive, or a mix of the two). In addition, ensure your writing is free of mechanical or typographic errors. Use the correct sentence structure, punctuation, and style format.

In the writing and editing context, 'style' can refer to the voice in general (including degrees of formality) and, more specifically, to the guidelines that cover formatting, punctuation, capitalisation, expression, dates, or units. In the social sciences, the three central style guides are the American Psychological Association (APA), the Modern Language Association (MLA), and the Chicago Manual of Style (CMS; University of Chicago, 2017). The American Psychological Association is perhaps the most commonly used style in the social sciences. The Chicago Manual of Style is a highly detailed style manual useful for most subject areas, whereas the Modern Language Association is primarily used in the humanities and liberal arts.

## References or bibliography

The style and format of references or bibliography depend on the disciplinary field. The primary consideration, however, is consistency. Follow the style chosen scrupulously throughout the document. The general structure in all the styles consists of four parts: author, year, title, publication channel, or publisher's name and publication place. MLA style puts the date after the publisher in the reference list without parentheses; APA puts the date after the author's name in parentheses. The format used helps readers to find their way through the thesis.

Check that your references are correctly formatted. Use your university or department guidelines. The reference section, titled 'References' or 'Bibliography', is placed at the end of the thesis. The reference list provides readers with the information to locate the sources you have cited in your thesis. A bibliography is also a list of sources referred to in scholarly work, but may contain other material of interest that has not been explicitly referred to in the thesis text. However, references are preferable in a thesis. The reference list allows readers to view the scope of your research and to judge the depth of your scholarship.

Some of the more advanced reference software systems can format. For example, some settings may allow footnote style (all references in footnotes or endnotes) or a numbered style (using numbers in the text to refer to a specific reference. There are also software packages used for reference management, such as EndNote, Reference Manager, and Mendeley. When using referencing software, enter the author's first name into the database, and the software writes a full name or initials as required. Next, the title should appear in the reference list as dictated by the referencing style used, and not by how it appears in the original source (e.g., some reference styles use minimal captitalisation, whereas the style of the original reference may use capital letters for all main words). Non-typical references include websites, blogs, personal communication, memos, reports, and unpublished manuscripts. Whatever style of presentation you adopt, apply it consistently throughout your references section.

Ensure that the in-text citations are accurate and correctly cited. Text citations must be listed in the reference section using the established reference style and appropriate referencing conventions in the field. Thus, citations in the text should match those in the reference list (by author(s) and date). Use your university's guidelines to format the references correctly.

## Footnotes

Sometimes it is justified to provide information that is not strictly pertinent to the text but that you want to bring to the reader's attention. In this case, you can use footnotes. Number content footnotes consecutively throughout the manuscript using superscript Arabic numerals (placed outside the punctuation), and include the accompanying footnotes at the bottom of the page on which they are referenced.

## Appendices

You can include supporting material in the appendices or annexes of the thesis. Appendices allow the inclusion of large and separate sections of material connected to the work (such as the questionnaire used in the study, detailed information on the interviewees, or the code list used in analysing qualitative data). They are numbered and titled and placed after the references section. Do not include any addenda that you do not refer to in the text.

Typical material that can be incorporated as appendices includes:

- A country profile, including maps that describe the economic, political, and social situation.
- Descriptions of cultural traditions of the people in the study area.
- The questionnaires used to carry out the study.
- Checklists.
- Letter of ethical approval.
- The fieldwork timetables.
- Descriptions which are too long or detailed for the text but are relevant to the findings.

Include material in appendices only if it supports the points you make in the thesis. Do not include material if it adds nothing to the work. If you have material as an appendix, you must refer to it in the main body of the text (e.g., see Appendix 3).

## A note on the oral defence (or viva) of thesis

Note that you will not have the manuscript of your thesis or any slides with you while presenting the oral defence of your work, but you can make short notes for yourself to guide you, but not to read. You will need to explain to the defence panel, preferably without using numbers, tables, or figures, a narrative of the following:

- The purpose and objectives of your study.
- What you did (briefly).
- What you discovered and the significant, memorable findings.
- What the findings mean. Why are the results significant/important/beneficial? How can they be used, and who can use them?

This presentation is usually 10 minutes. The trick here is to rehearse with colleagues or in front of a mirror.

## Using checklists in finalising your thesis

Creating a checklist to ensure you have completed all the necessary checks before you submit your thesis is a useful strategy to follow. There are several checklists you can refer to in the literature. The thesis checklist I have selected by way of illustration is from an article by Janice L. Hewitt, PhD, Rice University. The checklist is freely available and can be downloaded for free (Hewitt, 2001). It helps you to evaluate your thesis as you write it, and can be used as a final check before turning in the finished product. It is therefore an appropriate way to end this chapter, and the book, as you complete the final stage of your journey to thesis submission – the thesis checklist.

### Thesis/dissertation checklist from Rice University

_____ 1. The thesis contains all the parts your university requires (usually Abstract, Acknowledgments, Table of Contents, List of Figures and Tables, Introduction, Background/Literature Review, Materials

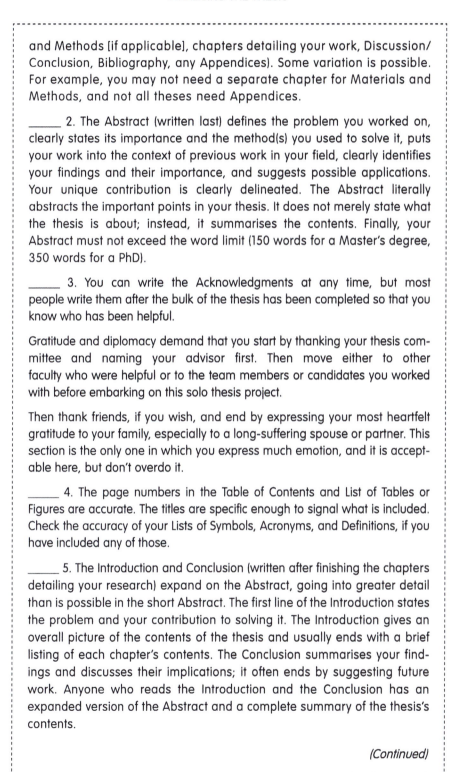

and Methods [if applicable], chapters detailing your work, Discussion/ Conclusion, Bibliography, any Appendices). Some variation is possible. For example, you may not need a separate chapter for Materials and Methods, and not all theses need Appendices.

_____ 2. The Abstract (written last) defines the problem you worked on, clearly states its importance and the method(s) you used to solve it, puts your work into the context of previous work in your field, clearly identifies your findings and their importance, and suggests possible applications. Your unique contribution is clearly delineated. The Abstract literally abstracts the important points in your thesis. It does not merely state what the thesis is about; instead, it summarises the contents. Finally, your Abstract must not exceed the word limit (150 words for a Master's degree, 350 words for a PhD).

_____ 3. You can write the Acknowledgments at any time, but most people write them after the bulk of the thesis has been completed so that you know who has been helpful.

Gratitude and diplomacy demand that you start by thanking your thesis committee and naming your advisor first. Then move either to other faculty who were helpful or to the team members or candidates you worked with before embarking on this solo thesis project.

Then thank friends, if you wish, and end by expressing your most heartfelt gratitude to your family, especially to a long-suffering spouse or partner. This section is the only one in which you express much emotion, and it is acceptable here, but don't overdo it.

_____ 4. The page numbers in the Table of Contents and List of Tables or Figures are accurate. The titles are specific enough to signal what is included. Check the accuracy of your Lists of Symbols, Acronyms, and Definitions, if you have included any of those.

_____ 5. The Introduction and Conclusion (written after finishing the chapters detailing your research) expand on the Abstract, going into greater detail than is possible in the short Abstract. The first line of the Introduction states the problem and your contribution to solving it. The Introduction gives an overall picture of the contents of the thesis and usually ends with a brief listing of each chapter's contents. The Conclusion summarises your findings and discusses their implications; it often ends by suggesting future work. Anyone who reads the Introduction and the Conclusion has an expanded version of the Abstract and a complete summary of the thesis's contents.

*(Continued)*

_____ 6. The Background/Literature Review situates your work within the larger context of your field. This chapter explains how your work grew out of earlier, related research and, in doing so, details the major developments and contrasting approaches in your specific field. You clarify the seminal work and then explain chronologically and thematically the important findings that preceded and motivated your research project. You identify key contributions, issues, and disagreements, and you show the 'links' between the research findings of others. Throughout the chapter, you indicate clearly why we are reading about a specific reference and how it relates to your own research.

This tightly argued chapter forms the basis for understanding and validating the importance of your work. It illustrates your skill as a scholar who can identify key papers in your field and then evaluate them.

Suppose your thesis relies heavily on your own previously published papers. In that case, you may want to incorporate the Literature Review in the body chapters for each of the papers to have a separate Lit Review for each paper. In any case, however, the Literature Review should be in much greater depth in your thesis than is possible in a short paper written for publication.

_____ 7. The Materials and Methods chapter contains sufficient details so that someone else could replicate your work. All chronology is clear.

_____ 8. The body chapters detail your research. The level of detail is sufficient so that your outside reader, who is not intimately familiar with your field, can understand your argument:

- What did you do?
- Why did you do it?
- How did you do it?
- What was the result?
- Why should we care about what you did? Why is the work important?

Those questions must be answered no matter what field you are in. For example, you cannot just string together a bunch of equations and let your reader figure things out.

Do not merely state; explain! You must lead your reader through your reasoning and your actions to your results. You must clearly identify your contributions, including the equipment or procedures you designed, as well as your research results.

_____ 9. Your Bibliography (or Works Cited) follows the format acceptable to your field. (If you're not certain what is preferred, check an edited journal in your field. APA and Chicago Manual of Style are common in science and engineering.) The Bibliography contains ALL the works cited in your thesis, including visuals, and nothing that is not actually cited. Proofread it for accuracy and consistency.

_____ 10. You have checked your sentences, paragraphs, sections, and chapters to see if the meaning is clear and logically sequential, not to you but your outside reader. If you sense that something is not clear, believe that it is not, and fix it. Ask someone else to read it and note any unclear sentences or sections.

_____ 11. You have checked for logical flow from sentence to sentence, paragraph to paragraph, section to section, chapter to chapter. You have topic sentences that signal a paragraph's content. Your introductions to each section and chapter signal their contents to the reader.

_____ 12. Visuals and figures appear within a page after they are mentioned in the text and not before they are mentioned. Titles are sufficiently detailed; the caption tells the reader what to notice so that it is not necessary to refer to the text to understand the illustration.

Similarly, the explanation in the text is clear enough to understand without referring to the visual. The visual should complement the text.

_____ 13. You have proofread for spelling and grammatical errors. Spellchecking will be easier if you add words to your dictionary every time you introduce a new one. Even so, you will need to proofread to see if you have used the right word. Do not rely on a grammar check program, which misses many errors and sometimes even suggests an incorrect usage.

_____ 14. Headings, sub-headings, lists, and captions are consistent in style and provide useful content. Font size and style, placement of figure and table titles, and margins meet university requirements and are consistent.

If you set up a style sheet when you first start writing, you will have fewer problems when preparing the final draft. If you use the required margins from the time you began writing, too, you will not now have trouble with graphs, tables, and equations wrapping. For example, Rice University requires a 1.5-inch left-hand margin for binding. You probably should not right justify it because it makes the text more difficult to read.

[It is easy to reset margins on Microsoft, but most LaTeX styles right-justify by default. To turn off the LaTeX right-justify command, type \raggedright near the beginning of the document.]

_____ 15. Ensure you have given author citations for all quotations, paraphrases, and borrowed or adapted visuals. Plagiarism is an academic crime.

_____ 16. Follow university regulations in setting up and publicising your defense.

*(Continued)*

_____ 17. Find out and follow the required steps for completing and submitting the thesis. Some deadlines are negotiable; others are not negotiable under any circumstances. For example, you may be able to give your committee the completed draft a couple of days after the suggested deadline. Nevertheless, the deadline for turning in to the university the completed copies with the title pages signed by your committee is completely rigid. All fees must be paid, and all the paperwork must be completed by the university deadline.

# Glossary

**Academic argument**  presents your standpoint, position, or claim on your topic, leading to your contribution to the current discussion on your topic.

**Academic writing**  is formal writing for scholarly purposes, used in universities and scholarly publications, including class essays, research papers, dissertations, and scholarly publications such as journal articles and books on academic topics. Academic writing is descriptive, analytical, persuasive, and critical.

**Annotated bibliography**  is a short descriptive text or comment (an annotation) for each source you have consulted in researching your topic in which you evaluate your sources and explain their importance for your research.

**Axiology**  is the study of judgement about values, i.e., what is wrong or right about what exists, what is worth studying to make an impact, and on whom it will make an impact.

**Bloom's taxonomy**  is a hierarchical model that defines and distinguishes the different levels of human cognition (i.e., thinking) and learning objectives. The six levels are: remembering, understanding, applying, analysing, evaluating, and creating. For example, learning can provide ideas to create lessons and assignments that help students to advance to more complex levels of thinking, such as analysis and evaluation.

**Critical review of the literature**  (or *critical review*) is an analysis and evaluation of numerous sources on a specific topic, providing your reader with an overview of the research you have done on your topic.

**Epistemology**  is the theory of knowledge which studies the nature, scope, and origin of knowledge. In epistemology, Evidence is used to justify belief by collating relevant sources in a particular field of inquiry.

**Ethnography** involves observing people in their environment to understand their experiences, perspectives, and everyday practices. It is an approach that relies on collecting data in the natural environment, i.e., how individuals' behaviour is influenced or mediated by the culture in which they live or the setting in which it occurs.

**Experimental designs** (or *true experimental designs*) are a research method that examines the cause of a certain phenomenon by controlling all the critical factors that might affect the phenomenon of interest. True experimental uses a completely randomised design, where each study participant is randomly assigned to either a treatment or a control group (a randomised controlled trial or RCT). In a blind RCT, the participants do not know whether they are assigned to the treatment or the control group, whereas in a double-blind RCT, neither the participants nor the researchers know who is assigned to the treatment or control groups. Double-blind RCTs reduce the risk of biased influences on the outcomes of the study by participants and researchers.

**Grounded theory** is a research method for discovering and developing new hypotheses and theories through the collection and analysis of real-world data.

**Hands-on exercise** is an activity which requires the student to practise performing a work task or procedure.

**Mixed methods** is a research approach for collecting, analysing, and 'mixing' quantitative and qualitative research methods in a single study to better understand a research problem.

**Ontology** is a fundamental belief about what exists and can be studied and what people know. In simple terms, ontology seeks the classification and explanation of entities.

**Phenomenology** focuses on individuals' interpretation of their experiences and how they express them, i.e., personal experiences of phenomena.

**Qualitative research** aims to gain a more focused or emotional insight into the research phenomenon. It is concerned with establishing answers to the whys and hows of the phenomenon. Cf. *Quantitative research*.

**Quantitative research** aims to discover how many people think, act, or feel in a specific way. Quantitative projects involve large sample sizes, concentrating on the number of responses. Cf. *Qualitative research*.

**Quasi-experimental research designs** are experimental research methods that aim to examine the cause of certain phenomena but where the treatment and control group participants are not randomly assigned. As it is often impossible to control all critical factors that might affect the phenomenon of interest, there may be several 'rival hypotheses' that explain the observed results.

**Reliability** is the extent to which a questionnaire, test, observation, or measurement procedure produces the same results on repeated trials and the stability or consistency of scores over time or across observers.

**Research design** is the overall structure, detailing how the chosen method will be applied to answer the research question.

**Research methods** are the tools, procedures, and approaches used to gather and analyse the data required to answer the research question(s).

**Validity** is the extent to which the instrument measures what it purports to measure, especially content validity, which relates to the degree with which the instrument thoroughly assesses or measures a construct (e.g., attitude).

**Writing genre** is a specific style of writing reflecting specific literary sub-classifications (or types of literature), more commonly known as literary genres. The primary genres in literature include comedy, tragedy, epic poetry, thriller, science fiction, romance, drama/play, essay, short story, and novel. The genres in academic writing include reviews, proposals, essays, papers, reports and theses.

# References

Agwor, T. C., & Adesina, O. (2018). Ethical issues for consideration in conducting research in the social and behavioural sciences. *The International Journal of Humanities & Social Studies*, 5(12).

Ajzen, I. (1991). The theory of planned behavior. *Organizational Behavior and Human Decision Processes*, 50(2), 179–211. https://doi.org/10.1016/0749-5978(91)90020-t

Ali Al-Khairy, M. (2013). Saudi English-major undergraduates' academic writing problems: A Taif University perspective. *English Language Teaching*, 6(6). https://doi.org/10.5539/elt.v6n6p1

Bastola, G. K. (2018). Teaching a five-paragraph essay. *Journal of NELTA*, 23(1–2), 174–178. https://doi.org/10.3126/nelta.v23i1-2.23365

Bazeley, P. (2012). Integrative analysis strategies for mixed data sources. *American Behavioral Scientist*, 56(6), 814–828. https://doi.org/10.1177/0002764211426330

Bloch, J. (2012). Plagiarism, intellectual property and the teaching of L2 writing: Explorations in the detection based approach. In *Plagiarism, Intellectual Property and the Teaching of L2 Writing*. Bristol: Multilingual Matters.

Bloomberg, L., & Volpe, M. (2012). *Completing Your Qualitative Dissertation: A Roadmap from Beginning to End*. Thousand Oaks, CA: Sage. https://doi.org/10.4135/9781452226613

Bottery, M., & Wright, N. (2019). *Writing a Watertight Thesis: A Guide to Successful Structure and Defence*. London: Bloomsbury Academic.

Bourke, S., & Holbrook, A. P. (2013). Examining PhD and research masters theses. *Assessment and Evaluation in Higher Education*, 38(4), 407–416. https://doi.org/10.1080/02602938.2011.638738

Brockmeier, M. (2006). *The Toulmin Model of Argument*. Science for All Americans Online.

Bryman, A. (2006). Integrating quantitative and qualitative research: How is it done? *Qualitative Research*, 6(1), 97–113. https://doi.org/10.1177/1468794106058877

Bui, Y. N. (2019). *How to Write a Master's Thesis*. Los Angeles, CA: Sage. https://uk.sagepub.com/en-gb/eur/how-to-write-a-masters-thesis/book250120

Burton, N., Brundrett, M., & Jones, M. (2018). *Doing your Education Research Project*. London: Sage. https://doi.org/10.4135/9781473921849

Cloutier, C., & Ravasi, D. (2021). Using tables to enhance trustworthiness in qualitative research. *Strategic Organization*, 19(1). https://doi.org/10.1177/1476127020979329

Cohen, J. (1988). *Statistical Power Analysis for the Behavioral Sciences* (2nd edition). Hillsdale NJ: Lawrence Erlbaum Associates.

Craswell, G., & Poore, M. (2011). *Writing for Academic Success: A Postgraduate Guide* (2nd edition). Thousand Oaks, CA: Sage.

Creswell, J. W. (2015). *A Concise Introduction to Mixed Methods Research*. Thousand Oaks, CA: Sage.

Cronk, B. C. (2019). *How to Use SPSS Statistics: A Step-by-step Guide to Analysis and Interpretation* (11th edition). Abingdon: Routledge.

Cumming, A., Lai, C., & Cho, H. (2016). Students' writing from sources for academic purposes: A synthesis of recent research. *Journal of English for Academic Purposes, 23*. https://doi.org/10.1016/j.jeap.2016.06.002

Cuneo, T., & van Woudenberg, R. (Eds) (2004). *The Cambridge Companion to Thomas Reid*. Cambridge: Cambridge University Press. https://doi.org/10.1017/CCOL0521812704

Davies, P. (1999). Paragraphs. In *70 Activities for Tutor Groups* (1st edition). Abingdon: Routledge. https://doi.org/10.4324/9781315264080-67

Ehninger, D. (1960). Toulmin on argument: An interpretation and application. *Quarterly Journal of Speech, 46*(1), 44–53. https://doi.org/10.1080/00335636009382390

Eldh, A. C., Årestedt, L., & Berterö, C. (2020). Quotations in qualitative studies: Reflections on constituents, custom, and purpose. *International Journal of Qualitative Methods, 10*(2), 229–248. https://doi.org/10.1177/1609406920969268

Ellis, T. J., & Levy, Y. (2008). Framework of problem-based research: A guide for novice researchers on the development of a research-worthy problem. *Informing Science: The International Journal of an Emerging Transdiscipline, 11*, 17–33. https://doi.org/10.28945/438

Evans, D., Gruba, P., & Zobel, J. (2014). *How to Write a Better Thesis*. New York: Springer. https://doi.org/10.1007/978-3-319-04286-2

Everett, E. L., & Furseth, I. (2013). *Doing Your Master's Dissertation: From Start to Finish*. Sage Study Skills Series. London: Sage.

Faryadi, Q. (2012). How to write your PhD proposal: A step-by-step guide. *American International Journal of Contemporary Research, 2*(4).

Few, S. (2012). Differing roles of tables and graphs. In *Show Me the Numbers: Designing Tables and Graphs to Enlighten* (2nd edition). El Dorado Hills, CA: Analytics Press.

Fisher, C. M., & Buglear, C. M. J. (2010). *Researching and Writing a Dissertation: A Guidebook for Business Students* (3rd edition). Harlow: Prentice Hall.

Garrard, J. (2017). *Health Sciences Literature Review Made Easy: The Matrix Method* (5th edition). Burlington, MA: Jones & Bartlett Learning.

Gill, P., & Dolan, G. (2015). Originality and the PhD: What is it and how can it be demonstrated? *Nurse Researcher, 22*(6), 11–15. https://doi.org/10.7748/nr.22.6.11.e1335

Gilmore, J., Strickland, D., Timmerman, B., Maher, M., & Feldon, D. (2010). Weeds in the flower garden: An exploration of plagiarism in graduate students' research proposals and its connection to enculturation, ESL, and contextual factors. *International Journal for Educational Integrity, 6*(1), 13–28. https://doi.org/10.21913/ijei.v6i1.673

Glasman-Deal, H. (2009). Unit 4: Writing the Discussion/Conclusion. In *Science Research Writing for Non-Native Speakers of English*. London: Imperial College Press. https://doi.org/10.1142p605

Golding, C. (2017). Advice for writing a thesis (based on what examiners do). *Open Review of Educational Research*, 4(1), 46–60. https://doi.org/10.1080/23265507.2017.1300862

Golding, C., Sharmini, S., & Lazarovitch, A. (2014). What examiners do: What thesis students should know. *Assessment & Evaluation in Higher Education*, 39(5), 563–576. https://doi.org/10.1080/02602938.2013.859230

Gopen, G. D., & Swan, J. A. (1990). The science of scientific writing. *American Scientist*. Retrieved 20 April 2022, from https://cseweb.ucsd.edu/~swanson/papers/science-of-writing.pdf.

Grant, C., & Osanloo, A. (2014). Understanding, selecting, and integrating a theoretical framework in dissertation research: Creating the blueprint for your 'house'. *Administrative Issues Journal: Connecting Education, Practice, and Research*, 4(2), 12–26. https://doi.org/10.5929/2014.4.2.9

Hart, C. (1998). *Doing a Literature Review: Releasing the Research Imagination* (2nd edition). London: Sage.

Hei, K. C., & David, M. K. (2015). Basic and advanced skills they don't have: The case of postgraduates and literature review writing. *Malaysian Journal of Learning and Instruction*, 12, 131–150. https://doi.org/10.32890/mjli.12.2015.7683

Hewitt, J. L. (2001) Thesis Checklist. Retrieved 18 May 2023, from https://www.owlnet.rice.edu/~cainproj/writingtips/thesischecklist.html

Hyland, K., & Shaw, P. (Eds) (2016). *The Routledge Handbook of English for Academic Purposes*. Abingdon: Routledge. https://doi.org/10.4324/9781315657455

Jacobs, R. L. (2011). Developing a research problem and purpose statement. In T. G. Hatcher & T. S. Rocco (Eds), *The Handbook of Scholarly Writing and Publishing*. San Francisco, CA: Jossey-Bass.

Kamler, B., & Thomson, P. (2014). *Helping Doctoral Students Write: Pedagogies for Supervision* (2nd edition). London: Routledge. https://doi.org/10.4324/9781315813639

Kelly, L., & Snowden, A. (2020). How to synthesise original findings back into the literature: A reintroduction to concurrent analysis. *Nurse Researcher*, 28(2). https://doi.org/10.7748/nr.2020.e1710

Kivunja, C. (2018). Distinguishing between theory, theoretical framework, and conceptual framework: A systematic review of lessons from the field. *International Journal of Higher Education*. https://doi.org/10.5430/ijhe.v7n6p44

Komba, S. C. (2015). Challenges of writing theses and dissertations among postgraduate students in Tanzanian higher learning institutions. *International Journal of Research Studies in Education*, 5(3), 71–80. https://doi.org/10.5861/ijrse.2015.1280

Kretchmer, P. (2021). Twelve steps to writing an effective results section. *San Francisco Edit*. Retrieved 17 May 2023, from https://www.sfedit.net/wp-content/uploads/2021/07/Results.pdf

Lajom, J. A., & Magno, C. (2011). Writing your winning thesis. *SSRN Electronic Journal*. https://doi.org/10.2139/ssrn.1429357

Langford, R. (2012). Qualitative research methods, by Monique Hennink, Inge Hutter and Ajay Bailey. *Critical Public Health*, 22(1), 111–112. https://doi.org/10.1080/09581596.2011.565689

Loseke, D. R. (2020). *Methodological Thinking: Basic Principles of Social Research Design* (2nd edition). London: Sage. https://doi.org/10.4135/9781071802700

Lunenburg, F., & Irby, B. (2014). Writing the literature review chapter. In *Writing a Successful Thesis or Dissertation: Tips and Strategies for Students in the Social and Behavioral Sciences* (pp. 137–164). Thousand Oaks, CA: Corwin Press. https://doi.org/10.4135/9781483329659.n7

Manchishi, P. C., Ndhlovu, D., & Mwanza, D. S. (2015). Common mistakes committed and challenges faced in research proposal writing by University of Zambia postgraduate students. *International Journal of Humanities Social Sciences and Education (IJHSSE)*, 2(3), 126–138.

Matheson, L., Lacey, F. M., & Jesson, J. (2011). *Doing Your Literature Review: Traditional and Systematic Techniques*. London: Sage.

McGee, I. (2017). Paragraphing beliefs, pedagogy, and practice: Omani TESOL teacher attempts to hold it all together. *International Journal of Applied Linguistics (United Kingdom)*. https://doi.org/10.1111/ijal.12136

Miles, D. A. (2019). Problem statement development: How to write a problem statement in a dissertation. *Doctoral Network Conference*. Retrieved 18 May 2023, from https://www.academia.edu/39588741/ARTICLE_Problem_Statement_Development_How_to_Write_a_Problem_Statement_in_A_Dissertation

Molasso, W. R. (2006). Theoretical frameworks in qualitative research. *Journal of College and Character*, 7(7). https://doi.org/10.2202/1940-1639.1246

Nishishiba, M., Jones, M., & Kraner, M. (2017). *Research Methods and Statistics for Public and Nonprofit Administrators: A Practical Guide*. London: Sage. https://doi.org/10.4135/9781544307763

Norris, J. M., Plonsky, L., Ross, S. J., & Schoonen, R. (2015). Guidelines for reporting quantitative methods and results in primary research. *Language Learning*, 65(2). https://doi.org/10.1111/lang.12104

Nygaard, L. (2017). *Writing Your Master's Thesis: From A to Zen*. London: Sage.

Patten, M. L., & Newhart, M. (2018). Introduction to validity. In *Understanding Research Methods: An Overview of the Essentials* (10th edition). London: Routledge. https://doi.org/10.4324/9781315213033

Petchko, K. (2018a). *How to Write about Economics and Public Policy*. Oxford: Elsevier. https://doi.org/10.1016/b978-0-12-813010-0.00010-7

Petchko, K. (2018b). Situating a study: The literature review. In *How to Write about Economics and Public Policy*. Oxford: Elsevier. https://doi.org/10.1016/b978-0-12-813010-0.00011-9

Petchko, K. (2018c). Data, methodology, results, and discussion: Models and examples. In *How to Write about Economics and Public Policy*. Oxford: Elsevier. https://doi.org/10.1016/b978-0-12-813010-0.00015-6

Petre, M., & Rugg, G. (2010). *The Unwritten Rules of PhD Research* (2nd edition). Maidenhead: Open University Press.

Qasem, F. A., & Zayid, E. I. M. (2019). The challenges and problems faced by students in the early stage of writing research projects in L2, University of Bisha, Saudi Arabia. *European Journal of Special Education Research*, 4(1), pp. 32–47. https://doi.org/10.5281/zenodo.2557036

Ramage, J. D., Bean, J. C., & Johnson, J. (2015). *Writing Arguments: A Rhetoric with Readings* (10th edition). New York: Pearson.

Reynolds, G. (2014). *Presentation Zen Design: A Simple Visual Approach to Presenting in Today's World* (2nd edition). Berkeley, CA: New Riders.

Robson, C. (2011). *Real World Research* (3rd edition). New York: Wiley.

Samuels, B., & Garbati, J. (2018). *Mastering Academic Writing* (1st edition). Thousand Oaks, CA: Sage.

Sawilowsky, S. S. (2009). New effect size rules of thumb. *Journal of Modern Applied Statistical Methods*, 8(2), 597–599. https://doi.org/10.22237/jmasm/1257035100

Scott, C. (2000). Health science literature review made easy: The matrix method. *Canadian Journal of Public Health/Revue Canadienne de Santé Publique*, *91*(1).

Sullivan, G. M., & Feinn, R. (2012). Using effect size—or why the p value is not enough. *Journal of Graduate Medical Education*, 4(3), 279–282. https://doi.org/10.4300/jgme-d-12-00156.1

Swales, J., & Feak, C. (2012). *Academic Writing for Graduate Students* (3rd edition). Ann Arbor, MI: University of Michigan Press. https://doi.org/10.3998/mpub.2173936

Sword, H. (2012). *Stylish Academic Writing*. Cambridge, MA: Harvard University Press.

Thody, A. (2013). *Writing and Presenting Research*. London: Sage.

Thompson, P. (2012). Thesis and dissertation writing. In B. Paltridge & S. Starfield (Eds), *The Handbook of English for Specific Purposes*. New York: Wiley. https://doi.org/10.1002/9781118339855.ch15

Thomson, P. (2014). connecting chapters/chapter introductions. *patter*. Retrieved 15 May 2023, from https://patthomson.net/2014/01/16/connecting-chapterschapter-introductions/

University of Arizona (n.d.). Template for writing an argumentative thesis. *Thesis Generator*. Retrieved 20 April 2022, from https://writingcenter.uagc.edu/thesis-generator

University of Chicago (2017). *Chicago Manual of Style* (17th edition). Chicago, IL: University of Chicago Press.

University of Wisconsin-Madison (n.d.). *How to Write Critical Reviews*. Madison, WI: The Writing Center, University of Wisconsin-Madison. Retrieved 20 April 2022, from https://writing.wisc.edu/handbook/assignments/crinonfiction/

Wakefield, A. (2015). Synthesising the literature as part of a literature review. *Nursing Standard*, 29(29), 44–51. https://doi.org/10.7748/ns.29.29.44.e8957

Wallace, M., & Wray, A. (2016). *Critical Reading and Writing for Postgraduates*. London: Sage.

Wallwork, A. (2011). *English for Writing Research Papers*. New York: Springer. https://doi.org/10.1007/978-1-4419-7922-3

Washington University. (2014). Paragraph Development. *Notes*. Available at https://faculty.washington.edu/ezent/impd.htm

Weinberg, L., & Kovarik, C. L. (2010). The WHO clinical staging system for HIV/AIDS. *AMA Journal of Ethics*, March. Retrieved 20 April 2022, from https://journalofethics.ama-assn.org/article/who-clinical-staging-system-hivaids/2010-03

Winchester, C. L., & Salji, M. (2016). Writing a literature review. *Journal of Clinical Urology*, *9*(5), 308–312. https://doi.org/10.1177/2051415816650133

Wingate, U. (2012). 'Argument!' Helping students understand what essay writing is about. *Journal of English for Academic Purposes*, *11*(2). https://doi.org/10.1016/j.jeap.2011.11.001

Woodrow, L. (2019). *Doing a Master's Dissertation in TESOL and Applied Linguistics*. London: Routledge. https://doi.org/10.4324/9780429504068

Yeh, C. (2010). New graduate students' perspectives on research writing in English: A case study in Taiwan. *New Graduate Students' Perspectives on Research Writing in English: A Case Study in Taiwan*, *4*(1), 1–12.

# Index